MW00827532

FICHTE'S TRANSCENDENTAL PHILOSOPHY
The Original Duplicity of Intelligence and Will

This is the first book in English on the major works of the German philosopher Johann Gottlieb Fichte (1762–1814). It examines the transcendental theory of self and world from the writings of Fichte's most influential period (1794–1800) and considers in detail recently discovered lectures on the *Foundations of Transcendental Philosophy*. At the center of that body of work stands Fichte's attempt to integrate the theories of volition and cognition into a unified but complex "system of freedom." The focus of this book is the intricate interplay between thinking and willing in the birth of experience out of the spirit of freedom.

Combining incomparable erudition, sensitive readings of some of the most difficult of philosophical texts, clarity in exposition, and an acute awareness of historical context, this book takes its place as the ideal introduction to Fichte's thought.

Günter Zöller is Professor of Philosophy and Chair of the Philosophy Department at the University of Iowa.

MODERN EUROPEAN PHILOSOPHY

This series contains a range of high-quality books on philosophers, topics, and schools of thought prominent in the Kantian and post-Kantian European tradition. It is nonsectarian in approach and methodology, and includes both introductory and more specialized treatments of these thinkers and topics. Authors are encouraged to interpret the boundaries of the modern European tradition in a broad way and in primarily philosophical rather than historical terms.

General Editor

ROBERT B. PIPPIN, *University of Chicago*

Advisory Board
GARY GUTTING, *University of Notre Dame*
ROLF-PETER HORSTMANN, *Humboldt University, Berlin*
MARK SACKS, *University of Essex*

Some recent titles:

Frederick A. Olafson, *What Is a Human Being?*
Stanley Rosen, *The Mask of Enlightenment:*
Nietzsche's Zarathustra
Robert C. Scharff, *Comte after Postivism*
F. G. T. Moore, *Bergson: Thinking Backwards*
Charles Larmore, *The Morals of Modernity*
Robert B. Pippin, *Idealism as Modernism*
Daniel C. Conway, *Nietzsche's Dangerous Game*
John P. McCormick, *Carl Schmitt's Critique of Liberalism*

FICHTE'S TRANSCENDENTAL PHILOSOPHY

The Original Duplicity of Intelligence and Will

GÜNTER ZÖLLER

CAMBRIDGE
UNIVERSITY PRESS

PUBLISHED BY THE PRESS SYNDICATE OF THE UNIVERSITY OF CAMBRIDGE
The Pitt Building, Trumpington Street, Cambridge, United Kingdom

CAMBRIDGE UNIVERSITY PRESS
The Edinburgh Building, Cambridge CB2 2RU, UK
40 West 20th Street, New York NY 10011–4211, USA
477 Williamstown Road, Port Melbourne, VIC 3207, Australia
Ruiz de Alarcón 13, 28014 Madrid, Spain
Dock House, The Waterfront, Cape Town 8001, South Africa

http://www.cambridge.org

© Günter Zöller 1998

This book is in copyright. Subject to statutory exception
and to the provisions of relevant collective licensing agreements,
no reproduction of any part may take place without
the written permission of Cambridge University Press.

First published 1998
First paperback edition 2002

Typeface Baskerville

A catalogue record for this book is available from the British Library

Library of Congress Cataloguing in Publication data
Zöller, Günter, 1954–
Fichte's transcendental philosophy: the original duplicity of
intelligence and will / Günter Zöller.
p.   cm.   (Modern European philosophy)
Earlier versions of the book's eight chapters were presented at
conferences between 1992 and 1996 at various academic institutions.
Includes bibliographical references and index.
ISBN 0 521 59160 0 (hb)
1. Fichte, Johann Gottlieb, 1762–1814. I. Title. II. Series.
B2848.Z64   1998
193–dc21   97-28811   CIP

ISBN 0 521 59160 0 hardback
ISBN 0 521 89273 2 paperback

Transferred to digital printing 2005

Für Marlena

CONTENTS

ACKNOWLEDGMENTS

I gratefully acknowledge the support of my work on this book and several related projects and publications through a grant and two fellowships: a grant from the National Endowment for the Humanities for directing a Scholars Workshop on theories of selfhood in classical German philosophy at the University of Iowa under its Project on Rhetoric of Inquiry (1992); a Fellowship for University Teachers from the National Endowment for the Humanities (1993–1994); and a Faculty Scholar Award from the University of Iowa (1994–1997). Additional support in the form of travel and equipment grants was provided by the College of Liberal Arts and the Office of the Provost at the University of Iowa and the Department of Philosophy at Princeton University. During my work on this book I held a number of honorary affiliations that provided me with a series of stimulating and supportive environments. For their academic hospitality I would like to thank the Project on Rhetoric of Inquiry at the University of Iowa, the Obermann Center for Advanced Studies at the University of Iowa, Queen's College (Oxford), Wolfson College (Oxford), the Philosophy Department at the University of Tübingen, the Ecole Normale Supérieure (Paris), and the Center for Literary and Cultural Studies at Harvard University. Special thanks for welcoming me at their institutions go to Susanne Bobzien, Manfred Frank and Jean-François Courtine.

Earlier versions of the book's eight chapters were presented at conferences and in colloquia series between 1992 and 1996 at the following academic institutions and events: the conference "Figuring the Self: Subject, Individual, and the Absolute in Classical German Philosophy" at the University of Iowa; the Second Biennial Meeting of the North American Fichte Society in Denver; the University of Illinois at Urbana-Champaign; Wellesley College; the conference "The Modern Subject: Classical German Idealist Conceptions of the Self" at the University of Notre Dame; Cambridge University; the University of Tübingen; the Congress of the International J. G. Fichte Society in Jena; the conference "Le Bicentenaire de la Doctrine de la Science de Fichte (1794–1994)" in Poitiers; the Eighth International Kant Congress in Memphis; the Third Biennial Meeting of the North American Fichte Society in Skakertown; the conference "Das Setzen in Fichtes erster Wissenschaftslehre" at the Instituto per gli studii filosofici in Naples; the conference "The Idea of a System of Transcendental Idealism in Kant, Fichte, Schelling and Hegel" at Dartmouth College; the conference "La Wissenschaftslehre y la unidad del sistema de Fichte" at the Instituto de Filosofía in Madrid; the University of Cologne; and the University of Wuppertal. I wish to thank my colleagues and friends at these gatherings for their helpful criticisms, comments and suggestions. I am especially grateful to Daniel Breazeale for his valuable advice on the manuscript as a whole. Thanks also go to Robert Pippin for including the book in the series Modern European Philosophy, to Terence Moore from Cambridge University Press for valuable advice, as well as to David Anderson, who copyedited the typescript with much diligence and care, and Louise Calabro, who oversaw the production of the book.

Four chapters of the book have previously appeared elsewhere. I would like to thank the editors and publishers of the following publications for their generous permission to reuse the material in slightly revised form: Chapter 2, "An Eye for an I," reprinted from *Figuring the Self: Subject, Individual, and Others in Classical German Philosophy*, ed. David Klemm and Günter Zöller, permission of the State University of New York Press ©1997; Chapter 4, "Changing the Appearances," reprinted from *Proceedings of the Eighth International Kant Congress*, Memphis 1995, ed. Hoke Robinson, permission of Marquette University Press ©1995; Chapter 5, "Willing as Thinking," reprinted from *New Perspectives on Fichte*, ed. Daniel Breazeale and Tom Rockmore, permission of Humanities Press ©1995; Chapter 6, "Ideal Thinking and Real Thinking," reprinted from *The Modern Subject: Conceptions of the Self in Classical German Philosophy*, ed. K. Ameriks and D. Sturma, permission of the State University of New York Press ©1995. My final thanks are to my wife and colleague, Marlena G. Corcoran, for being one as well as the other.

METHOD OF CITATION FOR FICHTE'S
AND KANT'S WORKS

Fichte's works are cited from the historical-critical edition of the Bavarian Academy of Sciences, which is nearing completion and already contains virtually all of Fichte's writings under consideration in this essay: *J. G. Fichte – Gesamtausgabe der Bayerischen Akademie der Wissenschaften*, ed. R. Lauth and H. Gliwitzky (Stuttgart–Bad Cannstatt: Frommann-Holzboog:1962ff.). The Academy edition proceeds chronologically in four parallel series: series I contains the works published by Fichte himself, series II contains unpublished works, series III contains the correspondence and series IV contains transcripts of Fichte's lectures from other hands. References to the Academy edition employ the abbreviation "GA," followed by a combination of Roman numeral, forward slash and arabic number indicating the series and volume, and one or more Arabic numbers indicating the page or pages referred to (e.g., GA I/2: 45).

Where a text cited is not yet available in the Academy edition, references are to the nineteenth-century edition of Fichte's works edited by his son: *Fichte's sämmtliche Werke*, ed. I. H. Fichte, 8 vols. (Berlin: Veit & Co., 1845–1846) and *Fichte's nachgelassene Schriften*, ed. I. H. Fichte, 3 vols. (Bonn: Adolph-Marcus, 1834–1835), reprinted together as *Fichtes Werke*, 11 vols (Berlin: de Gruyter, 1971) and referred to in the notes as "SW," "NW" and "FW," respectively, with Roman numerals indicating the volumes and Arabic numerals indicating the pages.

One of the key texts of this study, the transcript by Krause of Fichte's 1798–1799 lectures on the *Wissenschaftslehre nova methodo*, is not included in either edition of Fichte's collected works. It is cited from the following separate edition: *Wissenschaftslehre nova methodo: Kollegnachschrift K. Chr. Fr. Krause 1798/99*, ed. E. Fuchs (Hamburg: Felix Meiner, 1982; 2d ed. 1994), and referred to in the notes as "WLnmK."

The quotations from these editions provided in the notes preserve the original spelling and punctuation. Key terms and phrases of the German original inserted parenthetically in the main body of the text are modernized.

Citations of the German editions of Fichte's works are followed by citations of modern English translations, whenever they are available. Any modifications of published translations are indicated in the notes. All other translations are my own. The following abbreviations are used:

ACR: *Attempt at a Critique of All Revelation*, trans. G. Green. Cambridge: Cambridge University Press, 1978.

CCR: "A Crystal Clear Report to the General Public Concerning the Actual Essence of the Newest Philosophy: An Attempt to Force the Reader to Understand," in *Philosophy of German Idealism*, ed. E. Behler. New York: Continuum, 1987, 39–115.

EPW: *Early Philosophical Writings*, ed. and trans. D. Breazeale. Ithaca, N.Y.: Cornell University Press, 1988.

FTP: *Foundations of Transcendental Philosophy (Wissenschaftslehre) Nova Methodo (1796/99)*, ed. and trans. D. Breazeale. Ithaca, N.Y.: Cornell University Press, 1992.

IWL: *Introductions to the Wissenschaftslehre and Other Writings*, ed. and trans. D. Breazeale. Indianapolis: Hackett, 1994.

SK: *Science of Knowledge with the First and Second Introductions*, trans. P. Heath and J. Lachs. Cambridge: Cambridge University Press, 1982.

VOM: *The Vocation of Man*, ed. R. M. Chisholm. New York: Macmillan, 1986.

Kant's writings are cited from *Kant's gesammelte Schriften*, ed. Royal Prussian Academy of Sciences and its successors (Berlin, later Berlin and New York: Reimer, later de Gruyter, 1900ff.), abbreviated as "AA," followed by Roman and Arabic numeral(s) indicating volume(s) and page(s), respectively. The only exception to this method of citation is the *Critique of Pure Reason*, which is cited according to the original pagination of the second and first editions ("B" and "A," respectively). References to English translations of Kant's work are to modern editions indicated in the respective notes.

KEY TO FICHTE'S WORKS CITED

The following list allows the reader to trace references to the Academy edition of Fichte's works (GA), as provided in the notes, to the individual works cited. The list gives the German titles of the works along with their English translation as well as their year of original publication cued to series, volume and page numbers of the Academy edition. The list is arranged in the order of the Academy edition, omitting the series with correspondence (GA III), which is cited by addressee and date directly in the notes. Works by Fichte that are cited from other editions are specified in the respective notes (cf. "Method of Citation" above).

GA I/1:15–162: *Versuch einer Critik aller Offenbarung; Attempt at a Critique of All Revelation*; 1792.

GA I/2:1–14: *Rezension: Leonhard Creuzer, "Skeptische Betrachtungen über die Freyheit des Willens mit Hinsicht auf die neuesten Theorien über dieselbe"; Review of Leonhard Creuzer, "Skeptical Considerations on the Freedom of the Will with Respect to the Newest Theories on the Latter"*; 1793.

GA I/2:31–67: *Recension des "Aenesidemus"; Review of "Aenesidemus"*; 1794.

GA I/2:107–72: *Ueber den Begriff der Wissenschaftslehre oder der sogenannten Philosophie; Concerning the Concept of the Wissenschaftslehre or of So-called Philosophy*; 1794.

GA I/2:251–451: *Grundlage der gesammten Wissenschaftslehre; Foundation of the Entire Wissenschaftslehre*, 1794–1795.

GA I/3:143–208: *Grundriss des Eigenthümlichen der Wissenschaftslehre in Rück-sicht auf das theoretische Vermögen; Outline of the Distinctive Character of the Wissenschaftslehre with Respect to the Theoretical Faculty;* 1795.

GA I/3:235–271: *Vergleichung des von Herrn Prof. Schmid aufgestellten Systems mit der Wissenschaftslehre; A Comparison between Prof. Schmid's System and the Wissenschaftslehre,* 1795.

GA I/3:313–460 and GA I/4:5–165: *Grundlage des Naturrechts nach Prin-cipien der Wissenschaftslehre; Foundation of Natural Law According to the Principles of the Wissenschaftslehre,* 1796–1797.

GA I/4:183–281: <u>*Versuch einer neuen Darstellung*</u> *der Wissenschaftslehre,* con-sisting of "<u>Vorerinnerung</u>" (GA I/4:183–185), "[Er<u>ste]</u> <u>Einleithung</u>" (GA I/4:186–208), "Zweyte Einleitung in die Wissenschaftslehre" (GA I/4:208–270) and "<u>Ersthes Kapitel</u>" (GA I/4:271–281); *Attempt at a New Presentation of the Wissenschaftslehre,* Consisting of "Preface," "[First] Intro-duction," "Second Introduction to the *Wissenschaftslehre,*" and "First Chapter"; 1797–1798.

GA I/5:21–317: *Das System der Sittenlehre nach den Principien der Wissenschafts-lehre; The System of Ethics According to the Principles of the Wissenschaftslehre,* 1798.

GA I/5:347–357: *Ueber den Grund unsers Glaubens an eine göttliche Welt-regierung; On the Basis of Our Belief in a Divine Governance of the World;* 1799.

GA I/6:189–309: *Die Bestimmung des Menschen; The Vocation of Man;* 1800.

GA I/7:185–268: *Sonnenklarer Bericht an das größere Publicum über das eigentliche Wesen der neuesten Philosophie: Ein Versuch, die Leser zum Verstehen zu zwingen; A Crystal Clear Report to the Larger Public concerning the Actual Essence of the Newest Philosophy: An Attempt to Force the Reader to Understand;* 1801.

GA II/4:37–367: *Zu Platners "Philosophischen Aphorismen": Vorlesungen über Logik und Metaphysik; On Platner's "Philosophical Aphorisms": Lectures on Logic and Metaphysics;* 1792–1812.

GA II/5:103–186: *Rückerinnerungen, Antworten, Fragen; Recollections, Answers, Questions;* 1799.

GA II/5:319–402: *Neue Bearbeitung der Wissenschaftslehre; New Treatment of the Wissenschaftslehre,* 1800.

GA IV/1:7–148: *Collegium über die Moral . . . im Sommerhalben Jah. 1796; Lectures on Morals from the Summer Semester of 1796.*

GA IV/1:175–450: *Vorlesungen über Logik und Metaphysik . . . nach Platners Philosoph. Aphorismen 1ter Theil 1793 im Sommerhj. 1797; Lectures on Logic and Metaphysics after Platner's Philosophical Aphorisms 1st Part 1793 from the Summer Semester of 1797.*

GA IV/2:17–267: *Wissenschaftslehre nach den Vorlesungen von Hr. Pr. Fichte; Wissenschaftslehre According to the Lectures of Prof. Fichte,* 1796–1797.

GA II/6:135–324: *Darstellung der Wissenschaftslehre aus den Jahren 1801/02; Presentation of the Wissenschaftslehre from the Years 1801/02.*

INTRODUCTION

Thinking is doing.

Joseph Beuys

In 1800 Johann Gottlieb Fichte, then thirty-seven years of age and without a post after having lost his professorship at the University of Jena over charges of atheism during the previous year, published a treatise whose title can suitably be placed over its author's entire oeuvre: *Die Bestimmung des Menschen,* customarily translated as "The Vocation of Man," but perhaps best rendered in English as "The Destination of Humanity." The key word of the work's German title, "*Bestimmung,*" can mean both "determination," in the sense of an imposed limitation, and "calling" or "vocation," indicating the goal of some pursuit. Fichte's employment of the term in its finitist-finalist double meaning addresses the tension between what is fixed or given in human existence and what is open and yet to be realized about it. As Fichte sees it, the goal for which human beings are destined is not given to them like a determination that would limit them from the outside. Rather, the destination of the human being is precisely the freedom from all determinations except the ones that the human being gives to itself freely. Determination is to become self-determination, facticity is to be worked off through freedom.

Fichte's basic belief in the supreme value of free self-determination runs through virtually his entire life and works, manifesting itself in his notoriously controversial public persona as well as his philosophical thinking on

1

such diverse subjects as politics, law, ethics and religion. It was the cause of freedom that attracted him to the early phase of the French revolution just as it motivated his participation in Prussia's uprising against Napoleon's rule over Europe. The pursuit of freedom also underlies Fichte's pioneering defense of the liberal state and informs his moral theory of radical autonomy. Even Fichte's philosophical reflections on religion feature prominently the role of free recognition in the relation to the absolute.

Fichte's championship of freedom and self-determination is not limited to his public personality and his work in practical philosophy. It also animates and sustains his highly abstract and exceedingly demanding philosophical speculations on the origin, the limits and the objects of human knowledge, which he undertook over a twenty-year period under the working title *Wissenschaftslehre,* literally "Doctrine of Science" or "Doctrine of Knowledge."[1] Historically speaking, Fichte's project of a *Wissenschaftslehre* continues Kant's development of a transcendental philosophy; it aims at a comprehensive account of the principles governing human knowledge and its world of objects. Fichte locates freedom at the very core of human knowledge, thereby putting into question the rigid distinction between knowing and doing, or theory and practice. To be sure, the freedom that is part of the transcendental conditions of all human knowledge is not the freedom involved in deliberation and choice. Freedom as a transcendental condition of knowledge and its objects is spontaneity and as such the root of all other, overt forms of freedom.

Fichte's development of the transcendental theory of knowledge and its objects as a theory of freedom offers an intriguing but also highly puzzling combination of theoretical rigor and practical fervor. His writings on the *Wissenschaftslehre* show extreme technical detail of an extent and complexity unknown in philosophy up to that point. But they also exhibit a sustained concern with broader, more general issues, most notably with the prefiguration of the overtly practical dimension of freedom in the transcendental foundation of knowledge. In fact, the first and philosophically most important and influential period of the two decades that Fichte devoted to the *Wissenschaftslehre* (1794–1800) centers around the systematic attempt to vindicate freedom to the domain of transcendental philosophy. Fichte himself expresses the novelty of according a central status to freedom in philosophy as a whole by claiming to have provided "the first system of freedom."[2]

The systematic prominence of the speculative foundations of freedom in the *Wissenschaftslehre* goes together with a radical reevaluation of the relation between theoretical and practical philosophy in Fichte. More importantly, the respective object domains of these philosophical disciplines – knowing and doing – undergo a reevaluation as well. Fichte's novel thinking about the relation between the theoretical and the practical is most prominent in his account of the two key features that make up human rationality, viz., intelligence and will. In his redrawing of the borders between the cognitive and the conative, Fichte emphasizes the practical aspects of knowing as well as the theoretical aspects of willing. Yet while implicating intelligence and will in each other to a considerable degree, Fichte is careful not to collapse their distinction. Rather than simply identifying the two, he works out their original proximity, thus maintaining a delicate balance between unity and division, which he himself addresses as the mind's "duplicity" and specifically "original duplicity" (ursprüngliche Duplizität).[3]

The dual unity or unitary duality of intelligence and will in the *Wissenschaftslehre* thus provides a key to Fichte's overall project of integrating a transcendental theory of knowledge and a transcendental theory of freedom into a comprehensive account of the principal structures and strictures of human reason. And since on a transcendental account such as Fichte's the principal conditions of knowing and willing are also the principal conditions of the world of objects of such knowing and willing, Fichte's integrated double theory of intelligence and will also provides a principal account of the objects involved in thinking and willing. Indeed, much of that first, most influential phase of Fichte's work on the *Wissenschaftslehre* is a systematic attempt to trace the overt distinctions between the worlds of theory and practice, of knowing and doing, to their complex yet unitary ground in an intelligence that is also practical.

As a transcendental theory of the practical intelligence, the *Wissenschaftslehre* is mainly concerned with the nature and status of the acts and objects of that intelligence. For Fichte, intelligence and will are not, at least not primarily or originally, psychological abilities. Rather, they are considered to be the basic ways in which the human being exists. Moreover, Fichte emphasizes the active as well as the productive nature of thinking and willing: Intelligence and will are the principal ways in which the human being exists through its own doing and making – either as theoretical, cognitive activity or as practical, volitional activity. Finally, the dynamism of the self-constitution of the practical intelligence is coupled with a productionism regarding the objects of knowing and willing.

Yet the radically idealist orientation of the *Wissenschaftslehre* is counterbalanced by a thoroughgoing concern with the reality that the acts and objects of the practical intelligence have. Fichte seeks to elucidate the role of the given as the material basis and the ineliminable restraint on any making and producing through the practical intelligence. In addition, he stresses that the intelligent and practical activity is restrained internally, through the universal laws that govern it. In line with his basic point about the mutual involvement of the theoretical and the practical, Fichte is particularly attentive to the practical core of cognition in the form of feeling and to the cognitive core of volition in the recognition of some guiding law that is integral to the will.

The complex interplay of intelligence and will in Fichte's transcendental double theory of knowledge and freedom emerges gradually over the course of his lecturing and publication activities in Jena (1794–1799) and their afterlude during his first year in Berlin (1799–1800). The terminological and philosophical development of Fichte's systematic transcendental philosophy reaches from the first published presentation of the *Wissenschaftslehre*, the *Foundation of the Entire Wissenschaftslehre* (1794–1795), through its radically revised presentation in several lecture courses and related publications (1796–1799) to its masterly restatement under a less technical, more popular guise in *The Vocation of Man* (1800).

During this time period Fichte resorts with increasing frequency and subtle modifications to the distinction between the real and the ideal in order to capture the relation between intelligence and will. Over the course of those years, the ideal assumes the double function of the (retentive) cognition of what is and the (protentive) cognition of what ought to be. Analogously, the real comes to stand both for the objects of the already existing empirical world and for the yet to be brought about objects of willing. The mutual implication of will and intellect – that willing involves thinking and that thinking involves willing – is mirrored in the double roles of the ideal and the real. That which is ideal in the practical sense – the goal of rational willing – is also that which is *truly* real, whereas that which is real by the standards of theoretical cognition – the objects of experience – is also that which is *merely* ideal.

The emergence of a practical, volitional sense of the ideal in the Jena *Wissenschaftslehre* terminates in a conception of purely rational volition ("pure will"), which, although not empirically real, has the reality of an entity of necessary thinking, that is, of a noumenon. According to Fichte, that which can only be thought – and which moreover must be so thought – has a reality far more substantial *in a practical regard* than the one possessed by the objects of theoretical cognition. And yet Fichte's practical idealism-realism with its emphasis on pure willing as that which is most real rests on the very *thinking* of such a will; it is the intellect through and for which such a being has its reality or, for that matter, ideality. The mutual implication of intelligence and will remains. Something real that would not also be an object of thought, that would not be subject to the latter's conditions and forms, would be nothing to us. It is at this point in the development of the *Wissenschaftslehre* that Fichte realizes the need to supplement the account of intelligent and practical activity given so far with an account of the unthinkable ground of all thinking and willing, alternatively identified as "infinite will" in the popular language of *The Vocation of Man* or as "the absolute" in the terminology of the later *Wissenschaftslehre*.

The following chapters provide a detailed reconstruction of Fichte's sustained reflections on intelligence and will, theory and practice, the real and the ideal, as well as their complex relationships. Fichte's thinking on the matter is traced from the beginnings of the *Wissenschaftslehre* and its methodological specifics through the core doctrines of two of its magisterial presentations right to the threshold of the late *Wissenschaftslehre* with its problematic turn of Fichte's thinking toward the unthinkable. In the process, the chapters cover much of his main writings from the philosophically most influential phase of his philosophical career. In their entirety, the chapters seek to provide an account of Fichte's theory of theoretical and practical reason that locates him in the systematic tradition of transcendental philosophy.

By focusing on the fundamental role of willing and the precariously close relation between thinking and willing in Fichte, this reading seeks to identify his original position in the post-Kantian debate about the unitary structure of subjectivity. Fichte's insistence on the twofold origin or originary duplicity of the human mind avoids both reductive simplification and additive pluralization in accounting for the transcendental conditions of human mental life. His emphasis on the mutual implication of the two key constituents of human subjectivity provides an original model for dynamic conceptions of selfhood. Finally, Fichte's increased recognition of the ultimate instability of subjectivity so conceived, and the need he perceived to ground the subject in something else and entirely unlike itself, makes him the first to carry the conception of radically self-sufficient subjectivity, which he himself pioneered, to its limits and to start exploring in systematic form a radically different conception of the subject's ultimate ground.

The proposed Kantian reading of Fichte as a transcendental philosopher intent on vindicating freedom to the theory of the principles of knowledge and its objects is meant to supplement other recent attempts in Continental and Anglo-American scholarship at retrieving the philosophical potential of the *Wissenschaftslehre*. Those approaches have tended to stress Fichte's contributions to the theory of self-consciousness (Henrich, Neuhouser, Pippin), his pioneering development of a theory of interpersonality (Lauth, Philonenko, Radrizzani), his innovations in practical philosophy (Verweyen, Wood), his engagement of skepticism and relation to the early post-Kantians (Breazeale) and his position in relation to Schelling and Hegel (Girndt, Siep, Baumanns, Lauth). In building on much of that recent literature, the present work addresses the major, first phase of the *Wissenschaftslehre* as a whole, focusing on Fichte's systematic contribution to the transcendental project in general and his transcendental theory of thinking and willing in particular. In so doing, special attention is paid to the interplay between substantial doctrinal specifics and methodological, metaphilosophical considerations in Fichte. The goal is to present Fichte's sustained and probing thinking about the nature of self and world in its most powerful and original aspects – and to do so in clear and concise language that preserves the specific details and overall context of his distinctions and doctrines. As any reader of Fichte knows, criticizing him comes easy; the hard part is making him intelligible.

A distinctive feature of the present approach to Fichte is its orientation toward the second or "new presentation" (*neue Darstellung*) of the *Wissenschaftslehre* (1796–1799), which is viewed here as the crowning achievement of Fichte's Jena years. By contrast, the earlier, first and only detailed, presentation of the *Wissenschaftslehre* published by Fichte himself, the *Foundation of the Entire Wissenschaftslehre* (1794–95), which for a long time has been the standard version of the *Wissenschaftslehre*, emerges as an initial version that was immediately improved upon by Fichte himself. To be sure, the complete presentation of the *Wissenschaftslehre nova methodo,* as the new presentation was called in Fichte's Latin course announcements, is preserved only in two student lecture transcripts.[4] But between them, they afford a reliable and surprisingly clear picture of Fichte's new presentation of the *Wissenschaftslehre,* confirmed and supplemented by his own publications on the *Wissenschaftslehre* from the same period.

The growing recognition of the *Wissenschaftslehre nova methodo* among scholars and students of Fichte's thought is reflected in the appearance of translations of that work into Italian, Spanish, French and English,[5] the recent publication of a succinct French commentary on the text,[6] its increased use in surveys and general treatments of Fichte's work,[7] as well as a conference, a collection of essays and a journal issue devoted to it.[8] Yet so far there has been no book-length treatment of the *Wissenschaftslehre nova methodo* in English, nor has there been an in-depth study of this work's core concern with the relation of thinking and willing in any language. The present study is designed to fill this lacuna.

With its focus on intelligence and will in Fichte's transcendental philosophy from the Jena years, the book has to forego discussion of important further aspects of his thinking before, during and after that time period. In particular, it was not possible to address in any detail Fichte's relation to philosophical precursors other than Kant and Jacobi or to address in any form his relation to his critics and successors, from Novalis and Hölderlin to Schelling, Hegel and Schopenhauer. Moreover, there is one major philosophical text by Fichte from the period under consideration that is not discussed in greater detail in the present study, viz., the first detailed presentation of the theory of interpersonality in the *Foundation of Natural Law* (1796–97). Although there is no arguing with the many interpreters of Fichte who view his account of the origin of individual consciousness in interpersonal relations in general and his theory of recognition (*Anerken-nung*) and solicitation (*Aufforderung*) in particular as major philosophical contributions to social philosophy, it is far from clear that Fichte's theory of interpersonality supplants his own conception of transcendental subjectivity. Rather than constituting a social ontology outside of individual consciousness and its transcendental conditions, interpersonality emerges within the confines of his transcendental theory of the subject.[9] For this reason, the study addresses the crucial but systematically subordinate role of interpersonality in the context of Fichte's theory of pure willing in the *Wissenschaftslehre nova methodo* without tracing the emergence and development of interpersonality in his earlier writings or addressing the important role of interpersonality in his social philosophy.[10]

The book's eight chapters are organized in four parts with two chapters each. Part I provides an orientation about Fichte's philosophical project in the *Wissenschaftslehre,* emphasizing the relation to Kant and methodological issues. Parts II and III examine the close connection between knowing and doing and between thinking and willing, respectively, in Fichte's transcendental philosophy. Part IV focuses on the crucial role that willing in general and pure willing in particular assume in Fichte.

More specifically, the first chapter examines Fichte's self-interpretation as heir to Kant's transcendental project. It shows how Fichte extends and deepens Kant's transcendental idealism through a sustained methodological reflection on the nature of idealism as a philosophical system. The chapter focuses on the distinction between philosophy or "speculation" and ordinary consciousness or "life" and argues for the reconstructive, model-like nature of Fichte's transcendental account of consciousness and its objects. The second chapter places his basic account of the I as the nonempirical ground of experience into the context of his philosophical procedure. The chapter explores Fichte's self-interpretation of the *Wissenschaftslehre* as a scientific experiment conducted by the philosopher upon himself or herself.

The third chapter reconstructs Fichte's grounding of the distinction between theory and practice in the mind's deep structure with its characteristic activity of "positing." The chapter focuses on the origin of theoretical and practical determination in his account of the I as self-positing. The fourth chapter examines Fichte's account of the practical relation to the world by placing it in the systematic context of the *Wissenschaftslehre.* The stress here is on his theory of action and the transcendental function of the principle of morality.

The fifth chapter deals with Fichte's general account of the relation between thinking and willing. It shows how for Fichte willing is a form of thinking, and it addresses his conception of pure willing as what is ultimately real for the practical intelligence. The sixth chapter builds on this by reconstructing Fichte's puzzling reconceptualization of knowing and doing as ideal thinking and real thinking, respectively.

The seventh chapter traces the development of Fichte's thinking about the will. The focus is on his distinction between deliberative and predeliberative willing and his adoption of the Kantian conception of pure will as pure practical reason. The concluding chapter relates Fichte's theory of the pure will to his account of the unity of thinking and willing. The emphasis is on the relation between the sensible and the intelligible world and on the systematic role of faith.

The main works by Fichte discussed in these chapters are the first major presentation of the *Wissenschaftslehre* from 1794–95 (Chapter 3) and the second, radically revised, presentation of the *Wissenschaftslehre* from 1796–99 (Chapters 5, 6, 7 and 8). The treatment of those two main presentations of the *Wissenschaftslehre* is supplemented by the discussion of several of Fichte's other writings from the period that expand the *Wissenschaftslehre* by providing introductory reflections on its methods and goals or by applying its principles and results to specific areas of philosophical inquiry. Among the further writings considered are the "Theory of the Will" added to the second edition of the *Attempt at a Critique of All Revelation* from 1793 (Chapter 7),[11] the programmatic brochure *On the Concept of the Wissenschaftslehre* from 1794 (Chapter 1), the two introductions to the new presentation of the *Wissenschaftslehre* from 1797–98 (Chapters 1 and 2) published by Fichte himself, *The System of Ethics* from 1798 (Chapters 4 and 7), *The Vocation of Man* from 1800 (Chapter 8) and the *Crystal Clear Report to the General Public concerning the Actual Essence of the Newest Philosophy* from 1801, although written for the most part in 1800 (Chapter 1).[12]

The book is intended for a dual, though hopefully not duplicitous, audience. To philosophically inclined readers who have never read or never understood Fichte, it may serve as a survey and advanced introduction that presupposes some knowledge of Kant but little or no knowledge of Fichte. To students and scholars already familiar with Fichte, it offers a unified interpretation under a guiding theme. But it might be an exaggeration to claim, with Fichte, that this book "ought to be intelligible to all readers who are able to understand a book at all."[13]

PART I

THINKING ABOUT THINKING

COMPLETING KANT'S
TRANSCENDENTAL IDEALISM

Both systematically and historically, Fichte's *Wissenschaftslehre* represents a further development of Kant's critical philosophy, prepared and inspired by the latter's earlier reception through Karl Leonhard Reinhold, Gottlob Ernst Schulze, Friedrich Heinrich Jacobi and Salomon Maimon. Fichte's relation to his illustrious predecessor is a curious mixture of unconditional allegiance and metacritical distancing. By applying such hermeneutical devices as the distinction between the letter (*Buchstabe*) and the spirit (*Geist*)[1] of an author's philosophical system and the separation of the system itself from its various presentations (*Darstellungen*), Fichte establishes a precarious balance between loyalty and patricide in his relationship to Kant. In so doing, Fichte is supported by Kant's own claim, originally raised with respect to Plato, that it is possible for an author to be better understood by someone else than by himself or herself.[2]

The basic direction of Fichte's move with Kant beyond Kant points toward a completion of what is prepared, begun and partially executed in the latter's critical philosophy. Fichte's project aims both at a more radical foundation and at a more extensive elaboration of the investigation of reason initiated by Kant, thereby integrating Kant's work in the three *Critiques* into a comprehensive, systematically unified account of (finite) reason. Drawing on Kant's own architectonic distinction between the "propaedeutic" and the "system of pure reason,"[3] Fichte claims to transform the "*critique* of pure reason" into the "*system of pure reason*," which, Fichte maintains, Kant never provided.[4]

Yet in spite of the delegation of Kant's critical philosophy, and specifically the *Critique of Pure Reason*, to a mere preliminary stage of the *Wis-*

senschaftslehre, Fichte does not give up the Kantian project of preparing the ground for philosophy proper by way of introductory considerations, specifically designed to orient the reader about the task, subject matter and method of philosophy.[5] On the contrary, the first major phase of Fichte's work on the *Wissenschaftslehre* (1793–1800), roughly coinciding with his professorship at Jena (1794–1799), is characterized by a parallel process of critical or introductory writings and systematic writings. Fichte's sustained theorizing *about* the *Wissenschaftslehre* accompanies the latter's development during the Jena years like a running commentary, in which he articulates the nature of his philosophical project with increasing clarity as well as polemical force.

At the center of Fichte's critical thinking about the *Wissenschaftslehre* stands the conception of transcendental idealism as the doctrinal core that assures the ultimate identity of his system with that of Kant. Occasioned by the misinterpretations and misunderstandings that the *Wissenschaftslehre* encountered upon its first appearance, Fichte advances a self-interpretation of transcendental idealism that combines insight into the origin of transcendental-idealist reasoning with the recognition of the extension and specifically the limits of all such thinking. Fichte thus extends Kant's critical investigation of the possibility of objective knowledge and its systematic completion in the *Wissenschaftslehre* through a critical investigation of philosophical knowledge itself, thereby radicalizing the project of philosophical critique from philosophy's critique of object knowledge to the metaphilosophy of philosophical knowledge.

This chapter is organized in three sections. The first section assesses the nature and function of transcendental idealism in Kant's critical philosophy. The second one examines Fichte's self-interpretation of the *Wissenschaftslehre* as a system of transcendental idealism. This middle section is based on his programmatic brochure *On the Concept of the Wissenschaftslehre* (1794) as well as the (so-called First) Introduction to the fragmentary *Attempt at a New Presentation of the Wissenschaftslehre* (1797). The concluding section examines Fichte's metacritical assessment of transcendental idealism in the *Crystal Clear Report to the General Public concerning the Actual Essence of the Newest Philosophy* (1801).

1. The Systematic Significance of Transcendental Idealism in Kant

During the 1780s Kant's conception of a critique of pure reason evolved from the originally planned single work under that title (1781), suitably characterized as a "critique of pure speculative reason," to include two further installments in the form of a critique of practical reason (1788) and a critique of reflective judgment (1790). According to Kant, the unity of the critical trilogy is assured by the unity of reason in its threefold employment as theoretical understanding, practical reason and aesthetico-teleological judgment.[6] The three-step development of the critical philosophy shows clearly in the expansion of the central critical question "How are synthetic judgments a priori possible?" from theoretical judgments concerning nature through practical judgments concerning the grounds of volition to reflective judgments concerning the grounds of pleasure and displeasure.[7] In each case the answer to the question involves the appeal to a priori subjective conditions that first make possible one of the three principal forms of nonempirical judgmental synthesis.

The parallel grounding of specifically different claims to objective validity in universal and necessary but subjective conditions might suggest a generic idealism of epistemic, thelematic and hedonic forms.[8] Yet in Kant the extension of the transcendental question does not go hand in hand with an analogous extension of the doctrine of transcendental idealism. On the contrary, the latter remains specific to the first, theoretical *Critique* and its restriction of all (theoretical) knowledge to the realm of appearances, whereas the second and third *Critiques* supplement the phenomenal restriction of theoretical knowledge with the practical and reflective extension of knowledge beyond the limits of experience into the domains of moral and teleological thinking. Thus, Kant's theoretical transcendental idealism is balanced by a critically mitigated nonempirical realism on ethical and ethico-teleological grounds that rehabilitates metaphysics in a moral guise.[9]

But not only does Kant not extend the appellation of "transcendental idealism" to all doctrines involving a priori subjective conditions of claims for objective validity. Even within the *Critique of Pure Reason* he restricts the phraseology of transcendental idealism and transcendental ideality to those aspects of the work that appeal to the role of sensibility in the constitution of objective knowledge. In the Transcendental Aesthetic the predicate "transcendental ideality" is originally attributed to the a priori forms of sensible intuition and secondarily to that of which they are the formal principles, viz., the appearances. The introduction of the very term "transcendental idealism" in the "Paralogisms of Pure Reason" in the first edition and in the "Antinomy of Pure Reason" in the second edition traces the phenomenal status of empirical objects to the fact that they are intuited in space and time.[10]

Conversely, neither the a priori concepts of the understanding (categories) nor the a priori concepts of theoretical reason (transcendental ideas) *as such* are ever characterized in terms of transcendental ideality and transcendental idealism. On the contrary, both the categories and the transcendental ideas are shown to originate independent of sensibility and its forms and to have some significance beyond the confines of the realm of appearances. It is only through their (theoretical) cognition-geared application to the manifold of space and time that the categories become restricted to appearances. The categories as such (as a priori forms of thinking) are not affected by the conditions of sensibility.[11]

The strict dissociation of the term and concept of transcendental idealism from the core of Kant's critique of understanding, reason and judgment points to a fundamental distinction between the Transcendental Aesthetic of the first *Critique* and the rest of the critical trilogy, including the Transcendental Logic of the *Critique of Pure Reason*. As a doctrine concerning the forms of sensibility and the features of objects due to those forms, transcendental idealism does not directly pertain to the concepts, principles and object domains of the "upper," rational registers of the faculties of cognition, volition and feeling examined in the three *Critiques*.

To be sure, the doctrine of transcendental idealism is of fundamental importance in Kant's critical project in allowing the theoretical realization of the categories in some pure sensible manifold in the first *Critique* and in negatively delineating a conceptual space for nontheoretical cognition and faith in the second and third *Critiques*. Still, the presentation of the doctrine remains outside of the critique of the *rational* capacities – as indicated by the historical origin of the Transcendental Aesthetic in the semicritical theory of the form and principles of the sensible world in the Inaugural-Dissertation from 1770.[12]

Moreover, the very term "transcendental ideality," as employed in the Transcendental Aesthetic of the *Critique of Pure Reason,* points back to the precritical and pre-Kantian understanding of "ideality" as "nullity" (*Nullität*) and of "transcendental" as "concerning the absolute nature of things." Predicating "transcendental ideality" of space and time qua forms of sensibility means to deny that they have any "meaning" (*Bedeutung*) for the way things are independent of our forms of sensing or to assert that they are "nothing" (*nichts*) with respect to things in themselves.[13]

The unique position of the Transcendental Aesthetic and its doctrine of transcendental idealism within the critical trilogy can be traced back to a crucial difference between the *sensible* a priori conditions of appearances elucidated in the Transcendental Aesthetic and the various *rational* conditions of objective validity established in the three *Critiques*. Space and time are the a priori forms of the mind's undergoing affections; they are the ways in which the mind receives determination. By contrast, the a priori forms and principles of the understanding, of reason and of judgment are the ways in which the mind actively brings about determination: by determining the object, determining the will or determining the feeling of pleasure and displeasure, respectively.[14]

But Kant's continued insistence on the equivalence between the ideality or nullity of representations (with regard to their forms) and the mind's passivity or receptivity in having those representations not only introduces a fundamental distinction between the theory of sensibility and the theory of spontaneous reason: It even entails a distinction between the receptive and spontaneous sides of space and time themselves. Whereas the Transcendental Aesthetic treats of space and time as passive forms of *intuiting*, the Transcendental Analytic considers space and time as *intuited* or as objects in their own right that reflect the formative influence of some activity, thereby effectuating the required mediation between sensibility and the understanding.[15] It therefore comes as no surprise that the very doctrine that pioneered the transcendental turn in Kant, viz., his theory of a priori forms of sensibility, was to become a chief target of the post-Kantian revisions of his work.

In addition to the systematic, architectonic reasons for not subjecting the notion of transcendental idealism to a comprehensive enlargement and making its scope coextensive with that of the entire transcendental project, there may well have been strategic considerations that spoke against such a move in Kant's eyes. After all, it was the doctrine of transcendental idealism that attracted some of the most vehement attacks and misunderstandings in the early reception of the *Critique of Pure Reason,* which led Kant to advance the alternative appellations "formal" and "critical idealism" for his doctrine.[16]

The original restriction of transcendental idealism to the theory of sensibility in Kant is also evident in the fact that he does not resort to formulations such as "system of transcendental idealism" to characterize his overall project of a critique of reason.[17] Kant's extensive reflections on the architectonic of philosophy in general and that of the critical philosophy in particular[18] are not cast in any specifically idealist terminology. For Kant, transcendental idealism is a "doctrinal concept" (*Lehrbegriff*), designed to account for the peculiar status of space and time as nondiscursive yet a priori representational forms.[19]

Moreover, to Kant's ear the phrase "system of transcendental idealism" would not designate the sum total of transcendental philosophy. When used in connection with "doctrinal concepts" such as preestablished harmony and occasionalism, to which one might add Kant's own transcendental idealism, the term "system" in Kant retains its older meaning of an account developed in order to explain a certain range of phenomena, as in talk about the Ptolemaic and Copernican "systems" in astronomy. The specific range of phenomena to be explained by Kant's strict, narrow conception of transcendental idealism would not warrant any identification of that system with transcendental philosophy *tout court.*

2. The *Wissenschaftslehre* as System of Transcendental Idealism

The Kantian basic terms "critique," "system" and "idealism" figure prominently in Fichte's sustained reflection on the form, method and goal of the *Wissenschaftslehre*. Yet in Fichte those terms enter into a constellation that makes them differ in significant regards from their earlier usage in Kant.[20] The terms in question receive their revised meaning from their relation to the fundamental notion of the *Wissenschaftslehre* itself.

Fichte's choice of the term "*Wissenschaftslehre*" for his project of a radicalized transcendental philosophy draws on the etymological connection as well as the semantic proximity of the German words for "science" and "knowledge" (*Wissenschaft, Wissen*). For Fichte philosophy is concerned with the nature of knowledge as such and can be described as the search for knowledge regarding knowledge. More specifically, the knowledge peculiar to philosophy is the knowledge of the most general features of knowledge, a metaknowledge that can be termed "transcendental" in that it transcends the specifics of any particular kind of knowledge while remaining within the confines of knowledge in general.

Whereas the term "*Wissen*" ("knowledge") in Fichte primarily designates the epistemic modality of philosophy qua *Wissenschaftslehre,* distinguishing the latter from mere opinion (*Meinung*) as well as belief or faith (*Glaube*), the term "*Wissenschaft*" ("science") addresses the epistemic form or structure of philosophy and indeed of all knowledge. That form is "systematic form"[21] or the form of a system, in which individual instances of knowledge receive their character as knowledge (*Gewißheit*) from their relation to basic propositions or principles (*Grundsätze*) that function as the ultimate source of certainty in all knowledge. Fichte stresses that systematic form is not sufficient for knowledge in that the form of a system can also pertain to a body of beliefs built on some groundless and improvable principle such as the existence of aerial spirits.[22] Moreover, systematic form belongs to science only contingently. The form of a system is not the purpose of a science but only its means required by the contingent fact that human beings know very little with certainty and need to establish certain knowledge by tracking their beliefs to paradigmatic instances of certain knowledge.[23]

In Fichte's first conception of the *Wissenschaftslehre,* as published in 1794–95, the systematic form of philosophy involves the initial presentation of the supreme principles of all knowledge, which in turn constitute a subsystem of knowledge, and the subsequent derivation of the main features of all knowledge from those principles.[24] But soon Fichte came to replace the beginning of the *Wissenschaftslehre* by way of separately presented principles with an alternative presentation, first presented in lecture form in 1796–97, that takes its departure from the postulate of reflecting on the form and structure of one's knowledge, thus integrating the foundations of knowledge into the development of its principal structure.[25]

Fichte's use of the term "system" to designate the architectonic form of knowledge is not restricted to the system of philosophical knowledge. Fichte argues that the very possibility of developing a system of knowledge regarding knowledge in the *Wissenschaftslehre* presupposes that knowledge as such have systematic form; hence, "the object of the *Wissenschaftslehre* is . . . the system of human knowledge."[26] Thus, the term "system" designates both the form of philosophical knowledge and the form of the object of philosophical knowledge. What links the two instances is the systematic nature of knowledge in general, of which philosophical knowledge regarding knowledge is just one instance.

Fichte tends to transfer the designation "system" as applied to the overall system of human knowledge to the mind as such and to characterize the object of the system of philosophical knowledge as "the system of the human mind."[27] To be sure, not everything contained in the mind is part of the latter's system. Fichte distinguishes between the representations (*Vorstellungen*) in the mind that arise freely and arbitrarily and hence without systematic connection to the rest of the mind, on the one hand, and the representations that arise with necessity, thus exhibiting systematic connection, on the other hand. The mind qua system is the system of the latter kind of representations, which Fichte also terms "the system of experience,"[28] stressing the compulsory nature of objective representations.[29]

The task of philosophy is to determine the ground of experience so conceived. Since the ground of experience falls necessarily outside of experience, a basic distinction is introduced between knowledge regarding experience, including the sciences, and philosophical knowledge regarding the nonempirical ground of knowledge. According to Fichte, both kinds of knowledge admit of systematic form.

In determining the nonempirical ground of all empirical knowledge, the *Wissenschaftslehre* provides a representation (*Darstellung*) of the system of the human mind. Fichte captures the representational nature of the *Wissenschaftslehre* with respect to the mind qua system of knowledge in the following description of the philosopher's activity: "We are not lawgivers of the human mind but its historiographers; to be sure, not journalists but writers of pragmatic history."[30] While stressing the independence of the mind's system from its theoretization in the system of philosophical knowledge, the analogy to historiography still suggests the philosopher's active and purpose-oriented role in writing the transcendental history of the mind.[31]

In addition to designating both the scientific form of human knowledge in general and that of specifically philosophical knowledge regarding all other knowledge, the term "system" in Fichte also refers to any particular philosophical system developed as an account of the ground of experience. The procedure of reconstructing the nonempirical ground of empirical knowledge originates in the philosopher's freely chosen act of separating what is united in experience, focusing on one element of experience at the expense of any other, thereby ascending from the level of actual experience to that of the latter's structural condition or ground.

Since the only principal factors that are connected in and through experience are the experienced thing (*Ding*) and the experiencing intelligence (*Intelligenz*), the procedure of philosophy results in two and only two alternative accounts of the ground of experience. If the thing experienced is raised from its status as a factor of experience to that of the ground of experience and considered in abstraction from experience, then the thing is reconfigured as a "thing in itself" (*Ding an sich*); if the intelligence undergoing experience is elevated from the status of an ingredient of experience to that of its ground and considered in isolation from experience, then the intelligence is reconfigured as an "intelligence in itself" (*Intelligenz an sich*) or "I in itself" (*Ich an sich*).[32]

Fichte terms the procedure of accounting for experience by way of a thing in itself "dogmatism" and calls the opposite procedure of explaining experience by appeal to some "intelligence in itself" "idealism." In assessing the difference between the two philosophical systems, Fichte stresses that the thing in itself of the dogmatic system is a mere "fiction" (*Erdichtung*) that has no reality in experience as such and could only be validated through the successful derivation of the system of experience from the thing in itself. By contrast, the absolute intelligence or I of the idealist system is not merely a hypothetical device awaiting confirmation through its explanatory potential but figures within consciousness as the "immediate self-consciousness . . . that occurs in a free action of the mind."[33] As an object of philosophical consciousness, the "I in itself" is of a unique kind: it is neither entirely made like a fictional being nor is it entirely given like an independently existing thing. Rather, it is given in its existence, while being determinable through the free intelligence with regard to its determinations.[34]

Fichte maintains that neither of the two principal philosophical systems is able to refute the other one, but he still argues for the speculative as well as practical superiority of the idealist system over the dogmatic system. The materialist monism implied by dogmatism is unable to account for the structural difference between intelligent beings, which are what they are for themselves – thus exhibiting a characteristic duality of being and knowing one's being – and nonintelligent beings, which are what they are not for themselves but only for others.[35] Moreover, the delegation of all independence from experience to some thing in itself fails to do justice to the human interest in absolute independence to be realized through free self-determination.[36] Yet none of these arguments will convince the dogmatist, who – on Fichte's account – simply lacks the belief (*Glaube*) in freedom that motivates the systematic pursuit of freedom by means of idealism.[37]

For Fichte, the philosophical systems of idealism and dogmatism are not products of some detached, artificial reasoning but are deeply rooted in an individual's overall disposition. More specifically, one's philosophical system reflects which of the two one believes to be originally absolute and independent of the other, whether the thing or the self. As Fichte himself explains the matter in commenting on his well-known dictum that the philosophy one chooses – whether dogmatism or idealism – depends on the human being one is: "a philosophical system is not some lifeless household item one can put aside or pick up as one wishes, but is animated by the soul of the human being whose system it is."[38]

Fichte's outright existentialist grounding of the philosophical system in an individual's protophilosophical outlook, together with his own profession of a basic belief in the original independence of the self from all thingly reality, leads him to advance an idealist philosophical system centered around the notion of the self as spontaneous intelligent activity (*Tun*) that is originally independent from anything other than itself. Yet the freedom from all external influence that lies at the heart of Fichte's idealism is not tantamount to lawless irregularity or personal caprice. Rather, the intelligent activity operates according to laws that are part of its own being and that provide determination to its activity and to the products of that activity. The fundamental law (*Grundgesetz*) behind all particular laws of the intelligent activity is that the intelligent being "gives itself its own laws in the course of its acting."[39]

Fichte contrasts his own "critical or transcendental idealism," which presupposes the original determination of the intelligence through its own laws and thus admits of a "system of necessary modes of acting,"[40] to "transcendent idealism," whose presupposition of an absolutely lawless intelligent activity contradicts the very idea of a system of the mind.[41]

Within critical or transcendental idealism Fichte further distinguishes between a "higher, complete criticism,"[42] which actually derives the system of mental activities from the basic laws of the intelligent being, on the one hand, and an incomplete idealism, which merely abstracts those laws from the objects of experience, on the other hand.[43] The latter form of transcendental idealism is incomplete in that it explains only the formal relational properties of a thing through the laws of intelligent activity but leaves the very matter (*Stoff*) unexplained, thus inviting a dogmatic interpretation of the thing as originally independent from the intelligent activity. By contrast, in "complete transcendental idealism"[44] the thing qua matter as well as its formal properties are shown to originate according to the laws of the intelligent activity. Thus, the thing in its entirety is derived from the "total" legislation of the intelligent activity.

The systematically incomplete idealism is deficient in yet another regard. It is limited to the laws governing external experience, thus neglecting to address large parts of the "system of reason," notably practical reason and reflective judgment, and amounting to a "half criticism."[45] Although these criticisms could be taken to address Kant's work, Fichte takes great care not to identify incomplete transcendental idealism with Kant's own position but only with that of some of his followers – a move that allows Fichte to credit Kant with the insight that "the object is given neither entirely nor half but rather is made."[46]

The conceptual development of the terms "system" and "transcendental idealism" from their separate usage in Kant to their combined employment in Fichte's notion of a radically idealist system of the mind's activity structure also includes a revised understanding of the nature and place of "critique" within the overall enterprise of philosophy. Fichte contrasts the philosophical system proper with the introduction into the system, in which the philosophy presented in the system becomes the object of a philosophical inquiry into its possibility, conditions and rules. His title for such a metaphilosophical introduction into philosophy proper is "critique." He even grants the introductory investigations undertaken in a critique the status of a system in its own right.[47]

According to Fichte, the relation between critique and philosophy proper – the latter being alternatively referred to as "metaphysics" and "*Wissenschaftslehre*" – is analogous to the relation between the *Wissenschaftslehre* and the ordinary, nonphilosophical standpoint. In both cases philosophy – in its capacity as critique or as *Wissenschaftslehre*, respectively – critiques a form or level of thinking: In one case it is philosophical thinking itself that is being critiqued; in the other case what is critiqued is natural thinking.[48] The relation of double critique thus established between philosophical thinking and its object allows Fichte to retain the specifically critical stand of philosophy introduced by Kant, while enlarging the critical project by a metacritique of philosophy's critique of natural thinking.

In Kant, Fichte finds the two levels of philosophical critique confused and the so-called critique for the most part concerned with metaphysics. The inverse deficiency still holds, as Fichte himself concedes, for the *Wissenschaftslehre*, whose elaborations so far given include elements of an introductory or metacritical nature. Moreover, for Fichte, advances in metaphilosophical understanding and advances in the presentation of the *Wissenschaftslehre* go hand in hand. A complete systematic account of the procedure of the *Wissenschaftslehre* is only to be expected once a "pure presentation of the *Wissenschaftslehre* itself" becomes possible.[49]

3. The Metacritique of Transcendental Idealism

In addition to addressing the relation between the idealist and the dogmatist system of philosophy, Fichte's sustained metaphilosophical reflections also include extensive discussions of the relation between the viewpoint of philosophy and the viewpoint of ordinary consciousness. In response to objections and misunderstandings encountered by the first presentations of the *Wissenschaftslehre,* Fichte addresses the very nature of the *Wissenschaftslehre,* stressing the limits as much as the possibilities of his radically idealist system. The central concern of his metacritical self-interpretation is to dispel the contemporary perception of the *Wissenschaftslehre* as an ontological idealism that teaches the production of the world through the mind. Fichte clarifies the scope of systematic idealism by emphasizing the role of extraphilosophical reality and by focusing on the reconstructive nature of the *Wissenschaftslehre.*

Fichte's critical reflections on the relation between philosophy and reality are part of his response to the critique of the *Wissenschaftslehre* in two open letters addressed to him in 1799, each written by a leading figure of late-eighteenth-century German thought, Kant and Jacobi.[50] In his "Declaration regarding the *Wissenschaftslehre*" Kant distances himself from a self-proclaimed follower who had become a liability to the Kantian movement by getting embroiled in a series of professional scandals, culminating in atheism charges and the loss of his professorship at Jena. Kant turns Fichte's charge that the former had only provided a philosophical propaedeutics against the *Wissenschaftslehre* itself, arguing that, far from being genuine metaphysics, it is merely a logic, thus devoid of content and without reference to reality.

Jacobi's open letter treats the *Wissenschaftslehre* as a case study in the spiritual dangers of the Kantian revolution in philosophy. For Jacobi, the transcendental idealism introduced by Kant and radicalized by Fichte dissolves reality into a mere figment of the mind. Rather than combating skepticism, Fichte's *Wissenschaftslehre* is seen as supporting doubt in everyday reality by replacing the realist worldview of ordinary consciousness with the idealist production of a world that is nothing but appearances and hence appearances of nothing. In his earlier critique of Kant, Jacobi had already coined the term "nihilism," which he reuses in the letter to Fichte to brandish the metaphysical and moral implications of transcendental idealism.[51]

In the *Crystal Clear Report* Fichte responds to his prominent critics by claiming an identical "tendency" in Kant's, Jacobi's and his own philosophy, viz., the recognition that all thinking, whether philosophical or ordinary, has its basis as well as its end in experience.[52] Following Jacobi, Fichte designates the reality provided by experience through the term "life."[53] Both in Fichte and in Jacobi, the notion of life as the sustaining core of reality goes beyond the narrowly biological and conveys the presence of subjective mental, even spiritual, factors that animate reality. Fichte explicitly excludes an absolutist reading of life as detached from possible or actual consciousness.[54]

Fichte expands Jacobi's notion of life to include even the detached ("speculative") life form of philosophy. Rather than merely contrasting life and speculation, Fichte links the two by distinguishing them as gradations of life, termed "potencies" (*Potenzen*).[55] Ordinary consciousness and its world of objects is the first potency of life, on which all further gradations are based. In ordinary consciousness the self is completely immersed in its experience, to the point of forgetting itself and its role in the constitution of experience.[56] By raising itself to the level of reflection on experience, consciousness actualizes the second potency of life in which the consciousness present at the first level becomes an object for philosophical consciousness.

Fichte stresses that life in the first potency is fully functional and complete. The higher gradations of life, of which only the first one is philosophically interesting and all subsequent ones consist in empty iterations, do not complete the most basic, primary potency of life but supplement it through contingent mental efforts. Hence, the fundamental difference between the two potencies of life remains. The essential character of life in the first potency is its pregivenness: objects appear to consciousness as ready-made and as imposing themselves on the mind. By contrast, life in the second potency is entirely the product of the mind's spontaneous activity.[57]

Their radical distinction notwithstanding, ordinary and philosophical consciousness are also intimately related. Life in the second potency is about life in the first potency. To be sure, philosophical life does not simply repeat ordinary life. Rather, it provides an account of the latter that seeks to understand the inner, hidden workings of ordinary consciousness. Fichte likens the business of philosophy as conducted in the *Wissenschaftslehre* to the demonstration of a watch. Explaining the workings of a watch involves the exhibition of its design, which accounts for the systematic arrangement of the parts in a functioning whole. Analogously, the idealist explanation of experience exhibits the systematic constitution of experience by relating the principal parts of experience to some overall unifying conception.[58] Philosophical life is as little capable of replacing ordinary life as the demonstration of a watch can be a substitute for an actual timekeeper.[59]

Now, given the restrictions of human knowledge, the teleological explanation of the systematic features of experience through the *Wissenschaftslehre* cannot presuppose some actual cosmic artisan that would make the world of experience, as it were, tick.[60] Moreover, on Fichte's account, the elements and laws that constitute the system of experience are not of a merely mechanical nature but have the organic qualities of self-motion and self-generation (*Selbsterzeugung*).[61] Unlike the demonstration of a watch, which involves the theoretical reinvent of a previously invented artifact, the philosophical reinvention of experience involves the construction of a system that as such exists only in and through contingent philosophical reflection. More precisely, philosophical reflection does not actually produce that system but functions as the occasion for the self-generation of the system of experience out of a presupposed first principle.

To be sure, the consciousness thus generated under the philosopher's observing eye is not ordinary consciousness or life in the first potency itself but the latter's "image" (*Abbildung*).[62] The systematic structure of experience does not belong to experience *per se* but to experience speculatively considered. Fichte thus returns to Kant's usage of the term "system" to designate primarily a philosophical account of some object domain, or that object domain itself insofar as it is considered by philosophical reason. Accordingly, the term "image" as applied to the philosopher's account of ordinary experience should be taken to convey the formed, artificially shaped nature of that consciousness, due to which it serves as a model – in Fichte's view, as the only acceptable model – of experience in its systematic unity.

The model-theoretical understanding of the imaging relation between ordinary consciousness and its philosophical reinvention receives further confirmation from Fichte's account of the applicability and, indeed, application of the former to the latter. According to Fichte, the freely initiated but lawfully generated determinations of consciousness are not merely internally consistent but predictive of the determinations of actual consciousness and thus permit a priori knowledge of the latter's principal features.[63] Fichte compares the relation between the two sets of determinations to that between pure geometry and its application to field measurements. Just as the a priori geometrical relations that hold in pure space apply to empirical space, so the a priori features of philosophically reconstructed consciousness apply to ordinary consciousness.

As in the earlier analogy between philosophical activity and the demonstration of a watch, Fichte resorts to teleological thinking in order to explain the match between imaged and actual consciousness. This time an analogy is set up between the philosophical reconstruction of ordinary consciousness and spatial measuring as the geometrical reconstruction of some empirically given space. In both cases the reconstruction is carried out under the presupposition of an original construction that is to be reconstructed through judgment and measurement, respectively. And as in the analogy with the watch, the presupposition is a methodological device with no implication as to the actual existence of some divine watchmaker or spacemaker.[64] Actual consciousness is considered "as though" (*als ob, gleichsam, gleich als ob*)[65] it were the result of some actual construction along the lines of its virtual construction in philosophical consciousness.

Fichte outright calls the philosophical account of ordinary consciousness a "fiction" (*Fiktion*) that is not to be confused with a "narrative of some true event which occured at some particular time."[66] The original construction of ordinary consciousness, as presupposed in the latter's philosophical reconstruction, is an artificial model of ordinary consciousness that allows the prediction of the main features of experience. It should not be taken to imply a generation or construction on the part of actual ordinary consciousness. On Fichte's understanding, the life of ordinary consciousness is not a matter of generating or constructing, but of finding: "Our existing world is all ready. . . . Life is not a producing but a finding."[67]

Fichte's insistence on the facticity of actual life and on the fictional nature of philosophy point toward a system of transcendental idealism that is quite akin to the teleological interpretation of mind and world in the *Critique of Judgment* with its treatment of systematic unity on the basis of an analogy to human design.[68] His metaphilosophical reflections in the immediate aftermath of his Jena years place the systematic idealist account of knowlegde in the broader context of an account of human existence that acknowledges the presence of a dimension that sustains knowledge while resisting its grasp. The later developments of the *Wissenschaftslehre* are further stages in Fichte's realization of the ground and limits of the transcendental-idealist system.

AN EYE FOR AN I

Doxographical wisdom has it that Fichte is the "philosopher of the I." Such stereotypical characterization is usually accompanied by the reminder that Fichte possessed an ego worthy of his philosophical subject matter, a biographical fact that made him an easy target for satirical portrayal through friend and foe. Yet hidden behind the double screen of schematic labeling and smart caricature lies a powerful philosophical oeuvre marked by a singular blend of speculative enthusiasm and analytic rigor. To be sure, Fichte is not easy to understand; worse yet, Fichte is easy to *misunderstand.* He eschewed established philosophical terminology, continued to modify and revise the presentation of his philosophical position throughout his lifetime and made unprecedented demands for sustained concentration on the listeners of his lectures and the readers of his works.

So, why study an author as dark and difficult as Fichte? The answer is, in short, that in his theorizing about the I, Fichte made a number of methodological and substantial contributions to our understanding of the human mind and its relation to the physical and moral world that have lost nothing of their originality and intellectual power. This chapter is intended to convey some of that originality and power by presenting the main lines of Fichte's thinking on the I during his Jena period.[1] During those years Fichte published the works that established his reputation as the foremost successor to Kant and as the instigator of the post-Kantian philosophical tradition known as German idealism. In his later years, most of which where spent in Berlin, Fichte continued to revise the presentation, if not the substance, of his philosophy in several lecture series, most of which have only recently been made available in their original form and received closer attention.[2]

The account of Fichte's thinking about the I from the Jena period provided in this chapter will first address the very nature of Fichte's philosophy, from there move on to a section on Fichte's idealism, then turn to the method of Fichte's thinking about the I, and following that present Fichte's basic account of the pure I. The chapter concludes with a brief assessment of the status of Fichte's philosophy of the I as a theory of human subjectivity.

1. Philosophy as *Wissenschaftslehre*

Early on in his philosophical career Fichte coined the term "*Wissenschaftslehre*" to convey the status and function of philosophy in general and of his own philosophical work in particular.[3] In line with contemporary usage, the word "science" (*Wissenschaft*) stands for the concept of systematically grounded knowledge. According to Fichte, philosophy is the discipline that provides the principles for all other domains of rigorous, scientific knowledge, while also providing its very own foundations. Fichte's foundationalist conception of knowledge makes philosophy the eminent science, thus changing its nature from the "love of wisdom," as the ancient Greek term would have it, to that of ultimate knowledge, understood as knowledge regarding knowledge.

Fichte's *Wissenschaftslehre* closely resembles Kant's transcendental philosophy. Both deal with a type of knowledge that is central to philosophy and fundamental to knowledge claims in disciplines other than philosophy, viz., synthetic judgments a priori.[4] Yet while crediting Kant with the very idea of a scientifically rigorous philosophy, Fichte insists on the merely propaedeutic nature of Kant's three *Critiques,* which are said to have provided the building material but not the actual construction of the system of philosophical knowledge.[5] Fichte's efforts at completing Kant follow similar attempts by early followers of Kant, most notably Jacob Sigismund Beck and Karl Leonhard Reinhold, to lend a more complete form of presentation to the Kantian doctrines.[6] But the Fichtean transformation of Kantian philosophy goes well beyond the adoption of an alternative mode of exposition and deeply affects the structure of philosophy and its basic tenets.

Following Kant, Fichte presents the *Wissenschaftslehre* as a theory about empirical knowledge, in particular as an account of the nonempirical grounds of experience.[7] The key feature of experience singled out for explanation is the intentionality of representations, that is, their ability to refer to or be about objects. Fichte takes over Kant's analysis of knowledge in terms of the "objective validity" of representations.[8] The objectivity of empirical knowledge is understood as involving the accompaniment of certain representations by the feeling of necessity. Philosophy qua *Wissenschaftslehre* investigates the ground for the feeling of necessity that accompanies representations and makes them more than creatures of our whim. Fichte stresses that the necessity characteristic of empirical knowledge is not an absolute necessity. The necessity in question pertains only to our representing of empirical objects and does not affect the contingency of the empirical objects themselves.[9]

Throughout the Jena period, Fichte's presentation of the *Wissenschaftslehre* as a theory of experience is intervowen with an alternative conception of the *Wissenschaftslehre* as a theory of freedom. Fichte's philosophy takes the reality of human freedom as its starting point, thus using the basic conviction about human freedom as the ultimate resting point for the foundationalist enterprise of the *Wissenschaftslehre*.[10] Fichte's conception of freedom is thoroughly Kantian; freedom is understood as autonomy or rational self-determination. But the systematic function granted to freedom by Fichte far exceeds the confines of Kant's moral understanding of autonomy. Fichte thinks of freedom, more precisely of our belief in freedom, as the foundation of his entire philosophy, in its theoretical as well as its practical parts. Moreover, he soon came to see the very distinction between theoretical and practical philosophy as a problematic Kantian heritage that demanded serious revision through a more integrated account of human mental activity.[11] The innovative role of freedom as the starting point and the ultimate point of concern in Fichte's philosophy is aptly conveyed in his own description of his philosophical project as the "first system of freedom."[12]

The double task of grounding experience and asserting freedom in Fichte's *Wissenschaftslehre* can suitably be brought together under the title of a theory of finite rationality.[13] Fichte has transformed Kant's threefold "critique of pure reason" into a highly integrated, yet complexly structured, system of rationality. The term "rationality" conveys the normative nature of Fichte's enterprise, thus distinguishing it from psychological or anthropological accounts of the human mind. The term "finite" indicates that the norms or laws of mental operations are not of the mind's own, absolutely free making but reflect the irreducible contingency of a being that has reason without being its own ground or reason.

2. The *Wissenschaftslehre* as Idealism

Following a methodological practice of the early post-Kantian debate, Fichte presents his basic philosophical outlook as a "standpoint" (*Standpunkt*) from which to treat the philosophical subject matter of his work.[14] He adopts an idealist standpoint according to which all possible objects of the human mind depend in their reality on the laws and functions of the mind and are for that matter appearances (*Erscheinungen*). It must be stressed that Fichte's

idealism – like that of Kant, which it strongly resembles – is a *transcendental idealism*, an idealism that makes the reality of appearances depend not
on some absolute, superhuman mind or spirit but on the a priori conditions of human mental activity. Fichte explicitly rejects a "transcendent idealism,"[15] which would accord to the mind absolute powers in the production of representations.

Fichte's adoption of the transcendental-idealist standpoint is intimately
tied to his fundamental belief in the reality of freedom. He considers idealism the one and only standpoint from which philosophical reflection can
do justice to the reality of freedom. The goal of preserving the reality of
freedom thus provides a theoretical reason for the idealist standpoint. Yet
Fichte concedes that the effectiveness of the argument for idealism from
the vindication of freedom depends on one's prior conviction of the reality of freedom. The choice of the idealist standpoint presupposes the extraphilosophical conviction that humans have freedom as their essence and
end.[16] On Fichte's view, the lack of such prior conviction results in the adoption of a philosophical standpoint that is systematically indifferent and in
effect inimical to human freedom, viz., the dogmatic standpoint.[17]

For Fichte, idealism and dogmatism constitute the basic alternative of
philosophical standpoints. Both positions address the task of transcendental philosophy to seek the nonempirical ground of experience. The idealist locates that ground in the human mind, whereas the dogmatist locates
it in the thing understood as originally independent of the human mind,
that is, the thing in itself. The philosopher's choice between those two basic
standpoints is not a matter of weighing theoretical reasons. Nor is it a matter of optional preference. In Fichte's famous words, "What philosophy one
chooses depends . . . on what human being one is."[18]

On Fichte's view of the matter, there are just two kinds of human beings,
protoidealists and protodogmatists: One is either a human being deeply
convinced of the reality of human freedom and determined to preserve
that freedom in one's practical and philosophical endeavors, or one is a
human being lacking any such sense of freedom and hence incapable of
distinguishing between oneself and "a piece of lava in the moon."[19]

Fichte's own conviction of the reality of human freedom leads him to
develop an idealist theory of experience in which the human mind, understood as the cognitive faculty ("intelligence"), is the ground for the representations of the objective world. Fichte critiques Kant for retaining the
thing in itself as the inscrutable source of material diversity among representations.[20] In order to complete Kant's transcendental idealism in the
spirit of a "system of freedom," the representation of reality has to be attributed entirely to the human mind. In a striking political analogy Fichte states:

Just as France has freed man from external shackles, so my system frees him from the fetters of things in themselves, which is to say, from those external influences with which all previous systems – including the Kantian – have more or less fettered man.[21]

Fichte's radical rejection of any dogmatic remnant in his completed transcendental idealism does not stop at the elimination of the thing in itself from any role in mental representation. It also affects the philosophical concepts with which the intelligence itself is to be described. Any notions that apply primarily to the analysis of external objects ("things") are deemed unsuitable and in need of being replaced by concepts that adequately reflect the radical independence of the intelligence from factors external to it. In light of the foundational role of freedom, Fichte resorts to a thoroughly praxeological field of concepts when characterizing the mind. The intelligence is analyzed in terms of its activity, and specifically of its capability of producing representations. In fact, Fichte is so scrupulous about avoiding reifying the mind qua intelligence that he refers to it as "an activity" (*ein Handeln*) rather than as "something that acts" (*ein Handelndes*).[22]

Fichte's choice of the pronoun for the first person singular, "I," to designate the idealist ground of experience is best understood in this context of a radical rejection of dogmatic, thing-oriented philosophy. Fichte's account of the intelligence as the ground of representations systematically avoids the language of "things." Even the Cartesian notion of a "thinking thing" (*res cogitans*) cannot do justice to the pure *actuosity* of the intelligence. Yet the I considered as the nonempirical ground of experience is also entirely removed from the spatio–temporally located person or individual customarily designated by the pronominal "I."[23] Fichte's I is a technical term that stands for a structure designed to address the methodological requirement of thinking the ground of experience in a manner consistent with the systematic commitment to freedom.

The distinction between the I as an empirical person and the I as a nonempirical structure is reflected in Fichte's distinction between two levels of cognitive activity. On the level of empirical consciousness are the empirical representations – representations that are about the empirical world and that themselves have their place in the empirical world of mental facts. But there are also, on a different plane and accessible only to philosophical analysis, the features of the I as intelligence that are the very conditions for the formation of those empirical representations. In line with his praxeological understanding of the mind, Fichte thinks of the nonempirical conditions for empirical representation as active and processlike. The generic term he employs to designate the nonempirical dynamical structure underlying all empirical representing is that of "positing" (*setzen*).[24] The origin of this term in logic, where it designates affirmation in judgment, indicates that the intellectual acts in question are not to be thought of as empirical-psychological events but as the structural conditions that govern all mental life.

3. The Method of the *Wissenschaftslehre*

Its ultimate starting point in some extraphilosophical conviction notwithstanding, Fichte's *Wissenschaftslehre* operates at a level of abstraction and reflection far removed from the facts and objects of empirical consciousness. In his metaphilosophical reflections Fichte refers to the nonphilosophical basis of philosophy as "life," whereas philosophy itself is identified as "speculation."[25] "Speculation" – the term derives from the Latin word for "mirror" (*speculum*) – is said to be *about* life, without itself being part of life. But the copying or mirroring of life through philosophy does not take the form of simple duplication. In moving from the level of experience to the level of the nonempirical conditions of experience, philosophy leaves behind the shapes and forms of ordinary consciousness. Fichte himself attributes the lack of comprehension encountered by his philosophy to the lack of distinction between what philosophy is about ("life") and what philosophy itself is ("speculation").

In an attempt to convey how artificial and removed from life philosophy is, Fichte likens the business of speculation to conducting an experiment.[26] In an experiment some real-life process is isolated and studied under artificial, systematically simplified conditions. The experiment of the *Wissenschaftslehre* involves the principal object of Fichte's idealism, the I as the nonempirical ground of experience. The philosophical object in question is not given as such but needs to be gained by systematically disregarding what is merely empirical ("abstraction") and by focusing on that which is not empirical ("reflection").[27] On Fichte's account, the experiment of the *Wissenschaftslehre* involves two I's, the individual I of the philosopher conducting the experiment and the preindividual I upon which the experiment is conducted. This duality leads to the distinction of two series in the experiment. The first series is that of the observing, *philosophizing* I; the second series is that of the observed, or *philosophized* I.

A key feature of Fichte's transcendental experiment is the intimate relation between the observing I and the observed I. After all, the experiment does not concern some entity external to the philosopher's mind but a structure instantiated in the philosopher qua mind. Yet the observed I is not the philosopher's own, individual I as such. It is rather the set of structural conditions of experience that is invariantly present in human minds. The way to access this structure and make it the object of one's philosophical analysis is the performance of an experiment upon oneself. Fichte is deeply convinced that the only way to capture the I in its true nature, unaltered by reification, is through one's own speculative effort. No one can do

S's purifying reflection

the idealist experiment for you. Philosophical instruction – and that includes Fichte's own work – is limited to providing instruction on how to do it. But you must do it yourself. To put it in Fichte's own words with their characteristic blend of imperative and conspirative tone: "Think yourself, and notice how you do that."[28]

The intricate setup of the Fichtean experiment is further complicated by the peculiar nature of the I to be observed. That I is an object only for and to the philosopher. In and of itself the I is entirely different from any thing and is of the nature of pure activity. In order to do justice to the original nature of I, the philosophical experimentator must choose an experimental setting that lets the I engage in its original activity. Moreover, the I under investigation is not something that is, among other things, engaged in pure activity. Rather, the I is nothing but that activity. Observing the I's activity is therefore observing the I's own coming about. Speculation consists in the philosopher's observation of the I constructing itself.[29] In tracking the self-construction of the observed I under artificial conditions, the philosopher achieves a reconstruction of the I.

It is important to realize that the Fichtean philosophical reconstruction of the I is a representation (*Darstellung*) of the complex nature of the I. Fichte sharply distinguishes between the system of the mind and its representation through a philosophical system.[30] The philosophical representation of the I employs a developmental account of the I's complex structure, providing, as it were, a historiography of the human mind.[31] Such linear, temporally articulated representation is a reflection of the philosopher's finite intellectual capacities rather than a feature pertaining to the I as such. Fichte's continued revising of the *Wissenschaftslehre* can be seen as a sustained effort to extend the limits of philosophy in order to render more adequately the absolute structure of the I with the means of finite cognition. Not counting introductory and preparatory writings, fifteen different versions of the *Wissenschaftslehre* have come down to us.[32]

The self-construction of the observed I under the philosophical observer's eye is not limited to the reconstructed coming about of the pure I as such. Given the systematic function of the I as the ground of experience, the reconstructed self-construction is simultaneously the reconstructed construction of empirical consciousness and its world of objects. The I functions as the principle from which the forms and laws of all consciousness are derived, or, in Fichte's terminology, *deduced*.[33] A crucial step in this reconstructed development from the pure I to an an individual, empirically concrete I is the deduction of interpersonality. Fichte argues that the actualization of the individual I's potential for self-determination can only take place through dynamic interaction with other intelligent beings that provide the "solicitation" (*Aufforderung*)[34] to independent action.

The development of individuality thus requires community, in the form of an external, legal association or of a "realm of rational beings" (*Reich vernün-ftiger Wesen*).[35] The reconstruction of the I thus proceeds from an artificially isolated minimal starting point to the fully developed structure of individ-ual, social, empirically determined consciousness. Throughout the philo-sophical tracking process, the observed I follows definite laws that are recon-structed by the experimenter-philosopher. Those laws are certainly not of the philosopher's making. But neither are they of the I's own making. The freedom of the I is a freedom under laws.[36]

4. The Experiment of the *Wissenschaftslehre*

During the Jena period Fichte's idealist reconstruction of the I as the prin-ciple of all consciousness received two basically different formulations. The earlier of the two, the *Foundation of the Entire Wissenschaftslehre* from 1794 to 1795, remained, throughout Fichte's lifetime, the only published detailed presentation of the *Wissenschaftslehre* as a whole. Yet in his own assessment, that first version was soon superseded by the presentation of the *Wissenschaftslehre* according to a "new method," offered in three lecture courses at Jena between 1796 and 1799, and accompanied by the publica-tion of the rudimentary *Attempt at a New Presentation of the Wissenschaftslehre* in 1797–1798 as well as by Fichte's work on a somewhat more extensive, but still incomplete, manuscript, the *New Treatment of the Wissenschaftslehre*, written in late 1800 and, perhaps, early 1801.[37] One can appreciate the advancements in presentation, if not in substance, that Fichte made in his Jena period by contrasting the theory of the I set forth in the first published version of the *Wissenschaftslehre* of 1794–1795 with the subsequent presen-tation according to the new method.

The *Foundation of the Entire Wissenschaftslehre* proceeds – by way of a tran-scendental argument – from empirical consciousness to its a priori condi-tions. Fichte employs the philosophical tools of reflection and abstraction to move from "facts" (*Tatsachen*) of consciousness to the underlying tran-scendental "activity" (*Tathandlung*).[38] The latter is not given as such but must be added in thought in order to account satisfactorily for what is given. Fichte's starting point is certain mental acts that he takes to be universally performed and therefore to have the status of uncontested facts of con-sciousness. These mental acts are said to require some mental activity that belongs to consciousness as its necessary condition but that is not itself an object of consciousness, except in the attenuated sense of being inferred through philosophical thinking.

Fichte distinguishes three basic transcendental acts of the mind, each expressed as a principle (*Grundsatz*) of the *Wissenschaftslehre*. The first prin-

ciple states that <u>the I posits itself absolutely</u>.[39] The main point of this prin- *1)*
ciple is that the I does not rest on some presupposed being but is entirely
the result of its activity. <u>The I's very being consists in the activity of positing
itself.</u> The second principle has the I engaged in oppositing or counterpositing (*entgegensetzen*).[40] <u>The I absolutely counterposits a Not-I to itself.</u> *2)*
Here the point is that by its very nature the I is caught up <u>in a conflict</u> with
something that, although posited by the I, is yet other than the I. According to the third principle, <u>the I counterposits in the I the divisible I and the</u> *3)*
<u>divisible Not-I</u>, the point being that the conflict between I and Not-I is, in
principle, <u>resolved through the relation of mutual limitation between the
I and the Not-I</u>.[41]

Fichte considers the three basic principles and the kinds of transcendental activity they express irreducible to each other or to anything else.
<u>Together they make up the complex structure of the I</u>, in which the latter
figures in three different capacities: <u>(1)</u> as the <u>absolute</u> I or *subject* that does
the positing; (2) as the <u>I or *substance*</u> in which I and Not-I are counterposited;
and (3) as the <u>divisible I or *accident*</u> that is counterposited to the Not-I.[42]
Based on these principles, the *Wissenschaftslehre* of 1794–1795 proceeds by
exposing and removing the tensions, within the I qua substance, between
the I qua accident and the Not-I. <u>The I is seen as "striving" (*streben*) pro-
gressively to eliminate the Not</u>-I and to have the I qua substance approach
the condition of the I qua subject, that is, unopposed absolute I-ness.[43] The
<u>procedure of progressive removal of contradictory determinations is an
infinite process</u>, though, a task rather than an accomplishment. The I qua */*
absolute subject remains an idea that cannot be fully realized under conditions of human, finite rationality.[44]

Fichte's attempts at a revised presentation of the *Wissenschaftslehre* adopt *β*
a new method of presentation. The move from empirical facts of consciousness to the *construction* of a system of basic principles, with subsequent
dialectical extrapolations, is replaced by the initial postulation of the I's
absolute nature, followed by a series of presuppositions that specify the principal requirements for transforming the bare core of the I into a finite rational being relevantly structured like us.[45] <u>Fichte's new procedure may be
termed a phenomenology of the I, in both the Husserlian and the Hegelian</u> *genetic*
senses of that term. Fichte engages in the description of the pure acts of *Phänom-*
consciousness by tracking the different forms and stages of consciousness *enology*
on its way from a bare starting point to concrete individuality.[46]

The chief methodological device employed in Fichte's new, phenomenological account of the I is the philosopher's ability to intuit the nonem-
<u>pirical, pure activity of the I</u>, an ability for which Fichte chooses the ominous
term "<u>intellectual intuition</u>" (*intellektuelle Anschauung*).[47] Fichte's appeal to
a nonsensory as well nonconceptual source of evidence regarding the I
might seem to violate the Kantian heterogeneity thesis of intuition and

thought, according to which all humanly possible intuition is sensible and all humanly possible intellection is conceptual.[48] Yet on Fichte's view of the matter, the philosopher's intellectual intuition is not some rare and dubious accomplishment, but is the philosopher's ability to raise to consciousness the very processes through which the I comes about. In Fichte's usage the term "intellectual intuition" originally designates the structure of the I as such and only derivatively applies to the philosopher's grasp of the intellectual-intuitive nature of the pure I.[49] It is that condition in each finite rational being due to which consciousness is possible. Like Kant's apperceptive "I think," Fichte's "intellectual intuition" is, in principle, present in each and every act of representing. It is the feature that makes my being conscious of something *my* being conscious of something. Indeed, Fichte claims that his own understanding of intellectual intuition is in perfect agreement with the spirit, if not with the letter, of Kant's theory of apperception.[50]

Fichte's choice of the term "intellectual intuition" is moreover motivated by Kant's own understanding of that term. To be sure, Kant rejects the attribution of nonsensory, intellectual intuition to finite rational beings. Yet he admits, and even requires, the concept of an intellectually intuitive mode of knowledge as a limiting concept, designed to determine the confines of human knowledge by entertaining the thought of alternative modes of cognition not subject to the strictures of human finitude.[51] On Kant's view, a being that possesses intellectual intuition is a being in which knowing and doing coincide. Fichte's description of the I in terms of "intellectual intuition" can be seen as an adaptation of the Kantian notion of a mind in which acting and knowing are originally unseparated. On Fichte's understanding, the I of intellectual intuition is a doing that is also a knowing, and vice versa.[52]

The notion of an intellectual intuition provides Fichte with a new way of describing the absolute, autonomous nature of the I. Fichte's presentation of the *Wissenschaftslehre* of 1794–1795 had already stressed that the I as such, the pure I, is nothing but the activity of positing. The I is not a thing that underlies the positing. Nor is it a thing upon which the positing is exercised. Yet in order for there to be an I, and not just a thing, the positing cannot be the positing of just anything. Whatever else is being posited, the positing has to be at least the positing *of the I*, and this in the twofold sense that the I is both that which does the positing and that which is so posited. The I has to be the subject as well as the object of the positing. Otherwise the positing would be the positing of something else, possibly involving an already presupposed I, yet it would not be that which posits the I in the first place. But how could such an original positing of the I take place? After all, the positing in question cannot rely on a pregiven subject-I that does the positing, nor can it rely on a pregiven object-I to which to direct the positing.[53] Any such presupposition of an already constituted I would introduce a vicious circle into the original positing of the I.[54] Therefore the original positing must be such that the positing that posits the object is equally the positing of the subject as that which does the positing: it must be a doing that is a knowing and a knowing that is a doing.

This is where the notion of an intellectual intuition, with its unseparated oneness of doing and knowing, comes in. The I is what it is – the activity of positing – only in that it also posits the positing as such. It is a "positing as positing."[55] The original unity of positing and positing-as-positing makes the positing a self-positing, a positing in and through which the I comes about:

> The I posits itself *absolutely*, i.e., without any mediation. It is at once *subject* and *object*. The I comes about only by means of positing itself – it has no prior existence – rather its very being is to posit itself as positing. . . . Therefore *an intuition of the I acting upon itself* is possible. Such an *intuition* is an *intellectual intuition*.[56]

The intimate union of doing and knowing conveyed in the term "intellectual intuition" also stands behind Fichte's characterization of the pure I as "immediate consciousness" or "immediate consciousness of itself."[57] In the case of intellectual intuition, the consciousness of an object includes immediately, that is, without further reflection, a consciousness of this very consciousness. Fichte also refers to this immediacy of the I's intuition of itself as "self-consciousness" or "immediate self-consciousness.[58] The self-consciousness involved in intellectual intuition is thus prereflective and must not be confused with the mediated self-consciousness that is based on a self's reflecting upon itself. Moreover, the immediate self-consciousness expressed through the term of art "intellectual intuition" is the transcendental condition not only of empirical self-knowledge but also of all other forms of consciousness. Fichte's intellectual intuition thus takes on the function of the Kantian "I think" that must be able to accompany all my representations.

In addition to casting the prereflective unity of doing and knowing in the pure I through a suitably revised notion of intellectual intuition, Fichte repeatedly explains the unity in question through a comparison between the I (*Ich*) and the organ of sight, the eye (*Auge*).[59] The comparison first occurs in the Jena lectures on the *Wissenschaftslehre* "according to a new method" and is continued, in revised form, in several of Fichte's later works, including a sonnet.[60] Typically in these comparisons, the eye stands for the element of knowing ("seeing") that is originally and indissolubly united with the activity of the I. In one such instance, Fichte reconstructs the coming about of the I as the unification of the "blindly" felt drive to absolute independence with the "sight" provided by thinking, a process in which "eyes are, as it were, inserted into the drive that is itself blind."[61] The metaphor of the eye here serves to represent the moment of consciousness in the original activity of the I. Fichte's talk about eyes being inserted into the drive should not be taken, though, to suggest the implantation of some further organ into an already functioning organism. Rather the eyes have always already been inserted, just as the positing of the I is originally also a positing-as-positing. At one point Fichte even conflates the terminologies of positing and seeing by calling the I "an eye that posits itself."[62]

In a remarkable comparison from the Jena period, Fichte employs the eye metaphor in an effort to distinguish his theory of the subject from previous thinking about the I. Fichte contrasts the views of earlier philosophies that understand the I as a mirror, passively reflecting its objects, with his own conception of the I as originally productive and conscious of its absolute independence. According to Fichte, the image of the mirror, when employed to capture the nature of the I, leaves unexplained that the image mirrored by the I is also seen by the I. In the case of the I, the mirrored image is not provided to some external observer looking at the mirror. Rather the mirrored image is seen internally, by the I itself. The I is therefore "a mirror that mirrors itself"[63] – a mirror that can see – in short, an eye. Moreover, the object of the eye's gaze is not some external reality, as in the case of some mirror, but the very activity of the I itself: "we see everything in us, we see only ourselves, only as acting."[64]

The I is here portrayed as self-enclosed to the point of seeming totally self-sufficient and a world onto its own. Yet the self-sufficiency in question is not the ontological independence or self-sufficiency of a divine mind, but the epistemological isolation of a finite intelligence that originally knows only itself, including its own states, and that derives all other knowledge from the experience of its own finitude. Viewed that way, Fichte's account of experience is an effort to derive the consciousness of external objects from the limitations that the I encounters in its original, intellectual intuition.

In employing the language of acting and knowing, of doing and seeing, Fichte resorts to imagery that casts the preindividual nature of the I, the I-ness under investigation, in decidedly individual-psychological terms. Yet Fichte clearly states that the pure I as such, the I of intellectual intuition, is "no consciousness, not even self-consciousness."[65] The I in question merely constitutes the "*possibility* of self-consciousness," but "no actual consciousness comes into being as yet."[66] The I of intellectual intuition is thus not an instance of consciousness, but the ground or the pure form of consciousness. Its status is that of an inferred condition, grasped in philosophical thought by means of abstraction from what is empirical in consciousness and reflection on what remains after such abstraction.

Yet, although Fichte is eager to dispel the impression that the pure I is individual in nature and empirical in content, he also maintains that the pure I is somehow present in all acts of consciousness. On Fichte's understanding, the I in question is not only a structural condition or form underlying all consciousness, but also a form present in all consciousness. To be sure, the universal mental presence of the pure I does not take the form of the pure I being an object of consciousness. Not even philosophical thinking is able to objectify the pure I as such. The pure I eludes all objectification. But, for Fichte, this by itself does not establish that the I in question lies outside of all consciousness. To him it rather suggests that the pure I is present in consciousness in a manner totally different from the way objects are present in consciousness. The presence peculiar to the pure I is the presence that the subject of consciousness has in all consciousness: "The immediate self-consciousness is that which is eternally, unchangeably *subjective* and as such, and in isolation, it never becomes *object*, of some consciousness."[67] Thus, the pure I is the object of no consciousness and the subject of all consciousness.

The identification of the pure I with the transcendental subject of consciousness makes Fichte's account of the I an egology in the eminent sense. The pure I is not just the central topic of Fichte's philosophical theory: That theory has, moreover, the pure I as its *principle*. The pure I is the principle of Fichte's *Wissenschaftslehre* in that all forms of consciousness are derived from the pure I, whereas the pure I itself is not the result of some further derivation. On Fichte's view, consciousness as such is the consciousness of an I (subjective genitive), which in all consciousness of other objects (objective genitive) is always also conscious of this very I (objective genitive). Rather than dissociating the subject underlying all consciousness from the field of consciousness itself, Fichte maintains that the subject of consciousness is itself the original element of consciousness in all other consciousness. The pure I is not only the transcendental condition for all consciousness, but it is itself the archetypal instance of consciousness. According to Fichte, immediate self-consciousness "is . . . nothing else but the *being-with-itself* and *being-for-itself* of the very being that becomes conscious – something that is to be presupposed in all consciousness – the pure reflex of consciousness."[68]

Still, Fichte's earlier point that the pure I as such is not to be encountered in consciousness remains in effect. The I qua transcendental subject, while being the archetype of all consciousness, is never given as such. No objectification could capture its absolute status as the subject of all consciousness. The pure I can only be inferred through philosophical reflection on its actualization in empirical consciousness: "That immediate self-consciousness is not raised to consciousness nor can it ever be. As soon as one reflects on it, it ceases to be what it is, and it disappears into a higher region."[69] Fichte's *Wissenschaftslehre* is its author's lifelong struggle to keep up with the disappearance act of the pure I.

In insisting on the nonobjective and indeed nonobjectifiable status of the pure I, Fichte does not mean to characterize the pure I as a subject only. On the contrary, it is part of the very essence of the I's being a subject that this subject is what it is *to* and *for* itself. Otherwise the subject would not really be a subject, but would be a being for something or someone else, that is, an object. Thus, the pure I, while not being any other subject's object, is still an object to itself. To be sure, the objectivity of the pure I cannot be that of an object given to and contemplated by the I. That way the *explanandum* (the I) would be doubly presupposed in the *explanans,* in the subject-I as well as the object-I. Rather, the I must be for-itself or with-itself in a manner that excludes all mediation, externality and duplication. The term of art that Fichte introduces for the absolute unity of the subject in its being-for-itself is "subject-object": "self-consciousness is immediate: in it the subjective and the objective are indivisibly united and absolutely one. . . . The I is not to be considered as subject only . . . but as subject-object in the sense indicated."[70] Fichte also refers to the absolute unity of I under the terms "self-intuition" and "intuition of the I." In the latter formulation, the genitive construction is objective as well as subjective: The I is both and in one the *intuiting* and the *intuited.*[71]

5. Assessing the Project of the *Wissenschaftslehre*

Fichte's theory of the subject-objectivity of the I is not an isolated piece of speculation, devoid of context and full of wild claims, but a view that is firmly integrated into his thinking and that moreover forms the very core of his philosophy. Throughout the Jena period, and even beyond that first major phase of his work, Fichte's thinking aims at a comprehensive account of the human subject. Fichte is chiefly concerned with the very origin and basic structure of subjectivity. He asks what it is, in terms of the most elementary features required, to be a human subject, as opposed to being a thing or object. And he asks how that most original layer of human subjectivity expresses itself in and through the two principal forms of human existence, knowing and doing. The inquiry is guided by the systematic concern with capturing the radical independence of human subjectivity from external conditions. The subject is seen as having its ground strictly within itself, as coming about and developing entirely on its own. The autonomous activity of the subject is moreover originally united with the subject's cognitive dimension; the independent activity of the subject is always also an activity *for* the subject.

The monadic, active cum cognitive conception of the human subject might suggest a metaphysical reading of Fichte along the lines of an absolute idealism that would have things mental and physical originate in the activity of some absolute subject or spirit. Yet Fichte's continued insistence on the principal limits of human subjectivity mitigates against such a reading. The subject in question is profoundly restricted in its intellectual and volitional powers. It cannot even posit itself qua I without also positing the Not-I. Still, there is an idealist character to the subject's positing of everything for itself. The objects and other subjects so posited are deeply affected by the Fichtean forms of positing, to the point of seeming to be nothing but positions brought about in the process of the subject's original activity of self-positing. However, it has to be kept in mind that subjectivity in Fichte is preindividual in nature. It is a structure that is realized by the individual subjects so structured. The idealism implied by the universal positing is therefore not a solipsistic idealism, but one involving a plurality of subjects that instantiate generic subjectivity in so many individually specific ways and that are united in the Fichtean realm of minds or spirits. Fichte may be an idealist about that which is posited, but he is much more of a realist about the subjects that do the positing, and especially about the preindividual, nonempirical ground of those subjects. For Fichte, the reality of finite spirits or minds points to a higher reality yet, "the absolute," which he came to acknowledge as the unfathomable ultimate ground of every thing and every subject.[72]

The chief concern of Fichte's *Wissenschaftslehre* from the Jena period is the proper integration of the absoluteness and the finitude of the human subject. This project requires a delicate balancing act between two equally unacceptable extremes. Emphasizing the element of absoluteness at the expense of the dimension of finitude would let the theory degenerate into a dogmatic metaphysics of the subject, whereas the inverse strategy of emphasizing finitude at the expense of absoluteness would lead into empirical anthropology and psychology. Fichte sought to avoid either of those paths. In his ambition to steer a middle course between a supranaturalist metaphysics and a naturalist psychology, Fichte partakes in the Kantian project of a transcendental science. Transcendental philosophy as formulated by Kant and reformulated by Fichte is a study of the principal forms and conditions of human consciousness that is both respectful of the limits of human knowledge and faithful to the otherworldly nature of human mental activity.

PART II

KNOWING AND DOING

3

POSITING AND DETERMINING

Fichte's project of a transcendental theory of knowledge (*Wissen*), which he developed under the title "*Wissenschaftslehre*" over a period of some twenty years, eludes classification within the traditional system of philosophical disciplines. The knowledge that Fichte seeks to elucidate in its principal structure includes theoretical as well as practical knowledge, thus pointing to the basis of knowledge of all kinds in a common ground that precedes and prepares its subsequent differentiations. Moreover, Fichte's account of the ground of all knowledge is not only concerned with the forms and structures of knowing. It is as much an account of the principal structure of that which is known in all knowledge. Accordingly, Fichte's transcendental theory of knowledge of all kinds is at the same a transcendental theory of objects of all kinds.

With its comprehensive scope and radical intentions, Fichte's *Wissenschaftslehre* can lay claim to the old Aristotelian title of a "first philosophy." Yet whereas traditional first philosophy was a theory of the principal forms and kinds of being, Fichte's *Wissenschaftslehre* – following the precedent of Descartes and Kant – takes the form of a theory of the principal forms and the ground of the knowledge of all being. The object of first philosophy in Fichte is not being as such but the knowledge of being, more precisely, the necessary conditions of such knowledge. The epistemic turn in first philosophy, which is characteristic of transcendental philosophy in general, is more than a methodological device designed to start with what is best known. It is based on the substantial rather than merely methodological insight that it is not possible to abstract from one's knowledge or,

43

more generally, from one's mental involvement in the consideration of whatever there is and whatever being is. It is this uneliminable presence of principal mental accomplishments that Fichte addresses under the term "I" (*Ich*) in the various elaborations of his *Wissenschaftslehre*.

Given the role assigned to the I as the principal ground of knowledge and its objects, the I in question cannot be the empirical self of the concrete human individual. Rather, Fichte's I is a structural complex or a complex structure that precedes and renders possible all individual mental life. Yet, the terms and concepts employed by Fichte to address the nature and functions of the I as transcendental principle are often borrowed from the sphere of the empirical, concrete I – including the former's appellation as "I" in the first place. This strategy is certainly motivated and probably justified by the consideration that the empirical I is the closest nontranscendental counterpart of the I of transcendental theory or the transcendental I. Still, the terminological proximity between the transcendental ground structure and that which it grounds is potentially misleading. In fact, it misled many readers and was reassessed by Fichte himself in the later versions of *Wissenschaftslehre*.

In the *Foundation of the Entire Wissenschaftslehre* of 1794–1795, though, the egological terms and concepts thoroughly pervade Fichte's transcendental theory of knowledge. A distinguishing feature of this presentation is its division into the three "Principles of the Entire *Wissenschaftslehre*," on the one hand, and the further development of the complex relations between those principles in the "Foundation of Theoretical Knowledge" and the "Foundation of the Knowledge of the Practical," on the other hand. Whereas the three principles that open the *Foundation of the Entire Wissenschaftslehre* present the most abstract, general traits of all knowledge, the separate but linked treatments of theoretical knowledge and knowledge of the practical, which are based on the interrelations of the three principles, address with growing specificity the principal features of concrete mental life, thus lending increased plausibility to Fichte's choice of the language of the "I" for his transcendental account of knowledge.

But the relation between the three principles of the entire *Wissenschaftslehre* and the latter's theoretical and practical parts not only documents the crucial transition from the generic conception of the I to its principal specifications as theoretical I and practical I. It also documents, in the inverse direction, the origin of the specific forms of knowledge and the forms of mental life associated with each of them in some generic, transcendental ground whose three principal components are responsible for the basic structures of all knowledge and mental life. To use a musical analogy, the three principles of the entire *Wissenschaftslehre* provide the exposition of the themes that are subsequently subjected to a development that brings out their initially latent potential for multiple relations. The *Foundation of the Entire Wissenschaftslehre* has a truncated sonata form.[1]

The complex relationship of prefiguration and unfolding that holds between the ground of the entire *Wissenschaftslehre,* on the one hand, and the grounds of theoretical and practical knowledge, on the other hand, has found linguistic expression in Fichte's judicious employment of the terminologies of positing (*setzen*) and determining (*bestimmen*), which pervade the *Foundation of the Entire Wissenschaftslehre.* Both terms and their derivatives are sufficiently generic to address the overall ("entire") structure of knowledge or the I. Yet, they are equally susceptible to further specification in order to capture what is peculiar to some but not all aspects of knowledge or the I. Moreover, between them those two terms repeat the developmental tension of the *Foundation of the Entire Wissenschaftslehre,* with the terminology of positing especially dominant in the formulation of the three principles of the entire *Wissenschaftslehre* and the terminology of determining to be found chiefly in the specifically theoretical and practical parts of the work.

The four sections of this chapter address Fichte's accounts of absolute positing, the transition from positing to determining, theoretical determining, and practical determining and predicative positing in the perspective of the unitary structure of the *Foundation of the Entire Wissenschaftslehre* and its object of study, the I.

1. Absolute Positing   *see supra*

The principal feature attributed to the I in the principles of the entire *Wissenschaftslehre* is that of *positing,* more precisely, of *positing absolutely* (*schlechthin*). According to the first principle "[t]he I posits originally absolutely its own being."[2] The second principle states that the I posits absolutely something over and against itself, viz., the Not-I.[3] Finally, as the third principle claims, the I posits absolutely the I as well as the Not-I as divisible.[4] Although all three kinds of the I's principal positing are characterized as absolute, the second and third principal kinds of positing are partially conditioned. The form of the I's op-positing or counterpositing of the Not-I is unconditioned (not derivable from the original absolute positing), but the matter or content of the I's counterpositing is conditioned in that the opposed content is the opposite of the posited I, viz., a Not-I.[5] By contrast, it is the matter or content of the third kind of absolute positing that is unconditioned (the divisibility of I and Not-I is not derivable from their being posited and counterposited, respectively), whereas the form of this kind of positing is contained in the task of reconciling the opposed kinds of the I's positing in the first and second principle.[6]

Fichte's choice of the term "positing" to designate the absolute, grounding dimension of knowledge or the I receives no explicit justification in the *Foundation of the Entire Wissenschaftslehre*. Nor is there an explanation of the technical meaning of this term offered anywhere in the work. Since there is also no direct precedent for the specific use of the term in transcendental philosophy before Fichte, it seems indicated to interpret Fichte's use of "positing" functionally, as a coinage designed to name a conceptual space opened up in his transcendental theory of knowledge.

The emergence of the term "positing" in Fichte can be traced to his involvement in the contemporary debate about a philosophy based on a first principle (*Grundsatz*). The conceptual space filled by the notion of positing was first opened up through Fichte's encounter with G. E. Schulze's skeptical critique of Reinhold's attempt to provide a unitary foundation for Kant's critical philosophy. Under the title "proposition of consciousness" (*Satz des Bewußtseins*), Reinhold had advanced the following formulation of the allegedly self-evident highest principle of all knowledge: "In consciousness the representation is distinguished by the subject from the subject and the object, and related to both."[7] In his anonymously published treatise entitled *Aenesidemus* (1792),[8] Schulze had critiqued Reinhold's principle by showing how the latter is not unconditional but both formally and materially conditioned by concepts and principles that it tacitly presupposes.

In his review of *Aenesidemus* (1794),[9] Fichte had responded to Schulze's criticism of Reinhold's version of the first principle of all knowledge by conceding the inadequacy of Reinhold's particular choice of a first principle, while maintaining the overall goal of searching for the first principle and indicating that a true first principle would have to provide the foundations not only for theoretical philosophy but also for the "entire" philosophy and would therefore have to employ a more generic concept than the specifically theoretical notion of representation to capture the foundational stratum of knowledge.[10]

In the *Foundation of the Entire Wissenschaftslehre* the fragmentary hints at the pretheoretical, prerepresentational foundation of all knowledge to be found in the *Aenesidemus* review have been developed into a complex account of the I's threefold absolute positing, designed to provide a more promising successor to Reinhold's principle with its distinction and relation between subject, object and representation.[11] The key features of the principal ground of all knowledge (absolute I, absolute Not-I, divisible I and divisible Not-I) are presented in separate but related principles, and the term "positing" addresses the generic, transcendental nature of the I's principal ground.

Yet although the term "positing," as used to address the absolute structure of the I, has neither a specifically theoretical nor a specifically practical meaning, it nevertheless prefigures the subsequent differentiation of the I into a theoretical I or intelligence and a practical or striving I. Absolute positing in Fichte contains the protocognitive connotation of self-ascription or "taking" as well as the protopractical connotation of activity or doing. Indeed, it is the very unity of those two traits that characterizes the I as such. For Fichte, the I is originally theoretical and practical. Neither of the two traits is added on to the other. Each can only be what it is in unison with the other.

Still, there is a tendency in Fichte to express the complex nature of the I predominantly in terms of activity or doing. But this conceptual strategy is not designed to play down the cognitive or theoretical aspect of Fichte's I, or its prototheoretical antecedent in absolute positing. Rather, the main addressee of this move is an unduly reified, static understanding of the I as a thing or object. Fichte seeks to counter such an ontological misunderstanding with a comprehensive practical interpretation of the I that includes rather than excludes its cognitive or theoretical dimension. Theory itself is a mode of practice generically understood.

In addition to its prototheoretical cum practical character, the transcendental ground of all knowledge possesses as its essential feature that the I's original positing occurs absolutely or unconditionally. The I in its capacity as universal ground is not itself grounded in anything outside of it but is strictly self-grounded. The I's absolute positing is not based on some prior being of the I. Rather, it is only in and through the I's absolute positing that the I first comes into existence.[12] In the original I, then, positing and being coincide: The I posits its own being. Yet equally originally, the I posits the being of a Not-I. The Not-I, too, in no way precedes its being posited by the I; it first comes about in and through the I's formally absolute counterpositing.

But not only is there no being preceding the I's positing activity; neither is there a being succeeding this positing as its result or product. The absolute I qua self-posited is nothing apart from this very act of positing. Its being is its being posited and nothing beyond that. Fichte expresses this unique feature of the I that distinguishes it from any other activity through the neologism "*Tathandlung*"[13] – a philosophical term that he coins to go beyond Reinhold's inadequate reliance on facts (*Tatsachen*) of consciousness.[14] Fichte's coinage indicates the identity of the act (*Handlung*) and its product (*Tat*) in the case of absolute self-positing.[15] Not even the I's other act of absolute positing, viz., that of positing the Not-I, can count as a case of *Tathandlung*. For in the latter case the product, the Not-I, is not identical with the I's act but different from it and even opposed to the I.[16]

The I that performs the three kinds of absolute positing (self-positing, counterpositing of the Not-I, and positing of the I and the Not-I as divisible) is the I qua *absolute subject*.[17] It is important to distinguish the I in its absolute capacity of preceding all subsequent distinctions with respect to the I from two other forms under which the I appears in the system of supreme principles, viz., the I qua substance that is being divided (by the absolute I's positing) into divisible I and divisible Not-I, and the I qua accident that is opposed in the substance I to the divisible Not-I.[18] Nor is the I qua subject of absolute positing to be identified with either the theoretical I or the practical I that figure in the specific parts of the *Foundation of the Entire Wissenschaftslehre.*

Strictly speaking, the absolute I is not an I at all. On the basis of the three forms of positing alone, there is no consciousness or self-consciousness. The absolute I, like its correlates (substance I, accident I, accident Not-I) are merely so many moments that enter into the constitution of actual consciousness and self-consciousness.[19] Thus, the formally absolute positing of the Not-I does not amount to the consciousness of an object, and the materially absolute positing of divisible I and Not-I does not yet establish any of the specific relations between I and world, such as the relation of knowing or the relation of acting. The absolute ground of knowledge is an I only proleptically speaking, in anticipation of the I made possible by those very principles. Yet given the task to articulate the radical heterogeneity of the absolute ground of all knowledge from every thing grounded therein, the terminology and conceptuality of the I with its connotations of spontaneous, self-regarding activity might still be considered one of the less objectionable choices.

2. From Positing to Determining

The three kinds of the I's absolute positing provide only the most abstract scaffolding for Fichte's reconstruction of the conditions and forms of all knowledge. In particular, the relation of the three absolute acts to each other receives only the most general characterization. Neither the abstract combinatorics of materially and formally unconditioned, formally unconditioned and materially unconditioned positing nor the differentiation of the I according to the titles of subject, substance and accident addresses the *specific* features of the I's overall constitution.

The lack of specificity in the initial presentation of the I's activity of positing is due to the absolute nature of that activity. In each of the three original acts the I's positing occurs (totally or in part) absolutely, that is, without conditions and entirely spontaneously. Even the counterpositing of the Not-I is a formally unconditioned act of the I qua absolute subject; similarly, the positing of the I and Not-I as divisible is a materially unconditioned act of the absolute I. Their very unconditioned character renders the three absolute acts of the I and the absolute I itself infinite; they do not have boundaries that would make them one thing rather than another.

Yet although the threefold absolute positing of the I is unconditional and infinite, the absolute activity of the I includes the very positing of specificity as such. In the second principle the absolute I posits a Not-I, and in the third principle the absolute I posits a divisible I opposed to a divisible Not-I. The resultant constellation of substance I, accident I and accident Not-I is characterized by the feature of determination (*Bestimmung*) or limitation (*Begrenzung*).[20] The I qua substance provides a totality to be divided up in yet to be specified ways between the accidental I and Not-I, which thus stand in the relation of limiting or determining each other.[21]

By contrast, the absolute I of the first principle is both undetermined and undeterminable. Strictly speaking, the absolute I is not something at all.[22] It is merely its own positing, which in turn consists in nothing but that very positing of itself. Logically speaking, the absolute subject is without any predicate. Fichte introduces a type of judgment peculiar to the absolute I and its manifestations, viz., the "thetic judgment" (*thetisches Urteil*), in which the position of the predicate determining the absolute subject is left open *ad infinitum*.[23]

Whereas the thetic judgment concerning the absolute subject lacks any determinate, finite predicate that would in turn determine the subject, all other forms of judgment stand under the logical principle of ground or reason (*Satz des Grundes*), which is the formal-logical version of the transcendental principle of mutual determination.[24] All nonthetic judgments have their ground in a feature (*Merkmal*) that determines the relation between subject and predicate. Fichte distinguishes between two types of nonthetic judgment, synthetic and antithetic (or analytic) judgments. In synthetic judgments the predication is based on a ground of relating (*Beziehungsgrund*), with regard to which what is otherwise opposed to each other is identical. Antithetic judgments involve a ground of distinguishing (*Unterscheidungsgrund*), with regard to which what is otherwise identical is being opposed.[25]

Thus, the introduction of determination in the third principle marks the transition from an absolute, infinite I to an I that is finite or limited with respect to the Not-I. But the third principle of the entire *Wissenschaftslehre* marks equally the introduction of a limiting or determining I: The I qua accident determines the Not-I qua accident just as much as the Not-I determines the I. In fact, the precise nature of the mutual relation of limitation or determination between finite I and Not-I is the very subject matter of the remaining parts of the *Foundation of the Entire Wissenschaftslehre.*

But that relation can only be established with reference to the I's original infinite, unconditioned nature. Divisible I and Not-I are not equal partners with an equal claim to limiting or determining the other. Rather, the I's original absolute status provides the directional sense for the I-Not-I relation: Just as the absolute I is the source of all positing, so the finite I is determined to be the one that is determining rather than the one that is being determined in the I's relation to the Not-I.[26] The term "determi-nation" here takes on a finalist connotation, thus creating a telling finitist-finalist double meaning, which permeates much of Fichte's thinking on the determination or destination of the human being (*Bestimmung des Menschen*).

3. Theoretical Determining

The mutual limitation or determination of I and Not-I introduced in the third absolute principle divides into two half-statements, each of which functions as the principle for one of the two specific parts of the *Foundation of the Entire Wissenschaftslehre*. Either the I posits itself as determined by the Not-I, or the I posits itself as determining or limiting the Not-I .[27] The first is the case of the theoretical relation, in which the Not-I is supposed to bring about determinations in the I; the second is the case of the practical relation, in which the I is supposed to bring about determinations in the Not-I.[28] Fichte postpones the analysis of the practical relation between I and Not-I until after the treatment of the theoretical relation, arguing that any determination of the Not-I by the I presupposes the reality of the Not-I, which cannot be taken for granted at this point and would first need to be established in the theoretical part of the *Wissenschaftslehre* with its derivation of the Not-I as source of the I's being determined.[29]

As it turns out, the analysis of the principle of theoretical determination does not result in establishing the absolute, independent reality of the Not-I. The Not-I remains something posited by the I. But there is a more limited reality to be accorded to the Not-I, which can become the focus of the analysis of practical determination of the Not-I by the I.

Moreover, not even the first half-statement of the third absolute principle will stand up to closer scrutiny. The notion that the I is determined by the Not-I stands in flagrant contradiction to the basic understanding of the I as absolutely positing. After all, it is the I itself, in its capacity as absolute subject, that posits the Not-I's determining of the I. And although the I that is determined by the Not-I is not the I in its absolutely positing capacity, the I subjected to determination by the Not-I is still an I with its characteristic feature of spontaneous activity. Otherwise the Not-I would not be determining an I but another Not-I.

The task of the theoretical part of the *Wissenschaftslehre* is therefore to mediate between the apparent passive status of the I as the recipient of determinations through the Not-I, and the absolute nature of the I. Fichte introduces an elaborate apparatus of mediations between the absolute and the theoretical functions of the I, geared toward eliminating the contradiction between absolute independence and passive determination.[30]

Although this process manages to minimize the contradiction underlying theoretical determination, the contradictory opposition between the absolutely active and the merely passive moment in the I never vanishes completely.

Fichte correlates the successive attempts at eliminating the fundamental contradiction inherent in theory as such to a series of philosophical standpoints.[31] Those range from extreme, "dogmatic" realism, defending the total determination of the I through the absolute reality of things in themselves, to more moderate forms of realism and idealism that seek to balance the active-passive double nature of the I with the attribution of various degrees of independence to the Not-I. The point of this systematic critique of philosophical positions is to generate by way of negation the one standpoint on theoretical knowledge that does justice to the I's spontaneity and independence while preserving the insight that in the theoretical relation the I undergoes determination.[32]

In rough outline, Fichte's solution to the basic contradiction of the theoretical relation is twofold. For one, he reduces the role of the Not-I from that of the source of all determinations in the I to that of a mere "check" (*Anstoß*) that sets in motion a process of self-limitation or determination by itself on the part of the theoretical I.[33] The Not-I is not actually determining the I nor is the I being determined in specific ways. Rather, the I is determined in a most general, unspecific way to bring about its own determinations at the instigation of the check. Any specific determination of the I is the work of the I's own activity in response to the generic determination provided by the check. In the end, the Not-I is a product of the positing I, and the check merely provides the occasion for the I's self-limiting activity.[34]

Moreover – and this is the second part of Fichte's solution of the theoretical contradiction – the theoretical activity of the I, while originating entirely in the I, is not always present to the I. Fichte introduces a sharp distinction between the philosophical consciousness of the I's monopoly on determination and the ordinary consciousness of the I as always also determined by something other than the I. Only in sustained philosophical reflection does it become clear that even in the case of the theoretical relation the I is strictly speaking entirely self-determining (except for the minimal influence of the Not-I under the form of the check) – albeit unbeknownst to the ordinary I involved in the theoretical relation. What *appears* to the theoretical I as the Not-I determining the I is actually, as seen by the philosopher, the I's being both what does the determining and what is being determined in a self-relation of determination or relation of self-determination.[35] The apparent interaction of I and Not-I turns out to be a circle-like interaction of the I with itself.[36]

4. Practical Determining and Predicative Positing

Because the theoretical part of the *Wissenschaftslehre* has not resulted in establishing the absolute reality of a Not-I that determines the I, the practical part cannot presuppose an original I-independent reality to be determined by the I either. Rather, the examination of the practical relation between a determining I and a determined Not-I must itself derive or, in Fichte's preferred parlance, "deduce" the very reality of the Not-I. The account of theoretical knowledge in the second part of the *Foundation of the Entire Wissenschaftslehre* presupposes the knowledge of the practical in the work's third part.[37]

Given the absolute, independent nature of the I in general, the Not-I can only exercise determination upon the I qua theoretical I, if the absolute I has previously determined the Not-I. As in the case of theoretical determination, the I determines itself. But now, in the case of practical determination, the I's self-determination occurs indirectly, with the Not-I mediating between the absolute I that determines it and the intelligent I that it determines. The I's practical determination of the Not-I is a "detour" (*Umweg*)[38] within the I's overall itinerary of circulating strictly within itself.[39]

The question arises, though, as to what brings about this detour through the practical in the first place. More specifically, one wonders how the I qua absolute subject comes to "maintain itself open" (this is Fichte's metaphor)[40] for something other than its infinite self-positing. After all, at this point of the transcendental reconstruction of the I and its knowledge a recourse to a preexisting Not-I is not available. Any presence of the Not-I in or to the I, such as the "check," already presupposes the I's openness to such a "touch." The same impasse seems reached that halted the limitation of the basic contradiction in the theoretical sphere.

Fichte undertakes several attempts at answering the crucial question of how the I comes to limit or determine its own absolute and infinite activity. At one point, he refers to everyone's own experience of "something alien" (*Fremdartiges*) in us that remains quite unspecific but announces something other than the I in the I itself.[41] He also introduces "feeling" (*Gefühl*) as the factual, undeducible source of the I's determinacy. On the basis of the felt, subjective state of being determined the I is then supposed to posit a world of objects as the conditions of the possibility of such feeling.[42] Most importantly though, Fichte argues that it is an essential feature of the I itself, viz., its nature as intelligence, that brings about finitude and determination in an otherwise absolute activity. In order for there to be an I in the fully functional sense of the term, the activity *of* the I must also be an activity *for* the I. Fichte explains the difference between the two levels of the I's activity by distinguishing between the I's "positing itself for some intelligence other than itself" and the I's "positing itself as posited by itself."[43]

Fichte characterizes the positing-as, which is required for the full functioning of the I, as "retrieval" (*Wiederholung*) of the original absolute positing.[44] The relationship between first, retrieved positing and second, retrieving positing is not one of mere duplication. The second positing does not
repeat the first positing but returns to it, and this in such a way that the I
that is posited absolutely by itself is now posited *as* such an I. Although the
original absolute positing of the I by the I occurs thetically, the second,
retrieving positing has the form of predication. More precisely, the second
positing is autopredicative: The I posits itself as self-posited. In all other
predication, which is predication of something other than the I itself, the
retrieval does not concern the I that posits itself but the Not-I that is posited
by the I and that in turn is posited as such through the predication.

Fichte calls the predicative self-positing of the I its activity of "reflecting
on itself."[45] "Reflection" is to be understood as the I's constitutive trait of
attending to its own activity. The I's reflection on itself in predicative self-
positing is not a case of positing yet again, and for the second time, some
already preexisting I. Rather, the positing of the I as self-posited first brings
about an I that knows itself as such. Thus, the original reflection on the self-
posited I is productive and itself a case of the I's original positing activity.

Now, this essential reflective activity of the I provides the very occasion
for the occurrence of determination in the I. Through the positing of something *as* something, which is peculiar to predicative positing, there enters
into the originally undetermined self-positing activity of the absolute I the
feature of being determined *as* some such self-positing activity. And although
the absolute status of the I might suggest that the I is found to be not just
something but everything, viz., all of reality, that expectation has already
been undermined by the very fact of the I's own counterpositing. The I that
posits itself in original reflection is not a perfectly infinite being or God,
but an imperfectly infinite (and imperfectly finite) being, one that is finite
in its infinity and infinite in its finitude.[46]

In a perfectly infinite being, whose status as all-encompassing substance
eliminates any distinction between that which is being reflected upon and
that which reflects, no self-consciousness of the kind to be found in human
consciousness would be possible.[47] Only a determined intelligent being,
that is, an intelligence that is something but not something else – that possesses some determinations but lacks others – can posit itself in original
reflection as so determined.

Yet reflection can bring about such consciousness of determinacy only
if that which is determined as such by reflection already possesses determination, more precisely, determinacy. With respect to the determinacy of
the I that is presupposed by original reflection, Fichte distinguishes between
practical and theoretical determinacy. The practical determinacy of the I
consists in the sum of all that is given to the I as a task under the form of

the "series of the ideal." By contrast, the theoretical determinacy of the I consists in the givenness of the check, which involves the limitation of the I thorough the "series of the real."[48] The two sides of the original reflection of the I correspond to the fundamental double character of the I as practical-ideal and theoretical-real.[49] With regard to both series, Fichte returns once more to the thought of some irreducible and nondeducible givenness of elementary determination – practically as command or obligation and theoretically as check.

The introduction of predicative self-positing through original reflection as a principal feature of the I's positing activity at the end of the *Foundation of the Entire Wissenschaftslehre* reveals the uneliminable gap between the actual character of the I as finite or determined (more precisely, as self-determined in a "checked" way), on the one hand, and the notion of the I's absoluteness, which is now reduced to the status of an idea to be strived after, on the other hand.[50] In its capacity as practical I determining or limiting the Not-I, the I strives to assimilate everything Not-I to the I – in an attempt to realize the originary absolute nature of the I under conditions of finitude as revealed in counterpositing, check and feeling. Yet the practical I remains forever striving. There is no returning to the unconditioned status of I expressed in the first principle. In fact, the I seems never to have had that status in the first place. And whatever held that status was certainly not an I.

Where does that leave the practical determination of the I through the Not-I? To be sure, there is progress. But it is infinite.[51] The positing of the Not-I and its manifestations as check and feeling are so much part of the I's own constitution that they could only be worked off at the price of self-destruction. Moreover, the finite changes that are actually brought about by practical determination are ultimately only changes in the I's self-determination resulting in a different way of positing the Not-I. Our acting, even if it contributes to practical progress, is "ideal," that is, it takes place for us through the medium of representation.[52] But then again, the determining of the Not-I is no more and no less real than the positing of the Not-I. All reality, whether theoretical or practical, is posited by the I. Fichte was not to address what is ultimately real – beyond all positing and counterpositing, determining and being determined – until several years after laying the foundation of the entire *Wissenschaftslehre*.

4

CHANGING THE APPEARANCES

When Goethe has Faust retranslate the opening verse of the prologue to the Gospel according to John with the words "In the beginning was the deed" (*Im Anfang war die Tat*),[1] thus rendering "*logos*" in decidedly activist, practical terms, he could well have been referring to the latter-day example of his contemporary and acquaintance Fichte. For in Fichte philosophical speculation, and theory in general, is put into the service of practical concerns, and specifically of moral considerations, based on his conviction that reason itself is originally practical and that philosophical theory has to vindicate reason's practical nature by reconstructing the practical foundations of all knowledge in a comprehensive *Wissenschaftslehre*.

Yet whereas in Goethe's *Faust* the relation between life's origin in doing and the pallor of thinking is the matter of tragedy, in Fichte's case life and thought are brought into harmony in the existence of the scholar-teacher, who is active through lecturing and publishing and who thus acts vicariously, through his students. Still, there is a tragic note even to Fichte's scholarly existence. For the philosopher's influence on action is conditional upon the free cooperation and comprehension of his listeners and readers – and for the most part Fichte failed to secure that cooperation and comprehension. For much of his life Fichte, the preacher, orator and professor, who always regarded it as his vocation to act upon others and through others, was effectively without an audience. Yet he persisted in his philosophical efforts, thus creating a vast legacy for his posthumous listeners.

Fichte's urge to act on and through his audience is nowhere more present than in his ethical writings, chiefly among those *The System of Ethics* of

1798.[2] The very ground of Fichte's ethical theory is the firm belief in the absolute value of a human practice that is guided by the principle of morality; theory is there for the sake of practice, and practice, when properly guided, is there for its own sake. Yet for Fichte philosophical ethics, while being the theory of the practice par excellence, remains theoretical; moral knowledge and moral action have to originate freely and spontaneously in each and every human being. Ethical theory can and must appeal to the grounds of morality in everyone, but all such theory can do is point to the basis of morality in oneself.[3] Thus, Fichte's system of ethics is not so much a prescriptive or normative ethics as it is a sustained reflection on the conditions of moral knowledge and action – a transcendental theory of ethics.

In outlining the main features of Fichte's moral philosophy as contained in *The System of Ethics* of 1798, this chapter addresses, in turn, the place of the *System* in Fichte's project of the *Wissenschaftslehre*, the foundational role of morality in his account of human subjectivity[4] and Fichte's pioneering development of a transcendental theory of action in general and moral action in particular.[5]

1. *The System of Ethics* in the System of the *Wissenschaftslehre*

As the complete title of the work indicates, Fichte's *System of Ethics* is developed "according to the principles of the *Wissenschaftslehre*." Fichte had presented those principles in the *Foundation of the Entire Wissenschaftslehre*, which he had published in installments as a handbook for students to accompany his lectures in Jena during the summer semester of 1794 and the winter semester of 1794–1795. The title of the latter work indicates an important distinction between the foundational stratum of the *Wissenschaftslehre* and the complete edifice of the *Wissenschaftslehre* to be erected on that foundation.[6] Fichte proceeded to build upon the *Foundation of the Entire Wissenschaftslehre* by furnishing a two-part system of practical philosophy, consisting of the *Foundation of Natural Law* (1796–1797)[7] and *The System of Ethics*.[8] Further installations of the complete system of the *Wissenschaftslehre*, which would have comprised the philosophy of religion[9] and the philosophy of nature,[10] were abandoned when Fichte had to leave his academic post at Jena in 1799 in the wake of the atheism dispute.

Within the projected system of Fichte's Jena *Wissenschaftslehre*, *The System of Ethics* occupies a strategic place. As a theory of moral action it is particularly well suited to bringing out the practical and specifically moral orientation of Fichte's overall theory. Moreover, the task of deriving the conditions and forms of moral action moves the *Wissenschaftslehre* from its exceedingly speculative foundation to an account of concrete human activity, thus rendering increased plausibility to Fichte's claim that the *Wis-*

senschaftslehre is about the life of human consciousness. In fact, *The System of Ethics* already reflects the further development of the *Wissenschaftslehre*, away from the austere initial presentation of its foundation in 1794–1795 toward the new presentation to be found in his lectures on the *Wissenschaftslehre nova methodo*.[11]

The special status of *The System of Ethics* within the Jena *Wissenschaftslehre* is to be understood in the context of the novel character of Fichte's core doctrine. Historically speaking, Fichte's *Wissenschaftslehre* is a close successor to Kant's transcendental philosophy, as developed in the *Critique of Pure Reason*. Yet whereas in Kant the systematic exploration of the necessary conditions of consciousness and its objects remains limited to the sphere of theoretical consciousness, Fichte sets out to expand the scope of transcendental philosophy to encompass all forms of consciousness. Moreover, he seeks to unify the different forms of consciousness by retrieving the latent foundational layer of all consciousness, which underlies the latter's overt distinctions. Formally speaking, Fichte's *Wissenschaftslehre* is designed to integrate all forms of consciousness in a comprehensive account of the latter's origin as well as development.

Like Kant, Fichte focuses his explorations of consciousness on the a priori elements that are the necessary conditions of all consciousness and its objects. Whereas Kant identifies the set of a priori conditions of knowledge with reason (*Vernunft*), Fichte employs the term "I" (*Ich*) to designate the radical heterogeneity between the principal ground of all knowledge and the world of objects grounded thereupon. Fichte thus radicalizes Kant's subjectivist understanding of reason as a human faculty into an outright identification of reason with the transcendental core of human mentality. Fichte's choice of the nominalized pronoun of the first-person singular is not meant to relativize reason to human individuals but to articulate the ground of individual minds in some generic, supraindividual conception of reason. Fichte's I is a super-I. To be sure, it has to be a chief concern of Fichte's theory to elucidate the peculiar relation between human individuality and its supraindividual transcendental principles. In fact, *The System of Ethics* contains some of Fichte's most helpful reflections on that difficult issue.

Again like Kant, Fichte understands reason (or the I) as a self-sufficient domain that is originally independent of nature but that provides the very principles that govern the order of nature. In reason or the I there are thus combined the features of infinity and finitude. Reason is infinite in that it is not determined by natural causes. Rather, it is a spontaneous source of activity. Yet reason is equally importantly finite in that it stands under fixed laws that regulate the exercise of its spontaneity and function as the system of structuring principles of finite reality. Fichte's choice of the term "I" is designed to bring out the finite-infinite double nature of reason. Even as an infinite, absolute principle, the I is finite or limited – both in terms of the laws under which it operates and in terms of the sphere in which it realizes itself. Fichte's I is not the static sum total of a priori principles but a dynamic structure that comprises the drama of the I's ceaseless development from infinite, absolute origin through conditions of finite existence to some never-to-be-reached, thus infinite, goal. The I remains forever striving.

Its psychological terminology notwithstanding, Fichte's account of the I is not a tale about personal self-realization. In the first instance, the *Wissenschaftslehre* is concerned with the realization of reason. The sphere for that realization is human social reality, specifically the effects of human beings on nature and the interaction of human beings with each other. Individual consciousness is neither the starting point nor the end point in Fichte's account of the I. Individual consciousness is systematically positioned between the preindividual domain of the origin of all mental life (and its objects) and the supraindividual domain of the ultimate, yet unreachable end of all human efforts.

Accordingly, Fichte's pervasive discussion of the I in terms of consciousness and self-consciousness needs to be grasped in its nonpsychological dimension. Just as the I in the generic, transcendental sense is the principle of any and all individual I, so the consciousness and self-consciousness associated with the generic, preindividual I is the principle of all empirically concrete, individual consciousness and self-consciousness. Pure, preindividual consciousness and self-consciousness is not so much an instance of consciousness but its basic, principal form. The terms are used metonymically, in a transfer from the conditioned to the condition.

Now, in order to account for the manifold structure of consciousness as well as its objects, the underlying principle – the I – must be complex rather than simple; it must possess an internal articulation that prepares the external articulation conditioned by it. On Fichte's account, the principal inner constitution of the I prefigures the main organization of all empirical mental life and its world of objects. Accordingly, empirical reality can be seen as the unfolding or development of the I's transcendental core structure. Given the role of the I in the constitution of all forms of consciousness, the · *Wissenschaftslehre* is as much a theory of objectivity as it is a theory of subjectivity.[12] Fichte's characteristic emphasis on self-consciousness targets the role of the latter as the principle of all objectivity. In its original, pure form self-consciousness is already of a complexity that prefigures the overt differentiations of conscious life, chiefly among those the complementary polar opposites of the subjective and the objective.

Fichte employs the term "subject-object" to designate the principal form of self-consciousness, thus indicating the original orientation of the I toward objectivity.[13] To be sure, the subjective-objective originary structure of the

I is not open to introspective observation. Fichte has to employ artificial procedures, which he likens to the conducting of a scientific experiment, in order to capture the elusive absolute nature of the I in a model built upon the empirical structures brought about by that very I as their principal ground.[14] In the *Wissenschaftslehre* the role of the I as the principle for the derivation of all forms of consciousness is cast as a relation between self-consciousness and objective consciousness: Objective consciousness is said to have its principle in self-consciousness. The self-consciousness in question is not to be confused with empirical self-consciousness, or the reflective awareness of one's inner states.

A crucial stage in the development of the main forms of consciousness from the I as their principle consists in the differentiation between the theoretical and the practical side of consciousness.[15] Basically, the former consists in consciousness having its representations determined, whereas the latter consists in consciousness determining its representations on its own. But the distinction is complicated by the fact that the *Wissenschaftslehre* seeks to vindicate spontaneous activity to all forms of consciousness, including its apparently passive, merely receptive, manifestations: hence, the terminology of action, even freedom, that pervades Fichte's transcendental theory. Yet the practical, active aspect of consciousness is not only located in the generic stratum of the I, where it precedes any disjunction between the theoretical and the practical. Fichte locates eminently practical features in theoretical consciousness itself. In the *Foundation of the Entire Wissenschaftslehre* practical consciousness with its characteristic activity is shown to be a prerequisite for theoretical consciousness. The experience of objective determinations in theoretical consciousness is shown to involve the frustration of the I's efforts at exercising its own determinations. And the *Wissenschaftslehre nova methodo* goes even further in integrating theoretical consciousness into the specifically, not just generically, practical dimension of the I.

Yet with all their emphasis on the originally practical nature of reason, neither the first nor the second presentations of the *Wissenschaftslehre* address the moral dimension of human consciousness as such. This is where *The System of Ethics* further completes the *Wissenschaftslehre* by showing how not only practice in general but specifically moral practice is required to complete the conditions of consciousness.

2. The Moral Principle of Subjectivity

Fichte's chief strategy in integrating ethical theory into the system of the *Wissenschaftslehre* is to show that the principle of morality is both a condition and a consequence of a self-conscious rational being: a condition in that without the recognition of the moral dimension of human existence, consciousness is not yet fully functional – and a consequence in that the actual possession of functioning rationality on the part of a really existing human being implies the reality and indeed applicability of the moral principle. In fact, this argumentative strategy, reminiscent of the Kantian coalition of regressive and progressive arguments in theoretical transcendental philosophy, is further extended to include a whole set of assumptions that need to be made in order to account for fully functioning self-consciousness or, alternatively stated, that are warranted through the very fact of such consciousness. Fichte is quite frank about the merely conditional validity of any reasoning for the necessary requirements for, or the necessary consequences from, such a fact.[16] The arguments are valid relative to the best of our, human, knowledge, or "for us," as Fichte likes to put it. This is not to be understood, though, as a de facto limitation, possibly to be overcome by better knowledge, but as a principal limitation reflecting the uncircumventable fact that consciousness and its conditions can be assessed only in and through consciousness itself.

The conception of reason or I-ness (*Ichheit*) brought to bear on the derivation of morality involves two principal features, each representing one aspect of the double-natured subject-objectivity of the pure I: the act-character or agility (*Agilität*) of the I, according to which the latter is not a thinglike being with a predetermined essence but a doing that first brings about what it is; and its character as intelligence or of being-for-itself, according to which nothing can have being with respect to the I that is not *for* the I.[17] The two features are contrasted as *doing* and *seeing*, and they are intimately linked through the notion that reason or the I in its original form sees nothing but its very own doing. Now, in reason or the I as such – in the pure I – the features of doing and seeing are not yet fully developed. Their appellation occurs by anticipation of the full-blown forms that those traits assume in the conscious life of individual rational human beings. In the latter the doing emerges as force and the seeing as self-consciousness.

Fichte claims that the emergence of reason in human individuals includes first of all the discovery of oneself as willing: "I find myself, as myself, only willing."[18] Typically the individual in question has no insight into the generic, transcendental conditions of rational individuality. According to Fichte, the minimal form under which the I first encounters itself ("finds itself") is as engaged in volition. Fichte is not about to provide a real definition of the mental phenomenon of willing. Here, as in similar cases involving basic mental phenomena, he appeals to everyone's own familiarity with the experiences in question.[19] He offers a reconstruction of the unfolding of originary subject-objectivity into an I in which the subjective and the objective appear as separate poles of a unitary subject. The subjective pole consists in the moment of awareness, whereas the objective pole – rendered provisionally as "the objective I" – consists in that of which this awareness is awareness.[20] The poles are related like knower to known, with the subjective, ideal, intelligent side being aware of the objective, real, activity-like side.[21]

On Fichte's understanding, the interplay between the subjective and the objective side of the I is not an external relation between separately existing *relata*. It is merely a reflection of the limitations of finite intelligence in general and philosophical theorizing in particular that the absolutely unitary structure of the I, as it expresses itself in rational individuals, needs to be represented under the form of a succession of interactions between distinct parts.[22] In particular, it must be pointed out that the subjective I and the objective I, which enter into the relation of knower and known, are not cases of a genuine I endowed with the latter's characteristic dual features of (self-)consciousness and activity. Rather, they represent those very features in separation; only their joint consideration yields an instance of an I in the genuine sense. Fichte's reconstruction of the I's original self-experience as willing details just this coming about of the I through the interaction of its constitutive moments.

The relation between the subjective and the objective moment in the I is highly complex. In the first instance, the activity represented by the objective I is the object (hence the very term "objective I") for the subjective I, which as intelligence simply is the awareness of that activity. Moreover, as an activity pertaining to the I, the activity of the objective I is not an outwardly directed, worldly activity. At this point of its developmental history – at the point of origin – there is nothing for the I but the I itself. The I's activity is not other-regarding but self-regarding; the I acts upon itself. The identity of the acting and the acted-upon in the objective I is the practical counterpart of the I qua intelligence "seeing" only itself. But in order for there to be awareness of the objective I's self-reverting practical activity the latter must be taken up by the subjective I. Fichte's term of art for the I's taking note of something and thus making it something *for the I* in the first place is "positing" (*setzen*).[23] Now, the positing in question cannot just consist in the subjective I registering a self-reverting or self-regarding activity on the part of the objective I. That way, subjective and objective I would be separate entities, one doing something and the other noticing it. Rather, the one doing and the one noticing must be the same and – most importantly – must realize this very identity ("posit it as such").

This is where the subjective I no longer functions merely as the passive observer of the objective I's activity. In fairly dramatic imagery Fichte portrays the subjective I as seizing upon the objective I and appropriating the activity as its own. In making the activity an activity of the intelligence, the activity is intellectualized and the intelligence is realized. The resultant unitary I is a practical intelligence (*praktische Intelligenz*) in which the activity is brought "under the rule of the concept."[24] The activity of the I is the I's own activity in the twofold sense of being known by the I and of being done by the I. Doing and knowing coincide.

Fichte also portrays the act of the I's practico-intellectual self-constitution as its tearing itself away from itself, where this is being done by the I itself.[25] In imagery like this Fichte addresses the total independence of the I from things external to it. By (re-)integrating the internal externality of the I's own objectivity to itself (the "objective I"), the I becomes truly an I, a being in which everything happens through the I and for the I.

Yet the spontaneity (*Selbsttätigkeit*)[26] and independence (*Selbstständigkeit*)[27] of the I, while being absolute or unconditioned by another being, is not infinite. Moreover, the I is not only finite but finitizing: Everything thought or intuited by the I ("posited") is *eo ipso* something determinate (*Bestimmtes*), something that is what it is and is not also or instead anything else.[28] In fact, the I's activity is essentially the exercise of determination (*Bestimmung*), originally as the practical or real determination of an activity and subsequent to that also as the theoretical or ideal activity of determining an object. Both kinds of determination can be considered forms of self-determination (*Selbstbestimmung*) in that the source of agency is the I itself, either as the proximate source of agency in the case of practical self-determination or as its ultimate source in the case of theoretical self-determination. However, the practical determination of the I through the I is self-determination in the eminent sense.

The I exercises practical self-determination by bringing its own real activity under the rule of something ideal or thought, viz., the concept. In practical self-determination the ideal precedes the real.[29] Alternatively put, "real being" (*reelles Sein*) follows from "ideal being" (*ideales Sein*). Now, in the case under consideration – that of the I's original, pure practical self-determination – there is nothing external to the I yet (at least, nothing that would be for the I) that might provide the concept of an end to be realized through the I's activity. The determination in question has to originate entirely in the I as such. Yet there has to be determination, given the I's nature as intellectually self-finitizing infinite activity. Hence, the determination of the pure I is nothing other than the determinacy of the I by itself. The I is determined to determine itself, the determination is one to self-determination or absolute independence from anything other than the I itself.[30]

Thus, an integral part of the I's originally finding itself willing is the I's finding itself willing *something* – but not a particular object, not even a multitude of them, rather, willing the I's own radical independence, thus willing itself. Given the I's unconditional nature, its practical activity is determined by nothing except the very idea of being unconditioned; yet given that same I's finite nature, complete independence remains an idea, forever to be strived after but never completely obtained. Fichte follows Kant's practice and addresses the spontaneity of practical activity as "freedom,"[31] its generic determinacy as "ought" (*Sollen*) [32] and the specific determinacy of its pure activity as "categorical ought" (*kategorisches Sollen*). [33] In Fichte's formulation, the ultimate law governing the I's practical activity, or the "principle of morality," is "the necessary thought of the intelligence that it ought to determine its freedom according to the concept of independence, absolutely and without exception." [34] In the context of Fichte's comprehensive theory of the practical I, "morality" assumes the meaning of the *ethos* of freedom under which all human practical activity stands.

3. A Transcendental Theory of Action

After establishing the principle of morality as the basic law of human rational practice Fichte's *System of Ethics* proceeds to deduce the "reality" (*Realität*) or "applicability" (*Anwendbarkeit*) of the principle. The point is to integrate the purely rational standard of action into a general account of human action. Fichte thus revises Kant's conception of practical philosophy, which centers around the project of a metaphysics of morals, to include the theory of action in general. In line with his general project of a transcendental theory of consciousness and its objects (*Wissenschaftslehre*), Fichte derives the main features of human practical activity from a reconstructive account of the necessary conditions of consciousness. The resultant transcendental theory of action not merely supplements Kant's moral philosophy with an account of extramoral action but deeply affects the understanding of the nature of morality. Fichte moves away from the abstract and formalist character of Kant's ethics of universalizable maxims toward an account of morality as responsive to the contingent circumstances of actual human life. To be sure, in his attempt to render ethics *concrete* Fichte still insists on the absolute status of moral claims. To put it in Kantian terms, Fichte's innovation concerns not so much the validity status of moral claims but their conditions of origin.

Fichte derives the key features involved in practical self-determination as further conditions of individual self-consciousness that go beyond the minimal core of the I's pure willing. Although the I finds itself *originally* as willing, the I thus found is not yet the fully functioning I of individual human consciousness. The further requirements point beyond the notion of pure activity and even beyond the sphere of the I. The practical activity of the I consists in bringing about a change in the world and thus takes place in a context of specific ends and their attempted realization in the world of objects. To be sure, the immersion of the I as agent in a world that is not of its own making but yet amenable to its efforts at changing it is not a relapse of Fichte's theory into precritical realism. Rather, the worldliness of the practical I reflects the way things appear to ordinary consciousness as the latter emerges through practical activity. Speaking from the transcendental point of view, the world of empirical practice is a set of suppositions introduced by the I but typically unbeknownst to itself. The world is "posited" in order to explain the limitations of the I.[35] They are assumptions made from within consciousness and based on the laws of finite thinking, hence in no way evidence of a transcendent, I-independent reality.

In maintaining a sharp distinction between the way things appear to ordinary consciousness and the way things can be seen to come about from the transcendental perspective, Fichte does not seek to invalidate empirical reality and human activity in it. On the contrary, he views human practical activity and the associated belief in a world that provides the sphere for the exercise of such activity as genuine extensions of the I's original double nature as subject-objectivity. The world in which the I acts can be seen as the objective side of the subject-object writ large, whereas the free self-determination of the I represents the empirical realization of the subjective side of the subject-object. The absolute nature of the I is realized in and through individual human efforts, which taken in their entirety point toward reestablishing that original condition of the pure I in which the I is everything and everything is the I.

Introducing the transcendental perspective into the theory of human practice allows Fichte to develop an ingenious solution to the problem of human practical causality. Fichte casts the problem in terms of the subjective or ideal (thinking) determining the objective or real (being), claiming to be the first to have posed the problem of human practice as such.[36] His solution is modeled on his own earlier solution of the problem of human knowledge, viz., the problem of how the objective or real can determine the subjective or ideal. In an argument that built on Kant's identification of the necessary conditions of the experience of objects with the conditions of those very objects themselves, Fichte had accounted for the harmony between the knowing subject and the known object by tracing both of them back to the same original unity, of which they represent different but coordinated views or aspects. The analogous argument for the case of the acting subject and the acted-upon object makes the same point: The subjective, internal side and the objective, external side of the practical relation match because they are the same subject-objectivity, experienced subjectively in the one case and experienced objectively in the other case.[37]

To be sure, the alternative viewpoints on the same subject-object, both in the theoretical and practical relation, are not taken by some outside observer or reconstructor of the I ("the philosopher"), but they are views pertaining to the empirical I ("ordinary consciousness"), which experiences what is one and the same (for the observer-philosopher) as two different, magically matching states of affairs. Fichte's proposed solution to the problems of knowledge and action might be termed "the system of self-established harmony," if it is understood that the source of the harmony is not some individual, private self, but the I as such. Fichte can be seen as adapting Leibniz's system of preestablished harmony under the conditions of the Kantian emphasis on the spontaneity of finite reason.

Thus, the change involved in practical activity is a self-determination in more than one sense. To begin with, there is self-determination in that there is some change internal to the I, viz., the I's determining itself to some action. Moreover, the ensuing change in the world – the practical determination of an object – is also a form of self-determination, even if unbeknownst to ordinary consciousness: The worldly change is the objectified change of the I's experience of finitude. Given that the world is posited by the I in accordance with the I's experience of its own finitude, a change or further determination in the world is the posited counterpart of a change or further determination in the I – ultimately, both are changes of the I and by the I: "*My world* is changed means *I* am being changed; *my world* is further determined means *I* am being further determined."[38]

The details of Fichte's account of the necessary conditions for the application of the moral principle are too numerous to be included in this discussion of the general features of his theory of practice. Suffice it to enumerate the key theorems, which include the "deduction of an object of our activity in general" (section 4),[39] the "actual exercise of the faculty of freedom . . . [in] an actual free willing" (section 5),[40] the "deduction of the actual causality of the rational being" (section 6),[41] the "determination of the rational being through its inner character" (section 7)[42] and the "deduction of a determinacy of the objects without our doing" (section 8).[43] As is already clear from this listing, the transcendental requirements of applied morality concern not only the subject of action, which becomes increasingly more complex and ever more closely resembles the main outlines of individual practical consciousness. The requirements also concern the structure of the world of objects with which the subject interacts.

In its reliance on teleological considerations Fichte's discussion of the organic constitution of natural objects and their amenability to human purposes shows a strong influence of Kant's *Critique of Judgment*. Kant's characteristic caveat in teleological thinking – that we have to think "as if" some apparently contingent state of affairs were the result of design – is transformed into the system of necessary positings through which the I projects its own finitude as a world and into it.

In addition to providing an extensive treatment of the relation between agent and world, Fichte's deduction of the reality of the principle of morality offers innovative thoughts on the relation between the rational and the animal sides of human existence. Although Fichte maintains that rationality and animality are the two coordinated sides of our absolute nature as subject-objectivity, he recognizes, and indeed seeks to explain, the potential for conflict between the two, and more importantly the ground for a

nonconflictual integration of animality and rationality in line with his project of a concrete ethics.

Fichte addresses the convergence of nature and freedom under the
notion of "drive" (*Trieb*), which he takes over from contemporary biological theory, following the precedent of Reinhold's appropriation of the term
for the reconstruction of Kant's practical philosophy.[44] In its widest meaning in Fichte, the term stands for the tendency of a being to determine
itself. In natural beings the drives – then termed "natural drives" (*Natur-
triebe*) – operate without the element of freedom. But since such drives are
exercised from within the natural being, there is a measure of spontaneity
present even in such cases.[45]

In not-only-natural beings ("us") the drive appears in its basic form as
the natural, objective side of the I that "drives" (*treibt*) the intelligent, subjective I. The natural drive presents itself to the I as an entire system of drives
that constitute the animal nature of the human being, its drive nature.[46]
But although the natural drive may incline the finite rational being, it does
not by itself necessitate the being to act upon the drive. Any action taken
in response to a drive, be it one of following the drive or one of resisting it,
is the work of freedom.[47] Freedom in this function of electing whether or
not to give in to a drive or which of several competing drives to follow is
"formal freedom" (*formale Freiheit*) or the "freedom of choice" (*Willkür*).[48]

In addition to acknowledging the natural drive and its specifications,
Fichte recognizes a "pure drive" (*reiner Trieb*) in finite rational beings: the
drive for independent activity for its own sake.[49] The dynamical nature of
the pure I (pure activity) is thereby rendered in the pseudonaturalist language of drives. Now, transcendentally speaking, the natural and the pure
drives are just as little different as are the subjective I and the objective I.
The two drives are one and the same "protodrive" (*Urtrieb*), differently
viewed.[50] The point of action is to reintegrate the two drives into a "mixed
drive" (*gemischter Trieb*), which combines the unconditional impetus of the
pure drive with the specific content of the natural drive.[51] The resultant
mixed drive is *objective activity* geared toward absolute freedom.[52] And
although this goal of a total overcoming of nature remains forever unreachable, it can still be approached.[53]

Fichte goes on to identify the mixed drive with the "moral drive" (*sitt-
licher Trieb*). He explicitly criticizes an ethics that is based solely on the pure
drive, resulting in a "mere *Metaphysics of Morals* that is empty and formal."[54]
A true ethics (*Sittenlehre*) must remain "real" (*reell*) by synthetically uniting
the pure drive with the natural drive. The called-for integration of higher
and lower drives takes the following form: Among the several actions
demanded by the system of natural drives in a given situation, the one that
is simultaneously appropriate to the pure drive – and thus satisfies the
mixed, moral drive – is the one that forms part of an infinite series in the

pursuit of which the I were to become free in the radical sense of total independence from nature.[55] Thus, nature is conceived as providing the very material for surpassing it.

Given the materially concrete character of the mixed drive, Fichte's statement of the moral law is indexed to the specifics of a given situation: "Fulfill in each case your destination."[56] In the composition of the mixed, moral drive, then, the natural drive provides the material and the pure drive contributes the element of selection among competing natural drives carried out under the idea of total freedom. But this would limit the freedom of the moral agent to the merely formal freedom of choosing among naturally presented ends. Yet Fichte also attributes to the I freedom in a much stronger sense: material freedom (*materiale Freiheit*) that introduces "an entirely new series of actions from the point of view of content."[57] Unfortunately it is not made clear in *The System of Ethics* how this emphatic notion of freedom – which is obviously indebted to the nondeliberative freedom of the pure will (*reiner Wille*) in Kant – relates to the mixed nature of morality. There seems to be a tension here between Fichte's project of integrating nature and freedom into a concrete ethics and his allegiance to a supranatural conception of the I or reason for which nature inside and outside the I is merely a transitional stage between some pure origin and an equally pure final end of reason. Characteristically, the further development of Fichte's theory of freedom since the *Wissenschaftslehre nova methodo* accords increasing prominence to a conception of pure, nondeliberative willing and of freedom beyond choice.

PART III

THINKING AND WILLING

5

WILLING AS THINKING

The German philosophical tradition from Leibniz to Heidegger has more often than not centered its work around the study of that being that is closest to us and from the perspective of which everything else comes into view, viz., our own existence as conscious, world-related self or subject. Since Leibniz, the inquiry into the structure of subjectivity has moreover tended to employ a double characterization of the self as subject of cognition and subject of volition. More importantly, the cognitive and the conative elements of human subjectivity have typically been characterized in terms of each other, stressing both the volitional component in knowing and the cognitive component in willing. Finally, the post-Leibnizian German tradition has almost always regarded human subjectivity not as part of the natural world but as belonging to an order of its own, an order that underlies the natural world as the very condition of the cognizability of the natural order if not as its very ground of being. The latter feature has given the classical German philosophy of subjectivity the status of a "first philosophy," which can lay claim to being the successor discipline to the ontology of traditional metaphysics.

An important stage in the development of a first philosophy of subjectivity is marked by Fichte's project of the *Wissenschaftslehre*. In a series of daring lecture courses, most of which were never published during his own lifetime, Fichte provided innovative, highly complex and equally controversial accounts of the constitution of the subject and its world. Particularly important are his proposals for understanding the unity of the subject in terms of an originary structure that prefigures the subject's "later" differentiations into the dichotomies of self and world, self and others, mind and body, knowing and doing. At the center of Fichte's sustained reflections on the original unity of the self lies the problem of how to capture the intimate relation between knowing and willing. A closer look at the main features of his account of thinking and willing is thus apt to shed light on his often obscure claims about the origin of subjectivity in the *Wissenschaftslehre* and to provide some indications for Fichte's place in the post-Kantian dissociation of the will from the intellect. In this chapter the outlines of Fichte's transcendental theory of thinking and willing are traced by focusing on the relations between theoretical and practical reason, thinking and freedom, thinking and intuiting, thinking and doing, thinking and willing, and thinking and pure willing. Throughout, the affinities and differences between Fichte's and Kant's theories of the subject are addressed.

1. An Integrated Theory of Reason

Fichte presents his *Wissenschaftslehre* as the systematic emendation of Kant's critical philosophy. In particular, the *Wissenschaftslehre* follows its Kantian precedent in the subjectivist turn to an examination of the a priori potential of human reason. Kant's critique of pure reason had investigated the rationality potential of the human subject in three separately published *Critiques,* with the second and third coming as a surprise even to their author. The additive nature of the critical trilogy is reflected in the relation between the specifically different employments of reason discussed in the *Critique of Pure Reason* (1781), the *Critique of Practical Reason* (1788) and the *Critique of Judgement* (1790). That relation is one of coordination between the cognitive and conative employment of reason, first – in the "Postulates of Pure Practical Reason" – under the guiding concept of the highest good, and then – in the theory of reflective judgment – under the directive of reason reflecting on human cognitive, moral and cultural needs. In Kant the unity of reason amid its differentiation into theoretical and practical reason is thus not established by recourse to some unity of *origin* but through a unity of *end,* viz., the rational supposition of a teleologically articulated physicomoral harmony both within the subject and between the subject and its world.

By contrast, Fichte's *Wissenschaftslehre* aims at an originally and systematically integrated account of human subjectivity, an account that relates the complex structure of finite rational beings to their ultimate grounding in some original unity. That ultimate unity, though, is not some primitive element to which everything can be reduced. Rather, the unity in question has a structure to it that allows one to derive or deduce the main features of human subjectivity in a process that can be described as the internal selfcompletion of the subject from its original unity all the way to a complexly determined human being situated in its world along with other human beings. Accordingly, the subject's original unity is not conceived monistically but by recourse to a structure of intricately related _co-original_ moments that collaborate in the constitution of subjectivity. In particular, Fichte's nonreductivist, antimonistic theory of the subject identifies in the very origin of subjectivity a prototype for the distinction between theoretical and practical reason. The entire first phase of Fichte's work on the _Wissenschaftslehre,_ between 1794 and 1800, can be regarded as a series of attempts to rethink the relation between the rationality standards of theory and the rationality standards of practice in light of the mutual dependence of both forms of reason in the constitution of human subjectivity.

In Fichte's earliest published version of the _Wissenschaftslehre,_ the _Foundation of the Entire Wissenschaftslehre_ of 1794–1795, practical reason is shown to be a requirement even for the theoretical or cognitive employment of reason. Knowledge along with its object is said to depend for its very possibility on the practical nature of reason understood as "striving" (_Streben_).[1] Yet in Fichte's presentation of the matter, the theory of reason's cognitive employment is for the most part developed independently of specifically practical considerations. The latter only enter in to complete the account of cognition. This mode of presentation provides a close link between the reason of theory and that of practice, but it does not yet adequately reflect the radical unity of the two, nor does it sufficiently address the inverse side of the mutual dependence of theoretical and practical reason, viz., the necessity of theoretical reason for the very possibility of practical reason.

Fichte himself came to see the shortcomings in the presentation if not the substance of the first published _Wissenschaftslehre_ and soon began work on the revised presentation of the _Wissenschaftslehre._ He published only a fragmented version of the _New Presentation_ of the _Wissenschaftslehre_ (1797–1798),[2] consisting of a preface, two substantial introductions and the first chapter. But that torso is supplemented by the two complete transcripts of Fichte's lectures on the _Wissenschaftslehre nova methodo._[3]

A further text, published by Fichte himself, to be included in the corpus of the new presentation of the _Wissenschaftslehre_ is _The System of Ethics_ of 1798,[4] which contains an extensive opening portion on the general theory of practical reason.[5] The present treatment of Fichte's account of thinking and willing is limited to select passages in the "First Introduction" of the _New Presentation of the Wissenschaftslehre_ and to key sections of the _Wissenschaftslehre nova methodo._

The second, methodologically revised version of the _Wissenschaftslehre_ is characterized by increased attention given to metaphilosophical considerations concerning the very nature, the starting point and the procedure of Fichte's transcendental philosophy. Terminologically speaking, the texts from the period of the new presentation of the _Wissenschaftslehre_ feature

prominently the vocabulary of thinking, this both in their description of
the kind of mental effort required by the *Wissenschaftslehre* itself and in the
actual account of finite subjectivity in the *Wissenschaftslehre*. Moreover, in
the main texts of the new presentation the concepts of thought and thinking are typically developed in close connection with the terminology of will
and willing. By contrast, the terminology of "thinking" and "willing" is conspicuously absent from the earlier version of the *Wissenschaftslehre*.[6] Moreover, in the *Wissenschaftslehre* of 1796–1799 the artificial division of transcendental philosophy into a theoretical and a practical part, still to be
found in the *Wissenschaftslehre* of 1794–1795, is given up in favor of a "much
more natural path, beginning with the practical" and "drawing the practical over into the theoretical in order to explain the latter through the former."[7]

2. Freedom and the Laws of Thinking

The notion of thinking figures prominently in the metaphilosophical and
methodological reflections of the writings that constitute the new presentation of the *Wissenschaftslehre*. At the center of Fichte's thoughts about
philosophical thinking stand two issues, viz., the general logical procedure
involved in the thinking that is philosophy and the specific personal effort
of thinking that the *Wissenschaftslehre* requires.

In his description of the basic method of philosophy in general and that
of the *Wissenschaftslehre* in particular, Fichte retains the Kantian understanding of transcendental philosophy as a theory of experience.[8] More
precisely, philosophy is the theory of the a priori conditions or, in Fichte's
preferred parlance, of the "ground" (*Grund*) of experience. Experience is
here understood as the system of those representations that are accompanied by the feeling of necessity. The latter are opposed to the representations that are accompanied by the feeling of freedom. Fichte's technical
understanding of transcendental philosophy thus systematically disregards
all those representations that are felt to be based on the exercise of human
freedom – and this on the grounds that those representations depend on
choice and therefore would have been different had the human being in
question chosen differently. By contrast, the system of experience is made
up of representations that are not subject to choice but rather that reflect
certain lawful relations among representations.

Now, the ground of experience, insofar as it is the transcendental ground
of all experience and not some particular, empirical, ground for this or that
experience, falls necessarily outside of experience. The ground in question
is therefore never "given" (*gegeben*) but must be "thought" (*gedacht*).[9] It is
the result of the intellectual activity of applying the "principle of reason"
(*Satz des Grundes*)[10] to the case of experience as a whole. As Fichte puts it,

the thinking in question is an "adding-on-in-thought" (*Hinzudenken*) by which the mind qua intellect moves from what is given to that which is not given but which must be thought in order to account for what is given. The necessity involved is one of "laws of thought" (*Gesetze des Denkens*).[11]

Yet although the laws that govern the thinking of the ground of experience are necessary, it is not necessary that the ground of experience be thought. In fact, on Fichte's view it requires considerable intellectual skill ("speculation")[12] to think the transcendental ground at all, and it requires even further qualifications of a more moral nature to think the ground of experience correctly, that is, along the lines of a radicalized Kantian transcendental idealism.[13] The thinking of the ground of experience is a matter of freedom in the twofold sense of requiring the freedom of thinking – of abstracting from the given as such and reflecting on its conditions – and of requiring the thinking of freedom – the realization of the ultimate nature of the subject as one of radical independence from all external determination. An important feature of Fichte's thinking about thinking emerges here: It is a matter of freedom whether or not thinking takes place; but if thinking takes place, then it operates under necessary laws.

Fichte's second set of thoughts about philosophical thinking, viz., those concerning the tremendous intellectual requirement imposed by the *Wissenschaftslehre*, are epitomized in his initial instruction to the listener of his lectures and the reader of his writings to "think yourself, and notice how you do this."[14] Again Fichte appeals to the freedom of thought, this time being the freedom to abstract from any object of one's thought and rather to reflect on the subject of thinking. The object of philosophy obtained under that instruction is an object of thought, and like any object of thought it has "ideal being" (*ideales Sein*)[15] or a being that consists in being thought. It deserves mention in this context that the Fichtean imperative to "think yourself" (*denke dich;* accusative personal pronoun) is not intended to effectuate the transmission of any specific thought, not even that of the idealistically conceived absolute ground of experience. Rather, Fichte instructs his listeners or readers to think that thought for themselves. On his view of the matter, it is simply not possible to think one's own idealist thinking, or any thought for that matter, into another person's mind. Fichte's term for that impossible intersubjective transfer of thought is "*hineindenken*" ("thinking something into someone").[16] On his assessment, communication, and that includes philosophical instruction, ultimately depends on thinking for oneself (*selber denken*).

3. Thinking and Intuiting

In order to further elucidate the crucial role of thinking in Fichte's writings from the new presentation of the *Wissenschaftslehre*, one has to turn from the thinking required from the philosopher to the thinking that is being examined by the philosopher. Fichte likens the procedure of his transcendental theory of the subject to that of a scientific experiment.[17] The object under investigation in Fichte's transcendental experiment is the idealistically conceived absolute ground of experience, called "the I" (*das Ich*). The philosopher's original conception of that I is one of pure, self-reverting activity. Fichte typically resorts to the logician's language of positing (affirmation in judgment), calling the pure I "self-positing," and more importantly, "positing itself as positing."[18] Alternatively, the I in question is characterized in decidedly praxeological language, as an instance of acting, more precisely, "an acting that goes back onto itself" (*in sich zurückgehendes Handeln*).[19]

The pure I so construed is not to be confused with a spatio-temporally situated, concrete I or individual.[20] Yet the two are closely related. On Fichte's view, the pure I is the ground for all the further specifications that make up the individual I. In his experiment with the I, Fichte seeks to reconstruct the path from the original, pure I to the concrete, individual I. Moreover, that reconstruction is the image (*Bild*) of the I's own or self-construction. The philosophical experimenter only follows a process that takes place in the I itself. There is an important difference, though, between the original self-construction of the I and the philosopher's reconstruction. The philosophical rendition of the I's genesis is a temporal process suggesting a history of the I, whereas the I itself comes about instantaneously, in one highly complex act of self-constitution. Fichte attributes the need for a temporally articulated representation of the I to the finite, discursive nature of philosophical thinking.[21]

Yet although Fichte clearly distinguishes between the historical rendition of the I by means of philosophy and the I's own ahistorical nature, he equally stresses the fact that the I under investigation in the experimental setting of the *Wissenschaftslehre* is none other than the philosopher's, and everyone else's, egologically structured subjectivity. This indicates both that the pure I is already finite, even though it may be capable of absolute acts, and that philosophical reflection is not merely finite thinking but capable of grasping the absolute nature of the I. Fichte himself makes that point by adapting the Kantian notion of an intellectual intuition and using it to characterize both the ultimate nature of the I and the activity required for the philosophical reconstruction of the I.[22] "Intellectual intuition" stands here for the immediate, not conceptually mediated awareness of the I's original activity.[23]

Fichte's double usage of the notion of intellectual intuition as a tool for doing philosophy and as descriptive of the nature of the pure I might be taken to suggest a merely subsidiary role for thinking in the original constitution of the I as well as in its philosophical reconstruction. Yet not unlike

Kantian sensible intuition, Fichtean intellectual intuition is "blind" and in need of determination through thinking. That clearly holds for the case of philosophical reflection on the I, where thinking first provides determination to the philosopher's object, that is, the as yet undetermined pure I. But the need for conceptual determination equally holds for the case of the I's own coming about. It is by thinking itself in certain, lawfully governed ways that the I becomes what it is, viz., concretely determined individual subjectivity.

The generic notion of thinking in Fichte can thus be described along Kantian lines. Thinking provides the form of determinacy to some material that is given through intuition. To be sure, that material basis of intuition must not be understood as given from without the subject. Rather, any thought of externality, and the term "thought" is chosen advisedly here, is the result of conceptually transforming what is internally given (intuition) into something that appears external to the subject (thing). Fichte's internalist understanding of intuition leads him to defend an identity of sorts between thought and intuition. They are two alternative and mutually complementing ways of expressing the ultimate nature of subjectivity and its function as the ground of all objectivity. In that vein, Fichte contrasts and relates intuition and concept as activity and rest,[24] thus indicating that he understands intuition as the act of intuiting (*Anschauung* as *Anschauen*) and concept as the result obtained by supplying an object to the intuiting.

On Fichte's account, thinking in the technical sense of conceptually adding an object to a given, more precisely a self-given, intuition operates under a basic law, viz., the "law of reflection concerning opposites" (*Reflexionsgesetz des Entgegensetzens*).[25] This law governs the exercise of determination and makes the latter take the form of contrasting the determined (*Bestimmtes*) with something determinable (*Bestimmbares*).[26] In making determination proceed by way of contrast to something that is not itself determined but that underlies the determination in question, Fichte takes up Spinoza's insight that all determination is by way of negation (*omnis determinatio est negatio*). Yet Fichte provides an idealist reading of the principle by treating it as a necessary feature of *thinking* that something determinable is presupposed in all thinking.[27] The opposition of determining and determinable is thus one introduced by the activity of thinking itself. The determinable is that which is to be thought along with the determination (*mitzudenken*).[28] Notice the difference between the earlier principle of ground or reason, which tracks all determination to its determining ground – a ground that itself has determination – and the new principle of opposition or determinability, which introduces the necessary contrast between determination and determinability. Applying the principle of reason presupposes the law of opposition in that a sphere needs to be posited, op-posited to be precise, which can serve as the recipient for the transfer of determination in accordance with the principle of reason.

4. Intelligence and Practical Faculty

The thinking that is of special interest to the *Wissenschaftslehre* is the thinking to be found in the subject that underlies all forms and objects of consciousness, the "pure I" or the "I-hood" (*Ichheit*), as Fichte also calls it.[29] Fichte asks how the I must think itself. The question does not concern itself with whatever being the I might have independent of thinking itself or reflecting on itself. Rather, it asks only how the I in reflecting on itself has to think of itself. Fichte maintains that the I is to think of itself as an "agility" (*Agilität*)[30] which takes the form of "passing-over" (*Übergehen*). That passing-over is none other than the activity of determination, viewed now as the transition from determinability to determinacy. Moreover, the transition in question is the I's own activity. It is a case of "free self-determination" (*freie Selbstbestimmung*).[31] Finally, the acting of the I is immediately intuited by the I – this original presence-to-itself being the very nature of the I as "subject-object" (*Subjekt-Objekt*).[32] In fact, the only thing that is originally intuited in and by the I is its own acting or passing-over: "all we see is ourselves, and only as acting."[33] Any further intuition on the part of the I is the thought-mediated projection of its original self-experience into a temporal-spatial world of things.

There are thus two activities present in the I, one, termed "real," which performs the actual doing (*Machen*), the other, termed "ideal," which follows the first by reflecting on it (*Nachbilden*).[34] Fichte distinguishes the two by attributing to the I two different sides, which he also at times presents as two I's, viz., the practical faculty or the practical I and the intelligence or the theoretical I.[35] The duality of real and ideal activity runs through the whole structure of the I and constitutes the irreducible ideal-real double nature of the I, its "duplicity" (*Duplizität*) or "subject-objectivity" (*Subjekt-Objektivität*).[36] Yet although the two constituents of the I are irreducible to each other, they also require one another for bringing about the I. In Fichte's words, "The I cannot be ideal without being practical, and vice versa."[37]

Fichte regards the necessity of thinking both features of the I together and in mutual dependence as indicative of their "absolute identity."[38] The latter characterization should not be taken, though, to imply a strict identity between the two but to refer to the identity of the I that is brought about by their joint operation. Similarly, Fichte's frequent assertions that two apparently different features of subjectivity, such as intuition and thought, are "really" two aspects or views of one, and the same should be understand against the background of the I's original double nature.[39]

5. Thinking and Willing

The sense of "practice" (*Praxis*)[40] introduced in Fichte's account of the I as originally practical cum intelligent is decidedly intellectual. At this point of his analysis, Fichte is not concerned with the empirical realization of things mental. The practice in question is internal to the subject and refers to the latter's acting upon itself. The intellectualist restriction of the practicality of the subject holds equally for Fichte's usage of the term "willing" to describe the moment of resolve and concentration of force involved in the mind's passing over from indeterminacy to determinacy.

Fichte himself introduces the concept of willing through the contrast to deliberating (*deliberieren*).[41] In deliberation the intellectual determination ("thinking") is not yet tied down to any particular determination, whereas the act of willing imposes a "freely willed limitation" (*freiwillige Beschränkung*)[42] to one path of thinking at the expense of all the others. Fichte even seems to identify outright thinking and willing when he declares "willing is nothing but a [kind of] thinking."[43] He also speaks of the "thinking of the willing" (*Denken des Wollens*).[44] The genitive in the construction "thinking of the willing" is to be understood not objectively – as though the willing were being thought about – but subjectively, as referring to the kind of thinking that willing is. Fichte regards willing as determined, resolved thinking.

Yet Fichte also considers willing as something to be encountered by thinking, as something that is "found" and then taken up through thinking.[45] The relation between thinking and willing is thus not one of ultimate identity but one of mutual requirement. In Fichte's own words: "I will insofar as I think myself as willing, and I think myself as willing insofar as I will."[46] His point here seems to be that the "doing" of the willing needs to be "seen," that is, thought, in order to have reality for the I.

The precariously close relation between thinking and willing in the origin of subjectivity can now be described in two, mutually complementary ways. One can speak of the *intellectualist* nature of willing in the new presentation, stressing that willing is a form of thinking, viz., determined, and more precisely, self-determined thinking. But one can with equal justification speak of the *volitional* nature of thinking, stressing that making one's thinking determined requires willing. Put another way, in his theory of thinking, Fichte emphasizes the "real" side of the thinking activity. In his theory of volition, by contrast, Fichte accentuates the "ideal" nature of willing.

6. Pure Willing and Thinking

Fichte's account of the relation between willing and thinking in the new presentation of the *Wissenschaftslehre* is ultimately grounded in a distinction he draws between empirical willing and pure willing. The distinction follows closely the one introduced by Kant between *Willkür* ("choice") and *Wille* ("will"),[47] with the former standing for the power of deciding between alternatives and the latter referring to an original, pure self-determination preceding the opening up of any alternatives. Fichte argues that in order to be rational, the willing has to operate under the conception of the end that is being willed. This presupposes cognition, the very capability that was to be explained by his account of volition-in-thinking in the first place. At this point, Fichte concedes a circle (*Zirkel*) in his account of the I: no acting without knowing, and no knowing without acting.[48]

The circle concerns in particular the original self-determination of the I, its self-constitution as finite but free intelligence. In this process, the I cannot rely on any preceding knowledge of ways for the I to be. In that regard the I is free. Yet the I is not free to be just anything but is limited by the condition in which the I originally finds itself. Fichte brings together the feature of freedom or self-determination of the I and its "found," given character or facticity in the notion of the I's determination to self-determination: "This determinacy, which constitutes my basic character, consists in the fact that I am determined to determine myself in a certain way."[49]

On Fichte's account, the circle is ultimately circumvented through the introduction of a "pure willing" (*reines Wollen*),[50] antecedent to any choice. In pure willing the ideal and the real moment, the knowing and the resolve, are one – a volitional counterpart to the unity of "doing" and "seeing" in the case of intellectual intuition. In pure willing, an original act of self-determination takes place that combines two features into one: freedom and determinacy, or, alternatively put, absoluteness and finitude. To be sure, the freedom in question cannot consist in a choice between alternatives. No such alternatives have been established yet. Rather, the freedom in question will have to be absolute spontaneity or the "capacity to begin absolutely" (*Vermögen absolut anzufangen*).[51] Yet a beginning has to be made, and thus the freedom of absolute beginning is restricted to a particular starting point. Fichte introduces the required synthesis thus: "Our synthetic concept is freedom and determinacy in one, freedom insofar as a beginning is being made, determinacy insofar as the beginning can be made only that way."[52]

The original restrictedness of absolute freedom manifests itself as an "absolute ought" (*absolutes Sollen*),[53] which is akin to the moral ought of the categorical imperative. Yet Fichte insists that the ought in question is a categorical claim genuine to the transcendental theory of consciousness, in particular to the transcendental theory of willing, and is not to be confused with an ought that is specifically moral. He also calls the ought of pure, transcendental willing the "mere form of willing" (*bloße Form des Wollens*),[54] thus indicating the status of pure willing as a necessary but not sufficient condition for all empirical willing.

Pure willing as such, which Fichte also refers to as "pure will" (*reiner Wille*),[55] is not to be encountered in consciousness. Rather, it is presupposed, on the part of transcendental reasoning, as the "explanatory ground of consciousness" and has the character of a "hypothesis."[56] Yet this should not be taken to suggest a derivative status of willing, as though pure willing were "merely" the product of philosophical thought. Although the *concept* of a pure will first comes about through philosophical thinking, it is part of that very notion that pure willing is presupposed in all thinking. In Fichte's words, "Hence the pure willing does not come about through thinking but is already posited in advance of the latter."[57] On Fichte's account, then, pure willing or pure will is the original source of determination in all thinking. It is due to pure willing that the I finds itself determined to self-determination, viz., finds itself willing.[58]

Yet pure willing, although presupposed in all thinking, is itself affected by the conditions of thinking. In line with the intellectual nature of the I, pure willing is taken up by thinking; it is brought under the form of thinking. In the process, pure willing – the universally presupposed ultimate source of determination – is itself determined by being thought or reflected upon. Now, the willing can only be thought as determined by establishing an opposition to something determinable. On Fichte's view, the split between determination and determinability thus introduced into the willing amounts to the pluralization of the will. In thinking itself as willing, the subject takes up the will as its own will, opposing it to the will of others. Thinking here assumes the role of a "intermediate link" (*Mittelglied*)[59] between the absolute nature of the pure will – "the intelligible" (*das Intelligible*),[60] as Fichte also calls it – and the individual nature of the empirical will.

In the *Wissenschaftslehre nova methodo,* the mediating function of thinking is introduced under the title "synthetic thinking" (*synthetisches Denken*).[61] Thinking is the original synthesis of the real and the ideal that brings about the I in the first place. Fichte's choice of the term "synthesis" clearly indicates that the role of thinking – while certainly original – is by no means absolute. To be sure, thinking depends on the pure, preempirical givenness of willing. Yet that pure willing is never given as such but is always already thought. Moreover, the thinking involved in thinking the will is discursive and brings with it the division of the I's original activity into individual acts of thinking and willing that fall into time.

Fichte thus portrays the will as subject to a transcendental dynamics in which the will is being thought and thereby realized under sensible conditions. In status and structure, the process resembles the realization of the categories under sensible conditions in Kant's doctrine of transcendental schematism.[62] In both cases, something that is nonsensible in origin is given a sensory form in order to become empirically real. Yet whereas Kant's schematism of the categories remains formal or pure and limited to the a priori features of time, Fichte extends the "sensification" (*Versinnlichung*)[63] of the pure will down to the level of the empirical. The will is being "materially sensified."[64] The chief empirical specifications of the pure will, as deduced by Fichte, are the physical reality of the will as my own body (*Leib*)[65] and the reality of other perceivable, embodied beings outside me.[66] Fichte here argues that the task of thinking oneself as willing requires the assumption of a whole series of necessary conditions that specify the spatio-temporal dimensions of finite consciousness.

Yet as Fichte himself insists, this type of argument only establishes a conditional and relative necessity: conditional on the spontaneity of thinking the will and relative to the forms of such thinking. In Fichte's own words, "We can only explain things in accordance with our laws of thinking, and our answer must be shaped by the latter. Our explanation is thus not valid absolutely; for our question is this: how can a rational being explain its own consciousness.[67] This may seem a severe restriction. But on Fichte's view, it is the best that any finite intelligence can do. What might at first appear to be a postcritical metaphysics about the absolute will realizing itself in the empirical world is thus instead a critical inquiry into the transcendental conditions of volitional consciousness.

6

IDEAL THINKING AND REAL THINKING

Fichte's work on the *Wissenschaftslehre* from his Jena period centers around the role of the subject as the principle of consciousness and its objects. Taken as a doctrinal concept, the *Wissenschaftslehre* amounts to a systematically radicalized Kantian transcendental idealism according to which all objects of possible experience, and indeed all objects in general, are necessarily conditioned by some nonempirical activity of the subject. Notoriously, Fichte eliminates the transcendental-realist remnants of Kant's formal idealism, viz., the things in themselves, in favor of a complete transcendental idealism, which has the matter as well as the form of all objectivity originate entirely in the subject and its transcendental acts.

With its ambition toward a systematic theory of consciousness, the *Wissenschaftslehre* takes on the difficult task of accounting for the unity among consciousness and its objects, while preserving the diversity and divisions that make up the complex structures of mind and world. Given the foundational role of the subject in the *Wissenschaftslehre*, the delicate balance between unity and difference concerns most importantly the nature of the subject itself. Fichte refers to that unity-within-duality and duality-within-unity by the nominalized pronoun of the first-person singular, "I" (*Ich*), and coins for it such paradoxical terms as "subject-object" and "subject-objectivity."

The most advanced expression of Fichte's reflections on the complex unity of the subject is to be found in the writings of the new presentation of the Jena *Wissenschaftslehre* (1796–1799), chief among them the lectures on the *Wissenschaftslehre nova methodo*. Unlike the forbiddingly terse, highly condensed initial presentation to be found in the *Foundation of the Entire Wissenschaftslehre* of 1794–1795,[1] the new presentation features detailed explanations of the procedure, goals and nature of Fichte's enterprise that accompany the Fichtean text almost like a running commentary. Moreover, the new presentation of the *Wissenschaftslehre* employs a number of conceptual distinctions that are particularly well suited to articulating the complex, yet unitary deep structure of the subject – chief among them the concepts of the ideal and the real and the related distinction between thinking and willing. Tracing the intricate relations between those notions will show the extent to which the subject in Fichte is both irreducibly complex and indicative of some ultimate reality that emerges at the heart of even the most radical transcendental idealism.

This chapter provides a critical reconstruction of Fichte's account of the subject and of the ultimate reality presupposed by the latter in the *Wissenschaftslehre nova methodo*. The chapter proceeds in four sections on the ideality of philosophy, the ideal and real activity of the subject, the relation between ideal and real thinking and the relation between thinking and ultimate reality.

1. The Ideality of Philosophy

Fichte's project of a fundamental philosophy, presented under the programmatic title "*Wissenschaftslehre*," takes up Kant's systematic investigation of the nature of finite rational beings in the three *Critiques*. Like Kant, Fichte presents an account of the theoretical or cognitive dimension of human existence that is systematically linked to the practical and affective dimensions of being human. Yet whereas Kant treats the distinction between the theoretical, the practical and the reflective employment of finite reason as a given that is beyond further analysis, Fichte seeks to elucidate the very origin of the principal divisions that make up the basic structure of finite rational beings. This leads him to a highly integrated account of finite rationality, in which the transcendental theory of experience and the transcendental theory of freedom are thoroughly intertwined.

To be sure, the distinction between theoretical and practical reason, along with its associated divisions, is not simply replaced by some undifferentiated generic conception of reason. Such a move would leave the subsequent differentiation unexplained and indeed inexplicable. Rather, the deep structure of the finite rational being must be such that the later, overt disjunctions are already latently prefigured. Hence, the originary structure of the finite rational being is itself complex rather than simple. However, the elements that make up the core of finite rationality do not exist independent of and prior to their unification. Otherwise the unity of the subject would be merely derivative, even accidental, and the original structure of subjectivity would be a disjointed plurality. Fichte's own model for the mutual dependence of elements and whole in the constitution of the finite rational being is the living organism, understood along the lines of Kant's philosophical biology in the *Critique of Judgment*.

Given these requirements, the *Wissenschaftslehre* has a twofold task. It must elucidate the original, yet complex deep structure of finite rational beings, and it must relate that originary structure to the overt distinctions and differentiations of human mental life. In the first presentation of the *Wissenschaftslehre* the former task is assigned to the short and highly condensed First Part, which presents the three principles of the entire *Wissenschaftslehre*, and the latter task is carried out in the remaining Second and Third Parts of the work, which contain the "Foundation of Theoretical Knowledge" and the "Foundation of the Science of the Practical," respectively.[2] The new presentation of the *Wissenschaftslehre* provides a further step toward a unified theory of finite rational beings. The principles are no longer presented separately from the derivations of the principal forms of rational mental life, and the basic forms of theory and practice are presented together in order to bring out their original unity.

The numerous methodological reflections that accompany the doctrinal core of the *Wissenschaftslehre nova methodo* attest to the fact that the philosophical presentation of the structure of finite rational beings is a highly artificial undertaking, dependent on the successful and sustained employment of a number of technical devices. Neither the original unity of the finite mind nor its articulation into the principal forms of mental life are empirically given data. Rather, they are the very ground of any experience, and as such they elude all observation.

The investigations of the *Wissenschaftslehre* demand disregarding what is merely empirical in experience ("abstraction")[3] and focusing on the nonempirical conditions that underlie all experience ("reflection").[4] Fichte mobilizes the term "intellectual intuition" to designate the peculiar nonsensible awareness required for grasping the nonsensible nature of the finite rational being.[5] Yet intellectual intuition as such does not establish any insight or knowledge. The latter requires that the material provided by the philosopher's intuition be thought. Now, all finite, human thinking is discursive, that is, a synthesis of elements that are taken up successively and subsequently united.[6] Hence, in the *Wissenschaftslehre* the original, holistic structure of finite rationality is subjected to the necessary conditions of discursive thinking. The dimension of time, and specifically temporal succession, thus introduced into the account of finite rationality is a reflection of the philosopher's own finite mind. The *Wissenschaftslehre* provides a discursive representation (*Darstellung*) of the original nondiscursive constitution of the human mind.

Fichte conveys the peculiar status of philosophy and its objects by resort-ing to the term "ideal" (*ideal*).[7] The philosophical representation of the nature and operations of the finite mind is certainly not real, if reality is equated with sensorily observable, empirical reality. But neither does the philosophical account of human mentality capture the nonempirical, absolute reality of the mind, which after all eludes all discursive thinking. Fichte also expresses the ideality of philosophy in general and the *Wis-senschaftslehre* in particular by likening it to an experiment with its charac-teristic artificial setup.[8] The idealist, experimental reconstruction of human mentality can be seen as a cognitive approximation of the absolute nature of the human mind under the conditions of finite thinking. In fact, Fichte's never-ceasing work on the project of the *Wissenschaftslehre* suggests that the approximation process can never be completed. Philosophy as the supreme self-comprehension of the human mind is the endless struggle of the mind against its own limitations – a struggle that has to take place within those very limitations. That Fichte considered this struggle worthwhile attests to an idealism of yet another kind on his part.

The ineliminable tension between the philosophically reconstructed finite mind and the finite mind itself finds expression in the paradoxical, highly speculative descriptions of the mind that form the very core of Fichte's *Wissenschaftslehre*. The complex, organic structure of the mind involves a part-whole relation whose representation strains the capabilities of discursive thinking. What is called for is uniting the thought that the whole precedes the parts with the opposite thought that the parts precede the whole. More specifically, those two thoughts must be thought as belong-ing together and supplementing each other rather than contradicting each other. The only logical form in which this task of thinking can be achieved is that of the circle. Fichte's main effort in the *Wissenschaftslehre nova methodo* consists in not having the inevitable circularity of philosophical presenta-tion deteriorate into a fallacious circle.[9]

2. Ideal and Real Activity

At the basis of Fichte's transcendental philosophy of the human mind in the second Jena *Wissenschaftslehre* lies the insight that the subject of con-sciousness is its own immediate object.[10] Fichte argues that all conscious-ness of objects requires a subject that is conscious (*Bewußtseiendes*). Now, in order to be conscious of itself, the subject of consciousness itself must be an object of consciousness. Yet this would require a further subject of con-sciousness for which the first subject is object, and so ad infinitum. Fichte sees only one way to avoid the fallacious regress and to account for the fact that there is indeed consciousness by the subject of itself or self-conscious-

ness. The subject of consciousness is its own object without the mediation
of any further acts and entities of consciousness, that is, immediately.

The *Wissenschaftslehre* elucidates the structure of original, immediate self-
consciousness and relates it to the structure of all consciousness. Fichte
seeks to show that all consciousness of other objects is conditioned by immediate self-consciousness and, more importantly, that immediate self-consciousness is possible only in a being that is conscious of things and human
beings other than itself. On Fichte's account, immediate self-consciousness
is not an independently existing state of consciousness but rather the necessary ingredient or the ground that makes all other consciousness possible. It is not an instance of consciousness but its principal form.

In the *Wissenschaftslehre nova methodo* the peculiar relation between the
subject and the object of consciousness in immediate self-consciousness
and, a fortiori, in all other consciousness is articulated through the distinction between the mind's ideal and real activity. Fichte resorts to the
generic characterization of the mind as "activity" in order to capture the
radical difference between things that are for minds and minds that are for
themselves and other minds (*Fürsein*). More precisely, the activity or agility
of the mind is one of transition or passing-over (*Übergehen*) from the undetermined (*Unbestimmtes*) to the determined (*Bestimmtes*).[11] The activity of
the mind is spontaneous in that it occurs absolutely or unconditionally.
Once spontaneously initiated, though, the mind's activity follows strict laws
that reflect its finitude.[12] The spontaneity of the mind is thus limited to the
absolutely free beginning of series that then continue according to fixed
laws.

Fichte identifies the subjective side of consciousness with ideal activity
and its objective side with real or practical activity.[13] The real activity consists in the absolute transition from the undetermined to the determined,
which Fichte understands as an activity of self-affection.[14] By contrast, the
ideal activity is bound by the real activity and consists in internally imitat-
ing or copying (*nachmachen*) and imaging (*abbilden*) the real activity.[15] Fichte
also uses the term "positing" for the ideal activity, calling the latter "ideal
positing" (*ideales Setzen*), thus linking the notion of positing with reflection
and awareness.[16] The ideal activity of the mind in the *Wissenschaftslehre nova
methodo* thus continues the theory of the positing I from the *Foundation of
the Entire Wissenschaftslehre*. Both doctrines are concerned with the cognitive, or rather the protocognitive aspect of the mind. By contrast, the real
activity introduced in the *Wissenschaftslehre nova methodo* takes up the theory
of the striving I from the *Foundation of the Entire Wissenschaftslehre* with its
emphasis on the practical, self-determining nature of the mind.

It must be kept in mind that the real activity and the ideal activity are not
independently functioning instances of consciousness but moments that
only together make up consciousness. Fichte proposes an experimental,

"ideal" isolation for the methodological purpose of reconstructing the origin of consciousness.[17] On his view, consciousness involves an original division of mental life into an object of consciousness that takes the form of the mind's absolute but finite real activity and a subject of consciousness that takes the form of capturing the real activity in an image. Drawing on the etymological connection between "idea" and "sight" or "vision" in Greek and Latin (*eidos, idea, videre*), Fichte contrasts the two essential moments of consciousness as "seeing" and "acting."[18]

Although the occurrence of consciousness depends on the original separation, or rather separateness, of ideal and real activity, it is equally necessary that the two activities be connected – and that the connection take place right at the point of origin (*gleich ursprünglich*).[19] No unification of separates *ex post* would do.[20] Fichte refers to the relation between real and ideal activity as one of "identity."[21] That term should not be taken to refer to some predisjunctive primal oneness in consciousness but to indicate the ultimate proximity of the distinct moments that make up consciousness. Real and ideal activity mutually require each other.[22] In particular, the real activity of consciousness is in need of ideal activity in order to be for consciousness and thus for itself, and the ideal activity is in need of real activity in order to have something to be posited. Thus, the real or practical activity is always already posited, and the ideal or positing activity is always already positing some real activity: hence Fichte's basic characterization of the human mind in its ideal–real unity as "practical intelligence."[23]

Now, the relationship of mutual requirement between the real and the ideal activity of the mind threatens Fichte's account of the mind with a fallacious circle.[24] On Fichte's account, the real activity stands for the practical, productive feature of the mind, whereas the ideal activity stands for the mind's cognitive, reflecting side. The mutual requirement of real and ideal activity thus translates into the mutual requirement of practice or action and theory or cognition. But that way, the point of origin for consciousness remains elusive. It seems that consciousness would never come about, for want of a cognition that is not in need of some prior action or an action that is not requiring some prior cognition.

Fichte's solution to the dilemma of a mind that cannot be practical without being cognitive and that cannot be cognitive without being practical structurally resembles his earlier postulation of immediate self-consciousness. He introduces an original unity of theory and practice in which the practical is already theoretical and the theoretical already practical. The postulated theoretico-practical unity is introduced as predeliberative, "pure willing."[25] Such a willing is theoretical insofar as it is expressive of an insight that takes the form of the recognition of an ought (*Sollen*). It is practical insofar as it involves a self-determination or self-affection in accordance with that ought. The stipulation that the willing in question be independent of any deliberation is designed to avoid the regressive presupposition of some knowledge that is prior to the pure willing itself.

Fichte's postulation of a predeliberative willing that is under the command of some absolute ought is obviously modeled on Kant's conception of a pure will (*reiner Wille*) dissociated from choice (*Willkür*) and extrinsic motivation. Yet Fichte insists that the ought in question is not yet the specifically moral ought of the categorical imperative.[26] Rather, the pure willing in question is the generic, transcendental condition of all theory and practice, moral and otherwise.

As in the case of immediate self-consciousness, it is imperative not to hypostatize pure willing into an independently functioning state or instance of consciousness. Fichte is even apprehensive about using the related noun "will" to designate the original unison of the theoretical or ideal and the practical or real. He regards pure willing as the "mere form of willing."[27] Pure willing as the transcendental form or condition of theoretical as well as practical consciousness is never experienced as such. Its closest representation in actual consciousness is the moral ought of the categorical imperative.

In the postulated pure form of consciousness – immediate self-consciousness – and its volitional counterpart – the pure form of willing – the real and the ideal activity of the mind are united almost to the point of fusion. And yet in each case the original unity of the ideal and the real is also and equally originally their division. Without original unity, there would be no unity to the mind and hence no mind in the relevant sense. Without original division, there would be no consciousness to the mind and thus no mind either. Fichte's further efforts in the *Wissenschaftslehre nova methodo* are geared toward an account of that mental activity that is responsible for the simultaneous occurrence of unity and division in consciousness.

3. Ideal and Real Thinking

At the core of Fichte's transcendental theory of the subject in the *Wissenschaftslehre nova methodo* lies a theory of finite, discursive thinking. On Fichte's understanding, the activity or agility characteristic of human mental life is at its core the activity of thinking. In thinking the mind spontaneously brings about a determination (*Bestimmtheit*). The activity of determination (*Bestimmung*) follows strict laws that govern the way in which the spontaneity of thinking is exercised in finite minds. The basic law of thought (*Denkgesetz*) is the "law of reflection concerning opposites."[28] According to this law, all determination proceeds by way of opposition. In particular, the law states that determination can only be brought about by opposing or oppositing in one's thinking something undetermined (*Unbestimmtes*) but determinable (*Bestimmbares*) against the background of which the act of determination (*Bestimmung*) takes place. Fichte here draws Kant's discussion of the contrast between the determinable and the determined under the heading of the concepts of reflection (*Reflexionsbegriffe*), matter and form.[29]

A crucial element of Fichte's account of the oppositional nature of all thinking is the status of the undetermined-determinable. The latter is "found alongside" (*mitgefunden*).[30] Strictly speaking, it is "added through thinking" (*hinzugedenken*)[31] and thus a product of thought – a by-product, to be precise, given that the primary product of thinking is the determination brought about through the act of thinking. Yet the ideal, thought-produced status of the determinable is not always properly recognized. On the contrary, typically the undetermined but determinable basis for determination appears as something found and not made, as something existing prior to and independent of thought, as something real.[32]

On the surface, the law of reflection regarding opposition seems to introduce contrast and division into the life of the mind. Yet, when considering the ideal nature of the determinable and the relation of mutual requirement of determination and determinable, the law in question is as much the law concerning the unity of the opposites. What is opposed belongs together; nothing is an opposite all by itself. Fichte goes even further than that. He maintains the identity (*Identität*) of the opposites, arguing that the opposites are the same viewed from two different sides.[33] The identity claimed for the opposites is thus the identity of different, even opposed, sides or aspects of one and the same ("identical") entity or state of affairs. On Fichte's account, the opposed views of the same entity or state of affairs are inseparable (*unzertrennlich*). The complete nature of the entity or state of affairs shows itself only in the joint consideration of the opposites. Fichte repeatedly refers to this internally oppositional, yet unitary basic structure of the human mind as its "original duplicity."[34] For Fichte the primordial case of the identity of opposites is the I (*Ich*) in its originary structure as subject-object.[35] All other oppositions, including that between I and Not-I, must be regarded as the unfolding of the basic opposition in the I between the subjective or ideal and the objective or real. Consciousness in all its forms and shapes along with the world to which it relates through cognition as well as volition is the subject-object writ large.

The opposition of the real and the ideal introduced into human mentality under the basic form of subject-objectivity shows itself as a fundamental opposition within thinking itself. Fichte contrasts the thinking involved in the cognition of objects and the thinking involved in the formulation of ends.[36] The point is not to propose the independence of one form of thinking from the other. Rather, Fichte seeks to elucidate the complicated relationship of mutual requirement between the thinking of an object and the thinking of an end.

In a perplexing terminological move Fichte casts the opposition between the two basic forms of thinking as the opposition of real and ideal thinking.[37] The latter distinction is a distinction within thinking and must not be confused with Fichte's distinction between real and ideal activity. The term "ideal," as used in the locution "ideal thinking," refers to the thinking of some ideal, yet to be realized object. The image involved in "ideal thinking" is not the copy of some prior reality, as in the ideal activity of positing some real activity, but the design of something that is yet to be realized. The primary sense of "ideal" has shifted from that of an "after-image" (*Nachbild*) to that of a "fore-image" (*Vorbild*).[38]

The term "real" undergoes an analogous change in the move from "real *activity*" to "real *thinking*." The "real" in "real *activity*" refers to some actual activity that is then posited by the ideal activity. By contrast, "real *thinking*" refers to the activity of having one's thought determined by how the object is in actuality. In a complete reversal of terms, the *ideal* activity ("copying") is being reconceptualized as *real* thinking (thinking of the real), whereas the *real* activity ("self-determination") is being reconceptualized as *ideal* thinking (thinking of the ideal). Put another way, the feature of production – as opposed to mere reproduction – is no longer associated with the real (in "real activity") but with the ideal (in "ideal thinking").[39] The true, "real" activity of the I is its ideal activity of formulating and pursuing ends, that is, the thinking involved in willing.

The upshot of the conceptual reorientation in Fichte's usage of the terms "ideal" and "real" is that the real or practical activity of the mind is now understood in decidedly idealist terms. Willing is no longer something real that then becomes the object of some ideal activity or positing. Rather, willing itself is now something ideal, that is, of the nature of thought. Yet unlike the ideal activity of positing, willing is not the thinking of something already made, but the thought of something to be made, of something that ought to be. The real, as reproduced in positing, comes about as the product of thinking and willing the ideal. Thus, the primacy of the ideal over the real in the *Wissenschaftslehre nova methodo* provides a reformulation of the doctrine of striving and the associated primacy of practical reason from the first presentation of the *Wissenschaftslehre*.

4. Thinking and the Real

In the *Wissenschaftslehre nova methodo* the activity of thinking occupies the central position in the constitution of consciousness and its objects. Both in ideal and real thinking, some determination is brought about spontaneously, and this in such a way that something undetermined but determinable is presupposed by thought as a basis or substratum for the act of determination. Fichte's generic term for the intellectual activity of introducing the determinable along with the determination is "synthesis," and the thinking in question is called "synthetic thinking."[40]

Now, the joining of the determining and the determinable is not some external piecing together of two separate things. Rather, the two belong together *ab origine*. One cannot be what it is without the other. According to Fichte, the synthesis involved in synthetic thinking points to the original identity of what is to be synthesized. In fact, it is the very act of thinking that first introduces nonidentity or manifoldness through some act of analysis that is just as original as the synthesis: "The beginning of all consicousness is at once synthesis and analysis."[41] Thinking as the mind's primary activity is as much unifying as it is diversifying, and it must be both in order to be either.

Fichte traces the operation of synthetic-analytic thinking through the two series (*Reihen*) of ideal and real thinking. Real thinking (theoretical cognition) involves the presupposition of a realm of determinability in the form of the empirical world. Real thinking produces or generates the representations of this world. Moreover, it is characteristic of real thinking that in it those spontaneously produced representations are taken for existing independently of the mind's activity. To real thinking, the products of thought appear as found objects.

By contrast, ideal thinking (the thinking and willing of an end) carries with it the presupposition of a realm of determinability in the form of an intelligible world. Fichte refers to the objects of this world of ideal beings as "objects of thought" or "noumena."[42] The noumenal realm is comprised of other rational beings. The *Wissenschaftslehre nova methodo* contains a detailed theory of interpersonality according to which the constitution of a subject's individuality presupposes the activity of other individuals that call upon the subject to realize its potential for independent existence.[43]

The contrast between the sensible and the intelligible system of determinability is based on Kant's distinction between phenomena and noumena.[44] In Kant, though, the concept of an intelligible object is merely a "limiting concept" (*Grenzbegriff*), designed to trace the confines of sensible knowledge by demarcating an open conceptual space possibly inhabited by objects of pure reason. For Fichte, on the other hand, every act of ideal, volitional thinking involves the thought of a noumenal substratum of determinability. To Fichte, (ideal) thinking as such opens up the noumenal realm.

The noumenal realm also functions as the condition or ground for the empirical world.[45] For Fichte, our bodily existence in the spatio-temporal world comes about by having our intelligible being subjected to the laws of discursive thinking. That descent from noumenal to phenomenal existence is unavoidable and a reflection of human finitude. To be sure, preempirical, preembodied existence is not an actual experience but a necessary thought on the part of the subject, which thus interprets its own dual existence as noumenal and phenomenal being. The only thing that can be thought as belonging to the elusive noumenal preexistence of the I is the pure will, understood as a timeless activity of self-determination.[46]

The pure will thus takes on the function of the ultimate determinable for discursive thinking. Fichte distinguishes two degrees of determination with respect to the pure, "absolute" will; there is, first, the subjection of the will to the limiting concept of individuality, resulting in individual will, and, second, the concrete empirical determinations of the will to particular, empirical volitions.[47] Fichte also characterizes the ultimate determinable of all willing as the "absoluteness of reason in its entirety" (*Absolutheit der gesamten Vernunft*),[48] thus suggesting a distinction between the finitizing thinking of the discursive intellect and some nondiscursive, undetermined, thus indefinite, realm of pure reason. It should be emphasized that Fichte's introduction of the notion of absolute reason is very much part of his transcendental inquiry into the conditions of finite consciousness, and not some extraneous piece of speculative metaphysics.

The distinction between pure, preindividual willing and finite, individual willing and the identification of pure will with absolute, indefinite reason lead Fichte to claim a unique status for the pure will. On his account, particular acts of individual willing are themselves modes of thinking. They are instances of determined, resolved thinking and hence affected by the finitizing conditions of discursive thought.[49] By contrast, the pure will is considered to be "that which is originally real" (*das urspüngliche Reale*).[50] Paradoxically, it is the most intelligible of entities, viz., the determinable as such, that is here accorded the status of ultimate reality, whereas everything else is merely a product of thought, either of real or of ideal thinking.

It must be asked, though, whether the pure will qua sheer determinable is not itself significantly affected by discursive thinking. After all, the pure will is presupposed by finite thinking in the process of its activity of determination. Fichte himself seems to have realized this point, for in his popular treatise on the destination of humanity (*Die Bestimmung des Menschen*), which was begun in early 1799 and published in 1800, the ultimate reality of pure will or absolute reason is no longer an object of thought and knowledge (*Wissen*) but of faith (*Glaube*). Moreover, the later versions of the *Wissenschaftslehre* (after 1800) are so many further attempts to develop the thought of the ultimately real on the basis of a transcendental theory of the subject. The proper relation between the duplication and indeed the multiplication involved in all forms of consciousness and some original, absolute reality remained the focus of Fichte's thinking on the subject.

PART IV

PURE WILLING

DETERMINATION TO SELF-DETERMINATION

Among the most consequential innovations in the post-Kantian philosophical discussion is the inclusion of practical philosophy into transcendental philosophy. In Kant the transcendental theory of consciousness and its objects is still restricted to the sphere of theoretical knowledge. Practical knowledge as well as the acting based on such knowledge is dealt with outside of transcendental philosophy, in moral philosophy. Moreover, the concept of the practical in Kant is limited to the morally practical. In Kant a general theory of the practical – of acting and of the knowledge that guides it – is only to be found *implicite* and in fragments. For Kant, transcendental philosophy, which he understands as critically revised *prima philosophia,* serves as the conceptual preparation of the "second philosophy."[1] The concept of freedom, which remains merely problematic in transcendental philosophy, receives its moral-practical realization in a critically grounded metaphysics of morals.

Kant's systematic separation of transcendental philosophy and moral philosophy goes together with the unmediated juxtaposition of the theoretical and the practical use of reason in the human subject. To be sure, Kant insists on the unity of theoretical and practical reason,[2] but this assurance has the status of an idea that is not actually realized in his system.

The post-Kantian transcendentalization of practical philosophy takes its departure from Reinhold's attempt of a renewed, unified foundation of Kant's main doctrines.[3] Soon Fichte surpasses Reinhold in this enterprise, in terms of both radicality and originality. For one thing, Fichte complements the inclusion of practical philosophy into transcendental philosophy by incorporating genuinely practical moments into the theory of our cognitive relation to the world. Moreover, he works out a deep structure of the subject that precedes the latter's differentiation into theoretical and practical subjectivity. Thus, in Fichte's first published presentation of his transcendental philosophy, the *Foundation of the Entire Wissenschaftslehre*, only the "Foundation of the Science of the Practical" completes the foundation of theoretical knowledge; and the differentiation of the modes of subjectivity according to theory and practice is preceded by the original dimension of subjectivity in form of the absolute positing of I and Not-I through the I.[4]

But Fichte's first presentation of the *Wissenschaftslehre* in its foundation still falls short of the ideal of a totally integrated transcendental theory of consciousness. The foundation of theoretical knowledge is still presented in separation of the foundation of practical knowledge, and the doctrine of positing in the system of the "Principles of the Entire *Wissenschaftslehre*" is presented in a separate introductory part. It is only in his efforts at a new presentation of the *Wissenschaftslehre*, starting in 1796, that Fichte succeeds at integrating the principles section into the treatise proper of the *Wissenschaftslehre* and to present the theory of the practical together with the doctrine of theoretical knowledge.

At the center of this new presentation, as preserved in the transcripts of his lectures on the *Wissenschaftslehre nova methodo*,[5] stands Fichte's doctrine of the will as the original reality of all consciousness. He takes over the term "will" from the contemporary psychological and moral-philosophical discussion and employs it as the basic concept of his transcendental theory of the subject. It stands to reason that it was above all the pairing of the cognitive and the conative in Kant's conception of the will that made the term suitable for articulating the original unity of theoretical and practical subjectivity. Moreover, the concept of the will offered the opportunity to Fichte to bring out the radical primacy of practical reason among all other forms of finite rational subjectivity. Finally, through its social-philosophical use in Rousseau's doctrine of the formation of the political will, as well as through Kant's moral-philosophical ideal of the good will, the term was prepared for conveying the supraindividual and nonempirical constitution of the subject.

Fichte's choice of the notion of the will as the basic concept of the *Wissenschaftslehre nova methodo* is prepared in a number of his earlier works and still resonates in the doctrine of the infinite, divine will in Book 3 of *The Vocation of Man*. In the later versions of the *Wissenschaftslehre*, with their departure from the egological terminology and conceptuality, the term and concept no longer play a crucial role.[6] This chapter traces the crucial stages in the development of Fichte's concept of the will by presenting them in their historic and systematic contexts. The emphasis is on the role of the will in his transcendental theory of the subject.

1. The *Attempt at a Critique of All Revelation*

The second edition of Fichte's first publication, *Attempt at a Critique of All Revelation*, published in 1793, includes two new sections, the first of which offers a "Theory of the Will, in Preparation for a Deduction of Religion in General."[7] In its basic concepts as well as in a number of details, Fichte's early doctrine of the will is strongly influenced by Reinhold's *Letters on the Kantian Philosophy*, especially by the details of the Seventh Letter and the Eighth Letter in Book 2, which appeared in 1792.[8]

Right at the beginning Fichte provides the following definition of "willing": "To determine oneself to produce a representation with consciousness of one's own activity."[9] According to this definition, in willing the practical moment of spontaneous activity (*Selbsttätigkeit*) and the theoretical moment of the consciousness of that activity are united. Fichte explains further that willing is an actual event, to be distinguished from what makes it possible, viz., the faculty of desire.[10] Thus, in my willing there is the awareness that I am active, and this awareness is the consciousness of an actual activity. To be sure, the self-conscious activity, actual as it may be, is restricted to the production of representations. Here Fichte follows Kant's disengagement of willing as inner, mental spontaneous activity from external, physical causality. Fichte makes the same point in his review of G. E. Schulze's *Aenesidemus*, written in 1793: "the moral law is not at first directed at a physical force . . . but at a hyperphysical faculty of desire and striving. . . . The moral law is not at first supposed to produce any actions at all, but only the constant striving toward an action."[11]

Now, moral willing may indeed concern primarily intentions and be indifferent toward their physical realization. But willing in the generic sense, and specifically morally indifferent willing, seems to include the breakthrough from changing oneself to changing the world. Thus, Fichte faces the task of extending the causal efficacy of willing beyond the sphere of the formation of moral intentions and of relating it to the physical constitution of the practical subject.

In the *Attempt at a Critique of All Revelation* Fichte undertakes a first step toward this integration of willing and acting by resorting to the concept of "drive" (*Trieb*), which had been brought into the post-Kantian debate by Reinhold.[12] For Fichte the drive mediates between the natural determinacy of the subject and its supranatural self-determination.[13] Through the drive, the subject is presented with a matter (*Stoff*), which the spontaneous subject then endows with a form (*Form*).[14] Fichte first examines the case of the "sensory drive" (*sinnlicher Trieb*), in which the matter is presented to the subject under the form of sensory perceptions. The role of the spontaneous subject is here first of all merely indirect: By means of the faculty of judgment a manifold of sensory matter is brought under principles of unity that aim at the natural end of happiness. But even in the case of the sensory drive a stronger, direct influence of the spontaneous subject is required. In order to compare the different modifications of the sensory drive and establish an order among them, the subject must be able to "bring to a halt" (*aufzuhalten*) any determination through the sensory drive and its specifications and then, after applying the eudaimonistic calculus, to yield spontaneously to the prevailing manifestation of the sensory drive.[15]

Thus, the determination of the will with respect to the sensory drive already presupposes the absolute spontaneity of the will. Moreover, the latter cannot be understood as a case of volitional response to some matter given by the senses. Rather, to Fichte, the matter of the absolute determination of the will is the form of willing as such. The will is here driven by the nonsensory, pure drive "to will simply because one wills."[16] Fichte identifies the absolute spontaneity of willing and the allied "pure drive" (*reiner Trieb*) with the moral self-determination of the human being based on the drive to self-respect.[17] To be sure, the moral drive is not sufficient for moral willing. Just like the sensory drive, the pure drive requires for its efficacy the spontaneous assent of the subject. The practical spontaneity of the subject thus appears as choice and is grounded in the "freedom of choice" (*Freiheit der Willkür*) as the faculty of choosing between competing manifestations of the sensory drive as well as between the sensory drive and the moral drive.[18]

Furthermore, Fichte distinguishes between the freedom of choice, which is present in all actual willing, and the "absolutely first expression of freedom through the practical law of reason," which precedes all choice.[19] The latter kind of freedom – which Fichte also calls "transcendental freedom" – consists in the independence of the moral self-determination from the mechanism of nature. Such transcendental freedom first makes possible the freedom of choice in rational beings such as ourselves, who follow the practical law of reason not of themselves but only through a free decision with respect to an absolute law.[20] Fichte draws a distinction here between the transcendental freedom of pure practical reason as such and the freedom of choice of the finite rational subject.[21] The latter distinction involves two forms of spontaneity, viz., the absolute spontaneity of reason in the determination of the pure will and the spontaneity of the subject in the determination of its will to moral as well as amoral and immoral actions.[22] Accordingly, Fichte's further reflections on the will, in the context of the *Wissenschaftslehre*, are concerned primarily with determining the relation between the individual will of the rational subject and the supraindividual pure will. At the center of these reflections stands a conception of freedom that comprehends both the individual self-determination of the subject through free decision and the subject's being determined through the law of reason.

2. The System of Ethics

Fichte's further development of the theory of the will in connection with his work on the *Wissenschaftslehre* first occurs in *The System of Ethics according to the Principles of the Wissenschaftslehre* (1798). As the complete title of the work indicates, *The System of Ethics* is building on the *Foundation of the Entire Wissenschaftslehre* of 1794–1795. Fichte's ethics systematically explores the practical basic relation of the I determining the Not-I.[23] He argues that the determination of the objective through the subjective in the practical sphere requires the presupposition of an original unity of the subjective and the objective.[24] In the *Foundation of the Entire Wissenschaftslehre* the original unity of the subject had been presented under the idea of the pure I that is posited absolutely through itself. The pure self-consciousness thus introduced was not really a case of consciousness but rather an ideal unity underlying all actual consciousness. In *The System of Ethics* Fichte characterizes the deep structure of the subject as "subject-object," thereby indicating that the subject is immediately and as such for itself and that all forms of the subject as well as those of its objects are grounded in the subject-object as their ultimate principle. The different empirical determinations of the subject and its objects in theory and practice are only that many finite – more precisely, finitized – "views" (*Ansichten*) of the absolute unity, which in itself is infinite and as such nonrepresentable. To be sure, the insight into the connection between the presupposed ground of consciousness and the ways and forms of actually occurring consciousness takes place only in and through philosophical reflection. The object of such reflection is ordinary, nonphilosophical consciousness, especially the development of the forms under which the latter experiences itself.

Fichte identifies the phenomenological beginning of consciousness with the I's original self-experience as willing: "I find myself, as myself, only willing."[25] He maintains that the original fact of my consciousness consists in the experience of myself as willing, and in nothing else. Fichte starts from the concept of the I, which he understands as the identity of thinking (*Denken*) and that which is being thought (*Gedachtes*). In the case of the I, the object is nothing different from the thinking, but the subject of thinking itself. However, the I does not experience the identity of the thinking and the thought in it as such. Thinking, here understood in the widest sense of "representing, or consciousness in general,"[26] only comes to consciousness by opposing something to itself and thus becoming objective. In the case of the subject's original thinking – a thinking that is concerned strictly with itself – the I qua subject thinking itself finds itself qua thought under the form of willing or as willing. According to Fichte, in the consciousness of my willing, my thinking and that as which I think myself, that is, as willing, are united. Willing is the original form of self-experience, insofar that in it nothing other is being thought than I myself, although not as pure thinking as such but rather as something that is being thought by pure thinking and that therefore is different from pure thinking.

The notion of willing operative here is that of a "real self-determining of oneself through oneself."[27] Fichte considers it impossible to provide a "real explanation" (*Realerklärung*) of the concept of willing and appeals to everyone's immediate familiarity with the phenomenon, which is supposed to be given "in intellectual intuition."[28] Based on the generic form of the I as absolute identity of subject and object, Fichte complements the identity of thinking and thought in the case of the theoretical relation ("thinking") by introducing the identity of the acting subject and that which is acted upon, or rather enacted, in the case of the practical relation ("willing"). In the original experience of myself as willing, the absolute identity of the I appears under the conditions of objective, objectifying thinking.

The intimate unity of thinking and willing as the two *relata* of the original self-experience of the I finds expression in Fichte's volontaristic treatment of thinking and the corresponding intellectualist conception of willing. Following Kant's notion of the spontaneity of the mind, Fichte understands thinking as activity, and specifically as the ideal activity of determination. By contrast, he sees willing as a real activity that has been brought "under the rule of the concept."[29] In each case, the basic activity of the I is characterized by the absoluteness that is peculiar to the I as such: "The rational being, considered as such, is absolute, independent, absolutely its own ground."[30]

Strictly speaking, this characteristic only holds of the absolute I as the ideal I toward which our human, finite I always strives, without ever reaching it. In finite rational beings the absolute nature of the I manifests itself in the "tendency to independence for independence's sake."[31] With respect to the practical rational self-relation in willing, this means that volitional self-determination aims at the absolute independence of the I with the consciousness of such independence and based on that very conception.

Thus, the willing of the finite rational being stands *eo ipso* under the form of an autonomy or self-legislation. Fichte distinguishes three different regards in which the legislation of the willing can be called "autonomous."[32] There is, first, the fact that the I reflects freely on the law, which is presupposed here, and subsequently adopts the law into its will through a free decision. In this regard, Fichte follows Reinhold's understanding of autonomy as free choice. Second, the law itself under which the willing stands prescribes the absolute self-determination of the I. In this regard, Fichte follows Kant's conception of autonomy under the moral law. Finally, the necessary law for the determination of the will cannot be thought independent of the I but functions only as the necessary form in which the I realizes its own freedom.

Fichte's further development of the theory of the will, both with respect to Kant's conception of moral autonomy and Reinhold's notion of self-determination through free choice, shows most clearly in his doctrine of the drives. Throughout, Fichte maintains that a rational being is never determined through its drives to the point of necessitation: "Each satisfaction of the drive, insofar as it occurs with consciousness, occurs necessarily with freedom."[33]

Fichte replaces his own earlier distinction between the selfish and the unselfish drive, which had been taken from Reinhold, with the distinction between the "natural drive" (*Naturtrieb*) and the "pure intellectual drive" (*reiner geistiger Trieb*). The latter two are considered to be united in the comprehensive "protodrive" (*Urtrieb*).[34] Fichte resorts here to the school-philosophical distinction, still effective in Kant, between the "higher" and the "lower" faculty of desire. Yet unlike Kant (and Reinhold), Fichte views the two levels in the faculty of desire not as in opposition but as two sides of the one, identical protodrive or basic drive toward independence for independence's sake. This move on Fichte's part might be considered a critically mitigated return to the pre-Kantian monistic concept of a single basic force.[35] Yet unlike Wolff and his disciples, Fichte does not claim any direct knowledge of the ultimately basic force. Rather, he treats the protodrive as a transcendental condition that is to be presupposed necessarily but that is never encountered as such. According to Fichte, the presupposed protodrive appears as the natural drive insofar as I am a sensible being among other sensible objects. The protodrive manifests itself as purely intellectual drive, insofar as I am a nonsensory subject.

Fichte criticizes the emptiness and formality of a "metaphysics of morals" only concerned with the purely intellectual drive, contrasting it with his own concrete ethics that is oriented toward a (re-)unification of the higher and lower faculties of desire.[36] The proposed integration of sensibility and rationality in Fichte's conception of ethical willing is carried out in his doctrine of ethical action as willed appropriation of the natural drive.[37] According to Fichte, nature under the form of the natural drive contributes the force to action, to which the will then adds the impulse toward execution. In principle, this also explains the possibility of the causal efficacy of the will in the sensible world. Any action in the natural order is the natural drive itself, as set into motion by the will. The will acts upon the natural side of the finite rational being, and the latter being acts upon outside nature.

Yet the Fichtean program just sketched should not give the impression that Fichte envisions an emancipation of sensibility in the manner of Ludwig Feuerbach. Rather, in Fichte, nature in general and the natural drive of the human being in particular are already understood in the light of reason and thus in a practically teleological way. For Fichte nature inside us and nature outside us comprise the field for the realization of the rational ideal of absolute independence – and nothing besides that: "There is no nature in itself; my nature and all other nature which is posited in order to explain the former is only a special way of viewing myself."[38]

Nature is, in Fichte's notorious phrase, "the sensible material of our duty."[39] Thus, for Fichte the principle of reason (to seek absolute independence for its own sake), under its specification as the moral law, functions as a principle for the deduction of empirical reality. Throughout, Fichte draws inferences from the pregiven unconditional or absolute end to the conditions that are to be presupposed necessarily for the former's infinite approximation.[40]

In terms of the argumentative strategy employed, Fichte here follows Kant's doctrine of the postulates of pure practical reason.[41] In both cases theoretical positions are established on the basis of moral-practical certainty. Yet while in Kant the postulates concern the faith in the existence of God and the immortality of the soul as the conditions for the realization of the necessary object of pure practical reason (the highest good), Fichte subordinates the entire faculty of theoretical cognition to the practical knowledge of one's duties. As he states, "Only in consequence of the practical drive are there any objects for us at all."[42]

Thus, Fichte radicalizes Kant's doctrine of the primacy of pure practical reason, which is restricted to the rational faith in the reality of the concepts of reason, to a primacy *tout court* of practical reason over theoretical reason.[43] Accordingly, Fichte defends the priority of the will even and precisely in the foundation of theoretical cognition. He transforms Kant's theoretical idealism, which grounds empirical reality by recourse to the cognitive forms of the subject, into a practical, and ultimately ethical, idealism built on the basic law of rational willing.

The comprehensive idealist conception of the theory of willing and acting in *The System of Ethics* also accommodates Fichte's understanding of the causal efficacy of the will in the sensible world. Acting in the sensible world is ultimately a changing of the world through a change of oneself. It is not so much that the subject changes the world but that the subject changes itself and through that alone already changes the world bound up with the subject: "*My world* is changed means, *I* am changed; *my world* is determined further means, *I* am determined further."[44]

The System of Ethics already foreshadows the next stage in the development of Fichte's theory of the will in that he immediately qualifies the idea of an integration of lower and higher drives in the formation of the moral will. With respect to the drive to absolute independence he distinguishes between the independence of the I as such (pure I) and the independence of empirically individuated reason (empirical I). For Fichte, the ultimate end of the human efforts toward absolute independence is the realization of the pure, supraindividual I. By contrast, the individual is merely "tool

and vehicle of the moral law."[45] But this conception of an ultimately supraindividual I fits poorly with the notion of the will as an individual's faculty of
deciding with respect to a manifold offered through drives.[46] If the formation of the moral will aims at the pure I, then the will so constituted can
no longer consist in free election by choice. The will now has to participate
in the supraindividual status of the pure I. Fichte takes the step from the
will as choice to the pure will without choice in the new presentation of the
Wissenschaftslehre.

3. The *Wissenschaftslehre Nova Methodo*

The revised presentation of the Fichte's transcendental philosophy in the
Wissenschaftslehre nova methodo (1796–1799) takes its departure from the
double nature of the I as "subject-object."[47] The term indicates that the I
originally has itself and only itself as its object. Yet this "immediate consciousness" of the I is not consciousness proper, but only "a dull positing of
itself."[48] Only the I's subsequent, freely occurring act of attending to itself
(reflection) brings about a consciousness in which the I articulates itself in
differentiation from its posited counterpart (Not-I). Fichte brings together
the reflective subject-object relation of the I with respect to itself and the
practical relation of acting-upon-oneself. The I originally brings itself about
through an acting that also knows its acting. In the I there are to be distinguished a real, acting side and an ideal, knowing side, yet with the understanding that the two are separate aspects of the one, ideal-real I.[49]

The *Wissenschaftslehre nova methodo* reconstructs the further differentiation and gradual reintegration of the "original duplicity"[50] of the I in a phenomenology of subjectivity that runs from sensory perception through
empirical action up to the moral community of pure minds. A crucial role
in connecting the real and the ideal series of the I is exercised by the activity of willing. The transcendental analysis of the I reveals a precarious relationship of mutual conditioning between the real and the ideal I.[51] On the
one hand, there can be no ideal activity of the I (cognition) without there
being a real activity of the I (acting) to be observed by the ideal I. On the
other hand, the real activity of the I presupposes that an end is provided to
be pursued in acting. Yet the cognition of an end is an ideal activity, which
in turn presupposes the I's real activity. Thus, there is a twofold ideal activity of the I at work: the cognitive reproduction of some real activity that has
already occurred and the anticipatory formulation of some end for a real
activity that has yet to be initiated.

According to Fichte, willing is the transition from the comparative consideration of possible courses of action ("deliberating") to the decisive pursuit of a determined end.[52] In particular, Fichte contrasts reflecting on a

manifold of possible determinations in deliberation ("determinability") with the absolutely free decision that is characteristic of actually exercising a particular determination of the will. He terms willing "determined thinking" – in contrast to the undetermined, unresolved "mere" thinking involved in deliberation.[53] This identification of willing as a species of thinking (determined thinking) occurs against the background of a theory of thinking for which thinking as such is the transition from determinability to determination.[54]

Now, the conception of the will as the faculty to decide in absolute freedom still remains within the confines of the notion of the will (*Wille*) as choice (*Willkür*). But the fundamental role of the will in theoretical cognition already indicates an enlarged role of the will. In the *Wissenschaftslehre nova methodo* Fichte develops that role by linking the theoretical, cognitive determination of the spatial location of an object to the amount of effort that would be required of the observer to traverse the space separating observer and object. From the concept of the force Fichte then moves to the volitional effort required to apply the force in question.[55] Here he understands willing as "inner efficacious acting" (*inneres Wirken*) or "efficacious acting upon oneself" (*Wirken auf sich selbst*) on the part of the I. He explains this self-relation by referring to Kant's doctrine of the self-affection of sensibility through the understanding.[56] Yet unlike in Kant, where self-affection concerns the relation between the two stems of theoretical cognition, self-affection in Fichte is an eminently practical self-relation. Moreover, for Fichte the theoretical determination of the object presupposes the possibility of practical self-determination. To be sure, the inverse applies equally well. The will as the faculty of free choice can become operative only when supplied with an end provided by the I's ideal activity.

The relationship of mutual requirement between the ideal and the real series in the I threatens to introduce a vicious circle into Fichte's account of theoretico-practical subjectivity, since what is to be derived already has to be presupposed.[57] He avoids the circle by recurring to a type of willing that precedes all choice and that therefore also does not require a prior cognition of the ends to be willed among which to choose. The willing that unites the ideal and the real series in a nonfallacious manner is not some empirical willing proceeding by choice but a "pure willing": "we have now postulated a kind of willing which does not presuppose cognition of an object, but which carries its object within itself."[58]

To the pure willing there corresponds a conception of the will different from the one associated with deliberative willing. When freedom is thought "purely," the issue is no longer the freedom of choice between alternative ends proposed by competing drives. In developing the notion of a pure will Fichte leaves behind the restriction of will to choice and its reduction of practical freedom to the freedom of choice, to be found in Reinhold. Fichte now explicitly endorses Kant's critique of Reinhold on that issue and takes over the Kantian relation of equivalence between freedom and autonomy.[59]

For Fichte, the concept of pure willing originally unites the absolute freedom and the finitude of human reason. Reason is originally, before any alternative is opened up from which to choose, determined. But freedom is required for taking up and realizing that pregiven determination: "Our synthetic concept is freedom and determinacy in one, freedom insofar as a beginning is being made, determinacy insofar as the beginning can be made only that way."[60]

Following Kant, Fichte represents the original limitation underlying reason in the form of pure willing as an absolute ought or categorical demand. Yet he insists on distinguishing the latter as a manifestation of reason's absoluteness from the moral law, understood as the absolute demand in relation to the faculty of choice (*Willkür*).[61] Absolute freedom in the finite rational being now no longer manifests itself as the faculty of choice but as the faculty of self-determination in accordance with the law of reason. The determination of the human being in the double sense of originary limitation and final orientation consists in determination to self-determination: "This determinacy, which constitutes my main character, consists in the fact that I am determined to determine myself in a certain way."[62]

But in the *Wissenschaftslehre nova methodo* the will functions not only as the original point of unity for the ideal-real double series of the I. It also serves to bridge the Kantian opposition between sensible and intelligible world. On the one hand, there is an ascending movement from empirical consciousness and its objects to pure will. In that regard the will, and specifically the unity of freedom and determination through reason present in pure willing, has the function of a nonsensible, intelligible substratum of the sensible. On the other hand, there is a descending movement from the pure will to the world of sensible, spatio-temporally specific determinations. In that regard the pure, extratemporal will is rendered temporal and corporeal or bodily.[63] The position of the pure will at the summit toward which to ascend from the empirical and from which to descend to the empirical is evident in the architectonic of the *Wissenschaftslehre nova methodo* with its rise from perception to pure determination of the will in the first half and the subsequent return to the empirical in the second part of the work.[64]

It bears mentioning that Fichte's detailed considerations of the cosmological dimension of the pure will are strongly integrated into the context of his transcendental theory of the subject. The thought of the nonempirical ground of experience, which has to be thought along the lines of willing, is an integral part of the reflection of the human subject on the conditions and limits of its theoretical as well as practical relation to the world, as reconstructed on behalf of the subject by Fichte. The self-interpretation of the subject follows the necessary laws of thinking pertaining to all finite reason.[65] Central among those laws is the "law of reflection concerning opposites" according to which determinacy can only come about through oppositing or counterpositing, viz., by presupposing in one's thinking for each determination the existence of something determinable to be determined through the former.[66] What is most important here is the circumstance that the determinable as such is never given but always thought and added in through thinking.

In the case of the determination of the will, the law of thinking concerning opposition or counterpositing leads to a world that is necessarily to be thought (added in thought) – the world of thought or the intelligible world – and its beings – beings of thought or noumena. On Fichte's account, only such a presupposition explains the original determinacy of the individual subject and specifically that of its will.[67] Moreover, situating the individual human being in its world has to be thought as requiring an undifferentiated but determinable "mass" (*Masse*) of pure reason or pure will from which individuation proceeds.[68] This line of argument seems to reduce the realm of the noumenal, including the pure will, to the status of a mere thought entity or *ens rationis*. But one must remember that what is introduced here is something that is to be thought *necessarily*, if thinking is to take place. The being of the noumenal is that of an *ens rationis purae*, not just a *cogitabile* but a *cogitandum*. Indeed it is an integral part of the notion of the noumena that they are something to be presupposed in all thinking and hence to be thought as preceding all thinking: "Consequently, pure willing does not originate by means of thinking; on the contrary, it is already presupposed by thinking."[69]

To be sure, this radical presupposition of the noumenal with respect to all thinking occurs in and through thinking and according to the laws of thinking. In the *Wissenschaftslehre nova methodo* all reality, whether noumenal or phenomenal, has being only with reference to its objectification through finite, finitizing thinking.[70] In thinking the supraindividual, pure willing is put asunder, even dispersed into a manifold of individual determinations.[71]

Fichte identifies the original ground of the subject and its real as well as ideal activity to be presupposed in all thinking with "pure willing" or, alternatively, with the latter's hypostization, "the pure will."[72] Thus, he transfers the concept of willing from the theory of the subject, where it denotes the activity of free self-determination, to the ground of all such willing. When speaking of the "determination of the pure will"[73] in this context, Fichte is not talking about an activity of self-determination exercised by the subject. Rather, what is at issue is the pure, nonempirical determinacy of the subject encountered by the latter's reflection: The subject finds itself to be originally, "purely" determined with respect to its willing.[74] Hence, pure willing is a willing only in a tenuous sense. It is really the supraindividual "mere form of willing,"[75] the formal lawfulness under which all individual willing stands, and which is most adequately realized in moral willing.

Thus, Fichte's Jena *Wissenschaftslehre* culminates in the foundation of theoretico-practical subjectivity in a command of reason (determination) to free self-determination, which in turn points toward an intelligible order and its ground (pure will). The latter notion fits squarely with Fichte's contemporary efforts toward a moral-philosophical conception of God in the writings of the atheism dispute and with the doctrine of God in *The Vocation of Man*. In Fichte's ethico-theological extension of his earlier thinking about the subject, the pure will becomes the "divine will" and functions as the founder and guarantor of the intelligible order.[76] His project of bringing the *Wissenschaftslehre* to a conclusion in the "system of the intelligible world"[77] thus continues his earlier concerns with grounding the individually determined subject in a presupposed supraindividual noumenon that is to be thought as will.

8

THE UNITY OF INTELLIGENCE AND WILL

In a radical extension of Kant's intents and achievements, transcendental philosophy in Fichte aims at a systematically integrated account of the principal conditions governing human consciousness and its objects. The intended integration concerns equally the conditioning structure of consciousness and that of its correlated worlds, thus resulting in complementary transcendental theories of subjectivity and objectivity. For Fichte the structural integration of self and world does not take the form of a reduction to some simple origin. Rather, the manifest complexity of consciousness and its objects is retained even at the level of their principal conditions. The origin is complex rather than simple, albeit of the fundamental complexity of two principal conditions that stand in a relation of "original duplicity."[1] In the transcendental theory of the subject the original duplicity is that of thinking and willing. In the transcendental theory of objects it is that of the world of experience and the world of freedom.

Yet their original duplicity notwithstanding, intelligence and will as well as their correlated worlds remain intimately linked and exhibit genuine unity amid all principal differentiations. To be sure, the unity in question is not that of an identical origin in some undifferentiated primal stratum of either self or world. Instead, it is the unity of a functioning whole; the self and its worlds are united in the teleological perspective of their essential cooperation. The original duplicity is at the same time an original complicity. There is no thinking without willing and vice versa, just as there is no world of experience without the world of freedom and vice versa. Moreover, there is no self without world and vice versa.

In tracing Fichte's efforts at articulating the unity of intelligence and will amid their original duplicity, this concluding chapter pays special attention to the overall unitary structure that brings together the dual nature of the self with the dual nature of its correlated worlds. The chapter moves from Fichte's treatment of subjective and objective unity in the *Wissenschaftslehre nova methodo* in the first two sections to the discussion of both kinds of unity in *The Vocation of Man* in the last section. It thus ascends from the technical-speculative level of discussion in the *Wissenschaftslehre* proper to the popular presentation of the latter's results and the assessment of their significance for the human condition.

1. Transcendental Noumenalism

In the *Wissenschaftslehre nova methodo* the unity of thinking and willing is established by way of their mutual implication. It is not only the case that thinking cannot operate in the absence of willing and that willing cannot function in the absence of thinking. Thinking as such involves willing, and willing as such is already a form of thinking.[2] This suggests a strict parity of thinking and willing in the transcendental structure of finite subjectivity. Yet although intellect and will can be viewed as equally original, Fichte supplements his account of their original duplicity by further specifying the circumstances under which the two coalesce *ab origine*.

In Fichte's reconstruction of the originary structure of subjectivity, all consciousness already presupposes the joint operation of the mind's ideal-intellectual and real-volitional activities. More specifically, there needs to be some real, volitional activity for the intellect to reflect upon, and there needs to be some ideal or imaging activity of the intellect to do the reflecting. In the absence of either of those essential factors, no consciousness whatsoever can come about. Yet although there is strict parity between thinking and willing in terms of their origin, the two stand on less equal footing when it comes to their original cooperation. Willing is the object or the subject matter of thinking, and hence always already under the "form of thinking."[3] In addition to originary parity, a functional disparity exists between thinking and willing, as expressed in the difference between knower and known.

Now, it is exactly the measure of disparity thus introduced into the original relation between thinking and willing that assures the unity of thinking and willing. In taking willing as its original object, thinking assumes the unitary but complex structure of willing thought, thought willing or the thinking of willing. Moreover, the treatment of thinking as form, more specifically as formative activity, allows Fichte to specify a set of formal features that accrue to willing by its being originally thought. Willing qua thought is deeply affected by the principal structures that govern thinking as such.

The basic law of thinking is the "law of reflection concerning opposites."[4] According to this law, which governs all finite thinking, thinking consists in the transition from indeterminacy to its opposite, determination. Thinking is nothing but the act of determination, an act through which all determination is first brought about. Moreover, the determinable is never given as such but always is presupposed on the part of thinking as the substrate upon which the latter exercises its determination. The determinable is to be added in and through thinking.[5] More specifically, the determinable introduced by thinking is unified and objectified by the operations of productive imagination (which in turn rely on space as the universal form of sensible inituiting): "the imagination is the power to get a hold of the determinable."[6]

But the activity of thinking, jointly with imagination, does not only provide the determinable as the basis for determination. In bringing about determination, thinking also produces the objects so determined. On Fichte's idealist construal, objects are the determinations of thinking rendered objective and seemingly independent of thought by the work of the imagination together with the form of sensible intuition.

The domain so generated is the sensible world with its empirical objects (*Sinnenwelt*), which to Fichte, as before him to Kant, is a world of appearances pointing to a different realm that is closer both to the origin and to the ultimate destination of human subjectivity. Fichte marks the difference between the two realms by resorting to Kant's "critical distinction" between phenomena and noumena or beings of sense (*sensibilia*) and beings of the intellect (*intelligibilia*).[7]

In Kant the notion of noumena is merely a negative or limiting concept indicating the restriction of theoretical knowledge to the conditions of sensibility. From the theoretical perspective, that is, from within the theory of experience, the world of noumena remains empty, to be filled by subsequent practical, more specifically moral, considerations. By contrast and in line with the program of a radical integration of the transcendental theories of experience and freedom, Fichte assigns a positive, indeed fundamental, function to the noumena for the principal structuring of the empirical world.[8] He considers the activity of thinking as such to involve reference to noumena. All thinking, not just the thinking of nonsensible objects, is concerned with noumena or the intelligible: "What does 'thinking' mean? The manner in which noumena come about, is that thinking? To carry the intelligible into the sensible as the ground of the latter's unification, that is what thinking means."[9]

The shift from Kant's limitative conception of noumena to their positive function in the transcendental structuring of experience in Fichte also involves a stricter distinction between noumena and things in themselves than is to be found in Kant. Given their principal unknowability by means of theoretical cognition, Kantian noumena closely resemble things in themselves, the difference between the former's merely negative status and the latter's inscrutable role in the origination of sensory data notwithstanding. By contrast, Fichtean noumena are closer in status (being made rather than given) to Kant's transcendental object and its correlate, the transcendental subject, which function as the ultimate points of unification in the structuring of experience through the understanding.[10]

To put Fichte's redefinition of the noumenal or the intelligible in the scholastic terminology favored by Kant, one could say that Fichte identifies the intelligible with the intellectual by deriving the objects of the intellect (*intelligibilia*) from the latter's forms (*intellectualia*).[11] This assimilation of the intelligible to the intellectual turns on an understanding of noumena that departs significantly from that of Kant, who in turn had been influenced in this matter by the latter-day Platonism of Leibniz's "realm of grace." For Fichte, the intelligible world or the world of noumena is not a realm of supersensible objects given to the intellect in some speculative or moral-practical orientation reaching beyond the world sense or nature. Rather, the intelligible or noumenal is a necessary product of thinking and its laws. It is part of the coming about of experience and a reflection of human finitude rather than its transcendence.

Fichte's emphasis on the produced nature of the noumenal suggests a close affinity between the production of empirical objects ("positing") and the coming about of noumena. In both cases the objects result from the imposition of a priori subjective forms. Now, in Kant transcendental idealism is restricted, terminologically as well conceptually, to the subjectivity of sensible forms, thus leaving room for the nonsensible, ethico-practical realization of intellectual forms.[12] Fichte can be seen as complementing the formal idealism regarding phenomena to be found in Kant with an analogous formal idealism regarding noumena or a transcendental noumenalism. To be sure, the noumenalism thus attributed to Fichte is a noumenalism with respect to the world of sense. Noumena in the sense just described are the intellectual forms and features of the world of appearances insofar as the latter is more than a tempo-spatially arrayed sensory manifold.

The integration of the thinking of noumena into the world of sense provides considerable unity on both the subjective and the objective sides of Fichte's transcendental account of consciousness. The activity of thinking lies at the center of the subject, which thinks itself (as willing) and which thinks its objects (as the possible or actual ends of its willing). But the unification achieved by the threefold thinking of willing, phenomena and noumena goes even further. Fichte sees the thinking of phenomenal and noumenal objects as deeply intertwined both with each other and with the thinking that is willing. With regard to the former, he maintains that there is a relation of manifestation between the intelligible and the sensible. The intelligible is objectified in and through the sensible. With respect to the latter, he regards willing (or its nominalized equivalent, the will) as the ultimate reality to be presupposed in all thinking and its objects. The world is the objectification and the realization of willing or the will.[13]

Yet in line with Fichte's sustained emphasis on the principal limitations of human knowledge regarding the ultimate grounds of subjectivity and objectivity, his speculations on the absolute nature of subject and object should not be taken as an uncritical relapse into *transcendent* noumenalism. Fichte's noumenalism stays *transcendental* and critical, ever mindful of the fact that the prediscursive nature of self and world is still being thought by a finite, discursive intellect. It seems indicated to view Fichte's speculative efforts at grasping the absolute nature of the subject as part of his attempt to do justice to the nonfinite dimension of human existence as expressed in the latter's radical freedom.

Fichte's ascent to a (discursively mediated) consideration of self and world prior to and independent of their discursive representation in and through thinking is followed by the steps of a corresponding descent in the inverse direction.[14] The two phases can be likened to the juxtaposition of the *ordo cognoscendi* and the *ordo essendi.* In the ascending movement from the empirical to the nonempirical, Fichte passes from the empirical determinations of individual consciousness to their ground in the pure, intelligible character of the individual and from there to the latter's origin in some preindividual "mass" of determinability, identified as pure will.[15]

The reverse movement from the nonempirical down to the empirical takes the form of a two-step process of individuation: from preindividuality to pure individuality and from pure individuality to empirically determined individuality. Fichte distinguishes between "formal" and "material sensification" (*Versinnlichung*)[16] and identifies three gradations in the descent from the noumenal:

> (1) Pure will, or the absoluteness of reason in its entirety, the realm of reason.... (2) Individuality, which is [further] determinable (3) with respect to a single moment of consciousness.[17]

Methodologically speaking, the ascending movement of the *Wissenschaftslehre nova methodo* from empirical consciousness to its ultimate ground remains within the confines of Kantian transcendental philosophy with its characteristic regress from experience to the conditions of experience. By contrast, the subsequent descent from the nonempirical to the empirical exemplifies the post-Kantian project of a reconstructive "history of consciousness," pioneered by Fichte himself in the final part of the *Foundation of the Entire Wissenschaftslehre.*[18] It is worth noting that Fichte's transcendental history of consciousness also includes the transcendental history of the objects of consciousness and their worlds. If one were to consider the project a psychology, it would equally well have to be regarded as a cosmology.

In the twofold transcendental-historical transition from preindividuality to pure individuality and from pure individuality to empirical individuality, as reconstructed by Fichte, thinking exercises a crucial role. It is through determining thinking that the mass of determinability is subject to determination and that an individual as such is grasped out of the previously undifferentiated mass. And it is through the forms and principles of discursive thinking that pure, generic individuality receives specification. In particular, thinking introduces the dimension of time into specific individuality.[19] Fichte stresses that thinking is temporal insofar as its discursive acts occur in succession: "All thinking occurs within time."[20]

Moreover, thinking imparts its essential temporality to that which is being thought. In and through thinking the subject and its activities are temporalized:

> time, progression in time, comes into being only as a result of our thinking. I do not undergo any development in time; I am finished and complete all at once and forever. This entire being is apprehended in time, and only thereby does a process of development over time come into being for thinking.[21]

In Fichte's transcendental-historical perspective the sensory realm, including its a priori forms, is not just given. Rather, it is made or generated through thinking: "Sensibility is only [the] sensification [of the noumenal], nothing original."[22]

Although this may suggest the primacy of the atemporal intelligible realm over its temporalization through thinking, Fichte stresses equally the priority of the sensible over the intelligible, pointing out that the intelligible world is merely a product of thinking erected upon the sensible world: "The intelligible is added on . . . through thinking."[23]

The puzzling concurrence of the subordination of the sensible world under the intelligible one and of the subordination of the intelligible world under the sensible one is further complicated by the integrationist view discussed earlier, according to which the intelligible is a constituent part of the world of sense. Yet rather than charging Fichte with inconsistency in his account of the relation between the sensible and the intelligible, it seems indicated to identify the grounds for each of the views offered and to understand them in the context of their respective methodological and substantial orientation.

The rivaling supraordination and subordination of the sensible with respect to the intelligible may be understood in light of the difference between the order of empirical knowledge and the order of transcendental knowledge. From within empirical knowledge the sensible world has priority over the nonsensible world. From that viewpoint the sensible world, and it alone, appears as given. Yet from the transcendental perspective both worlds are the product of spontaneous, albeit unconscious activity and to that extent equal in status (as made rather than given). Still, within that very same perspective the intelligible takes precedence over the sensible due to the former's explanatory potential for the overall structure of finite subjectivity and its objects. The world of sense can be derived from the intelligible order: "Only the intelligible is original, the world of sense is a certain way of looking at the former."[24]

Finally, the integrationist account of the intelligible as residing *within* the sensible may be regarded as an attempt on Fichte's part to minimize the *chorismos* between the two worlds, while not actually collapsing their distinction. Considered that way, the spectrum of relations between the sensible and the intelligible, reaching from subordination and supraordination to integration, marks Fichte's manifold attempts at articulating the unitary yet complex structure of the subject and its worlds.

2. Synthetic Thinking and the Pure Will

Fichte's detailed account of the unity of consciousness and its objects is built around the notion of synthetic thinking. According to Fichte, thinking as such is synthetic activity, an activity that involves the extension of thinking through the very activity of thinking. Unlike synthesis in Kant, which takes the form of a combination of an antecedently given manifold,[25] the synthesis of thinking in Fichte includes the very introduction of the manifold that is to be determined by thinking. In fact, Fichtean synthetic thinking is as much the synthetic production of a determinable manifold as the latter's determination through thinking. The synthetic self-extension of thinking encompasses real, object-oriented thinking (knowing) as well as ideal, end-oriented thinking (willing) and extends further to the syntheses of the respective object domains or worlds.

For Fichte, the comprehensive meaning of the concept of synthetic thinking as the universal structure underlying self and world is to be derived from its originary meaning as pure will thought. First and foremost, synthetic thinking is the finite, finitizing reflection of pure willing from which every other principal feature of self and world is derived. Synthetic thinking in the latter understanding is originary in a twofold sense: It is the point of origin for synthetic features of subjectivity and objectivity, and that very origin is itself already synthetic. Original thinking is synthetic in that the distinction between thinking and willing does not precede their unification. Unification and distinction are equally original; the original synthesis of thinking and willing is also their original analysis:

> the thinking that introduces distinctions and the thinking that provides uni-
> fication are one and not to be separated from each other; through synthetic
> thinking the thinking that introduces distinctions is not simply unified but
> first divided in such a way that it cannot be united.[26]

More specifically, original synthetic thinking consists in the I's thinking
of itself as determining itself. In this thinking, the I is both the object of its
thinking and the end of its self-determination, thereby representing a unity
of thinking and willing in which there is only a minimal difference between
what something is (object) and what it ought to be (end). It is the occurrence of thinking and willing in the I's "one" consciousness as self-determining that Fichte terms "synthetic thinking" in the term's originary meaning:

> in this thinking [synthetic thinking] the I thinks of itself as determining itself,
> which thought moreover is inseparable [from the I]; the I is an I for itself.
> Here we have a thinking of the object and a thinking of the end. Though
> these two are distinct from each other, they necessarily occur together in one
> consciousness, and the latter is called "synthetic thinking."[27]

The self-determination involved in original synthetic thinking exhibits
a dual character. The resultant determinacy (*Bestimmtheit*) marks the limitation of the I, whereas the act of determination (*Bestimmung*) indicates the
I's freedom. By separating the two originally unified features, the I differ-
entiates its thinking into constraint thinking and free thinking. Yet these
opposites represent only the separate but complementary aspects of the
underlying original duplicity of thinking and willing:

> If we attend to the determinacy, then the I appears to be constrained. This
> sort of thinking is called "objective thinking," and a specific feeling is con-
> nected with it. If, on the other hand, we attend to the freedom involved in
> such an act of determining, then it appears to be an act of willing. The think-
> ing of an end and the thinking of an object are really the same, only viewed
> from different sides.[28]

Thus, the original duplicity of thinking and willing results in a sustained
"duplicity of aspect" (*Duplizität der Ansicht*)[29] regarding self and world.

The duplicity of aspect assures the ultimate unity of such principal opposites as knowing and willing, mind and body, self and world. In each case,
the opposites are opposite sides on one underlying complex, "duplicitous"
unity: "Everything is one and the same, only always under different
aspects.[30] It should be stressed that the opposites arise in natural thinking,
whereas their identification as alternative but complementary aspects of
one and the same is the work of the philosophical thinking.[31]

The thoroughgoing duplicity of ideal and real aspects also shows in the parallel emphasis on the finitude of human volition and cognition: "With respect to reality, I am not everything; with respect to ideality, I am unable to grasp what I am all at once."[32] Although Fichte stresses that thinking imports temporality into anything so thought, he already attributes finitude or limitation to pure willing as such, thus indicating a pure, extratemporal volitional core constituent of the I (pure will) that is further finitized by being thought into time. To be sure, the finitude of pure willing as such, prior to its temporalization through objectifying thought, is itself a product of thinking – albeit of a negative thinking that systematically disregards any temporal dimension with respect to pure willing.

The finitude or limitation of pure will makes up the I's pure, preempirical individuality or its basic character. The latter is not so much a specific set of character traits as the fundamental law governing the exercise of human freedom, that of being determined to self-determination:

> This determinacy . . . consists merely in a task to act in a certain way, in an ought. The determination of the human being is not something that the human being gives to itself; instead it is that through which a human being is a human being.[33]

Fichte's specification that the determination involved in human agency is "a task to act in a certain way" suggests that pure individuality is not generic and the same in all humans but specific to the individual human being. Thus, the pure or basic character would be the extratemporal prefiguration of an individual's temporal characteristics. Such an account may seem to threaten the possibility of human freedom. But freedom is preserved through the practical nature of the pure character. The latter gives the law for how to act but does not necessitate the action.[34]

For Fichte the original determinacy or "original limitation" (ursprüngliche Beschränktheit)[35] of the pure will provides the "explanatory ground of all consciousness."[36] Specific acts of volition as well as specific acts of cognition are so many different ways to express in empirical terms the pure, nonempirical facticity of the will. In a rare use of pronouns of the first person singular, Fichte even calls originally determined pure will "my true being" (mein wahres Sein),[37] thereby suggesting a contrast between the core of a human being and its temporo-spatially fragmented manifestation. Yet the primacy of pure willing over its temporal refractions in an individual's life does not amount to a detachment of pure will from thinking. On the contrary, the two remain linked, and calling pure willing "my true being" also carries the epistemological sense of its being "true being" for me. While maintaining a primacy of sorts with respect to pure willing, Fichte insists on the ideality of all willing, including pure willing: "Every act of willing is an appearance, pure willing is merely presupposed as an explanatory ground."[38] Or, as he puts the point in its most universal, and least specific, statement: "Everything is appearance, including I myself."[39]

Its ultimate ideality notwithstanding, pure willing and its temporalization through thinking are the very stuff that the world is made of. On Fichte's account, the pure facticity of willing and its reflection in finite thinking appear to the human being as limitations encountered in its cognitive and conative activities. In the cognitive attitude the individual's basic limitation is encountered under the form of feeling (*Gefühl*): "*De facto* feeling is what comes first and is original."[40] Feeling and its systematic pluralization (*System der Gefühle*) exercise a constraint on thinking (*Denkzwang*),[41] resulting in the positing of a world of objects external to and independent of the cognitive subject.[42]

Fichte supplies an analogous derivation of the human subject's relation to the world of other human beings in the conative attitude. The original encounter of other persons occurs through the thought that the individual's basic practical limitation reflects the claims of other individuals to the exercise of their respective volitional activities. Unlike the constraint on thinking imposed by feeling in the cognitive attitude, the limitation on willing imposed by the claim of others is not a strict necessitation. It is experienced as a basic appeal to the individual to limit its volitional activity. Fichte terms the appeal a "solicitation to freedom" (*Aufforderung zur Freiheit*),[43] thereby indicating that realizing the claims of others first awakens the individual to the exercise of its free self-determination. Fichte even considers the solicitation to lie at the origin of an individual's entire overt mental activity, practical or otherwise, and to be more fundamental yet than the cognitive encounter of objects on the basis of feeling: "The first representation I can have is that of being solicited, as an individual, to engage in an act of free willing."[44]

Now, it might seem that the doctrine of the solicitation and the recognition through other individuals and their restrictive claims on an individual's free self-determination provides a realist grounding to Fichte's otherwise decidedly idealist treatment of self and world. The solicitation appears to disclose the reality of other human beings and thereby ground objectivity in something more than the cognitive and conative activities of an individual subject. Yet the solicitation is not really an appeal issued from outside the individual but is the individual's "clandestine" representation to itself of its own finite being under the form of the solicitation. The world of other human individuals opened up by the solicitation is still a world that originates in an individual's thought-reflection on the latter's originally limited practical activity. The other individuals are noumena or entities of thought, both in the sense of being entities of thinking and in the sense of being entities that are thought to be, themselves, thinking entities:

I do not perceive the reason and the free will of others outside of me; this is something I only infer from an appearance in the sensible world. Consequently, these other rational beings belong not within the sensible world, but rather within the intelligible one, the world of the noumena.[45]

To be sure, for the individual itself the solicitation and the rational agent or agents behind it assume independent status. The realm of reason in general, along with the other rational individuals in it, appears to the individual as prior to itself and as a necessary condition of its own individuation. But upon deeper analysis, it becomes clear that the necessary dependence of a given individual on the solicitation through another individual does not really explain how rational individuality comes about in the first place. If no individual is self-sufficient in the realization of its rationality, then there remains the problem of accounting for the first, unsolicited solicitor. It is at this point that Fichte argues that the ultimate foundation of individuality lies not in some other individual but in something altogether different from finite individuals and perhaps incomprehensible to them: "No individual is able to account for himself on the basis of himself alone. Consequently, when one arrives – as one must – at a first individual, one must also assume the existence of an even higher, incomprehensible being."[46]

In the framework of the *Wissenschaftslehre nova methodo* the necessary presupposition of a supraindividual ground of individuality consists in the thought of the highest determinable to all possible determination. Fichte's attempt to elucidate this ultimate ground seeks to reconcile two insights: that the presupposition of the absolute ground is still a thought produced by the individual in accounting for its own original determination, and that it is yet the thought of something radically different from and independent of all finite thinking, something on which all finite thinking is supposed to depend.

It should be emphasized that the ultimate ideality of other individuals in the *Wissenschaftslehre nova methodo* does not diminish Fichte's historical achievement of introducing the concept of interpersonality into the transcendental theory of consciousness.[47] Yet although the possible or actual relation to other finite rational beings is a constituent feature of individual consciousness, interpersonality is not able to function as the principle of subjectivity. Interpersonality provides the crucial intermediary layer between the absolute ground of consciousness and individual consciousness, between subjectivity in general and the concrete human subject. But rather than replacing subjectivity with *intersubjectivity*, interpersonality remains a form of subjectivity, of *intrasubjectivity* to be precise. By contrast, the ultimate ground of subjectivity, as sought by Fichte, is not an other consciousness but something other than consciousness altogether.

Incidentally, the specifics of the interpersonal relation remain largely unaddressed in the *Wissenschaftslehre nova methodo*. To judge by Fichte's own testimony, he was just about to address the "synthesis of the world of spirits"[48] when the outbreak of the atheism dispute distracted him from that project and eventually led him to address it in a more popular vein in the Third Book of *The Vocation of Man*.[49]

In the confines of the *Wissenschaftslehre nova methodo* the theory of interpersonality is thus part of Fichte's comprehensive transcendental account of consciousness and its objects, as conveyed in that work's culminating conception of the fivefold "synthetic periodus" (*synthetischer Periodus*)[50] linking original synthetic thinking, its alternative realizations as ideal thinking and real thinking and their respective worlds (nature and the realm of freedom) into a circular, self-enclosed structure. There are two series consisting of two elements each (real thinking and its world, and ideal thinking and its world) stretching in different directions from their common point of origin, viz., original synthetic thinking. The joining of the extreme ends of the two series (world of nature and world of spirits) turns the reconnecting series into a self-enclosed structure that runs in cycles (*periodus*). Fichte introduces Latin and Greek letters to designate the relationships between the five elements of his periodic table of consciousness:

> To make our account easier to follow, let us designate the central synthesis *A;* let us designate the immediately adjacent real term on this side *b;* and let us designate the extreme or outermost real term on this side, which is connected to *b, g.* Looking at the other side of the synthesis, let us designate the immediately adjacent element β and the outermost element as γ.[51]

The crucial connection between the extreme ends of the real and ideal series is provided by the interaction of the two worlds. The supersensible ends of free volition are realized in the empirical world, and the empirical word exhibits teleological structures that make it an "*analogon* of freedom."[52]

It remains for one to ask whether Fichte's account of the fivefold periodic structure of consciousness is not circular in a deficient sense by closing the subject and its worlds off from a reality that might underlie and support the self-generation of self and world. The transcendental theory of the *Wissenschaftslehre nova methodo* might need to be supplemented by the introduction of something unthought, and even unthinkable, that would provide a stable point of reference to the ceaseless circling of the I in and around itself.

3. Faith as the Unity of Intelligence and Will

Fichte's systematic concern with the overall structure of consciousness in general and the relation between thinking and willing in particular receives

its most dramatic rendition in *The Vocation of Man*. Written in Berlin immediately after his involuntary removal from Jena and published in early 1800,
this work occupies a unique place in Fichte's literary production. It provides a lucid restatement of the main tenets of the Jena *Wissenschaftslehre* in
a nontechnical presentation that employs the literary devices of meditation
and dialogue. The very organization of *The Vocation of Man* marks the sta-
tions of a philosophical psychodrama from doubt (*Zweifel*) through knowledge (*Wissen*) to faith (*Glaube*), as indicated in the headings of the work's
three books.

In its dramatically unified structure *The Vocation of Man* integrates the
methodological and metaphilosophical issue of the alternative between dogmatism and idealism, addressed in the various introductory writings to the
Wissenschaftslehre, with the latter's core doctrine of the original complex relation between thinking and willing. The work traces the development of
insight from the dogmatic standpoint of a deterministic, materialist "system
of nature" through the idealist system of knowledge in which everything
and everyone, including the self ("I"), is a mere representation or "image"
(*Bild*)[53] in consciousness, to the "system of freedom" in which the reality
and certainty of self, world and others is reestablished on moral grounds.

By separating the presentation of theoretical knowledge, now termed
"knowledge" *simpliciter*, from that of knowledge based on moral-practical
grounds, now termed "faith," Fichte seeks to undercut some of the criticisms addressed against the *Wissenschaftslehre*, chiefly among those Jacobi's
charge that transcendental idealism annihilates all reality by reducing the
latter to mere representations in consciousness.[54] Fichte manages to deflect
the nihilism charge from the *Wissenschaftslehre* proper to its incomplete sur-
rogate, *theoretical* transcendental idealism, while claiming some of the key
features of Jacobi's philosophy of faith (*Glaubensphilosophie*) for his own position of complete, *practical* transcendental idealism.[55] In fact, the Third Book
of *The Vocation of Man* contains entire passages that are unidentified and
unmarked quotations from those parts of Jacobi's open letter in which
Jacobi describes his very own position.[56]

In integrating key elements of Jacobi's seemingly opposed position into
the *Wissenschaftslehre* and relegating the position critiqued by Jacobi to that
of a pseudo-*Wissenschaftslehre*,[57] Fichte is engaged in more than a polemical maneuver. The appropriation of Jacobi in the Third Book of *The Vocation of Man* actually retrieves the influence that some of Jacobi's earlier
works, among them the novels *Allwill* and *Woldemar* and the books on Spinoza and Hume,[58] had exercised on the formation of the *Wissenschaftslehre*.[59]
Jacobi's limitation of the claims of reason and knowledge in favor of feeling and belief or faith supplements Fichte's systematic allegiance to Kant
and may well account for the proto-romantic or even proto-existentialist
aspects of his philosophical thinking.

The triadic sequence of dogmatism, theoretical transcendental idealism and practical transcendental idealism in *The Vocation of Man* lends considerable drama to the relation between thinking and willing and their respective faculties, intelligence and will. In line with the popular vein of the work, Fichte contrasts the two as understanding (*Verstand*) and heart (*Herz*). The dogmatist system of nature as an all-encompassing hierarchy of forces, reaching from inanimate nature through vegetative and animal life to human mental life, thoroughly satisfies the cognitive interest of the understanding. But it leaves unaddressed and even thoroughly frustrates the practical interest that the heart takes in the freedom of human existence from the deterministic system of nature. The meditator of Book 1 is suspended in a state despair ("doubt"),[60] unable to decide between two competing conceptions of human existence that each address only a fragmented part of the entire human being.

The system of theoretical transcendental idealism seeks to redress the situation by deducing all reality from the laws of the intelligence, here understood in strictly cognitive terms to the exclusion of the practical nature of the intelligence. Yet the attempt at a *theoretical* system of freedom results only in negatively freeing thinking from all external constraints and totally disengages the activity of thinking from any reality to which it might refer or that might provide support to that activity, effectively casting into doubt the very integrity of the I. Again the meditator's reaction is one of despair.

It is only when the meditator turns from the sphere of (theoretical) knowledge to that of acting and its grounding in the will that a system of self and world comes into view that preserves the basic human interest in freedom. This move at the beginning of Book 3 of *The Vocation of Man* is based on the insight that "[theoretical] knowledge cannot provide its own foundation and proof."[61] The nontheoretical grounding of knowledge occurs in a practical perspective through an intervention of the will, which in turn is informed by the consciousness of the moral law. From a merely theoretical point of view, self and world remain forever subject to skeptical doubt about their reality. But turning from the perspective of the knower to that of the actor brings in a different kind of certainty, viz., the certainty bound up with conscience (*Gewissen*)[62] or the consciousness of the practical laws governing human conduct.

The recognition of a system of practical laws is not merely a matter of knowledge. If that were the case, the skeptical doubts concerning the reality of theoretical knowledge would reemerge in a practical guise as doubts about the binding force of the practical laws. Rather, the recognition in question includes the eminently practical moment of a decision to affirm the reality of the practical laws. It is this cognitive-conative unity resulting from the "decision of the will to recognize the validity of the [practical] knowledge" that Fichte terms "faith."[63] Thus, faith assures the very "unity and completion . . . of human nature."[64]

The role of the will in assenting to the practical knowledge of what ought to be done might suggest a decisionist grounding of knowledge in an ultimately arbitrary act of willing. But the role of willing does not consist in the determination of the practical laws themselves but only in the voluntary assent to them. Willing completes rather than substitutes the recognition of the practical laws.

On Fichte's understanding, the practical standpoint with its grounding of knowledge in faith is not the result of philosophical speculation but represents the "standpoint of natural thinking."[65] The assenting intervention of the will puts an end to the artificial reasoning of theoretical idealism and marks a "voluntary acquiescence in the view which is naturally presented to us."[66] Moreover, the natural standpoint in question is not the natural standpoint of the theoretical belief in things in themselves that underlies philosophical dogmatism but the standpoint of the moral belief in human freedom that forms the basis of the *Wissenschaftslehre*. The difference between the natural practical standpoint and the standpoint of faith lies in the latter's adoption through a conscious, free decision: "With freedom and consciousness I have returned to the standpoint in which also my nature had left me."[67]

Its striking mise-en-scène notwithstanding, the "system of freedom" developed in Book 3 of *The Vocation of Man* is for the most part a restatement of Fichte's previously developed and published position on the primacy of the practical over the theoretical. The juxtaposition of knowledge and faith repeats in a different terminological guise the distinction between theoretical and practical reason to be found in Fichte's writings since the review of *Aenesidemus* (1794) and the *Foundation of the Entire Wissenschaftslehre* (1794–1795). The move from a generic conception of the practical to its specifically moral-practical form can be found in *The System of Ethics* (1798).[68] The conception of faith as the unity of thinking and willing occurs in Fichte's essay "On the Basis of Our Belief in a Divine Governance of the World" (1799).[69] Finally, the key idea of legitimating theoretical knowledge claims on the basis of moral knowledge by arguing that the former are the necessary conditions for the exercise of moral obligations is equally present in the last-mentioned essay and figures prominently in the lectures on the *Wissenschaftslehre nova methodo* (1796–1799).[70]

The harmonious unity of head and heart achieved in the Third Book of *The Vocation of Man* is nothing other than the unity of thinking and willing in pure practical reason or pure rational will. In its relation to theoretical reason, pure practical reason or pure rational will possesses primacy: freedom and its laws (morality) have original certainty and epistemic authority for theoretical knowledge claims: "Practical reason is the root of all reason."[71] Yet considered in is internal constitution, pure practical reason or pure rational will exhibits original duplicity: It is thinking and willing in primordial, yet differentiated, unity.

In addition to its function in the free assent to moral constraints, the will plays yet another role in the concluding book of *The Vocation of Man*. Based on the distinction between the sensible and the intelligible world, Fichte draws an analogy between the role of motion (*Bewegung*), understood as moving force, in the former and that of the will in the latter: "The will is what is active and alive in the world of reason, just as motion is what is active and alive in the world of sense."[72]

The point of the analogy is that whereas physical moving forces exercise causal efficacy in the sensible world, the will as intelligent moving force possesses efficacy in the intelligible world, the will's frequent inefficacy in the sensible world notwithstanding: "I am a member of two orders; a purely spiritual one, in which I reign merely through the pure will, and a sensible one, in which I act through my deed."[73]

Yet even in the intelligible world, with all physical hindrances of the sensible world removed, the will cannot be efficacious strictly on its own. In the intelligible world the will is supposed to act upon the will of the other members of that order. Fichte argues that the interpersonally efficacious will of the intelligible world is not, at least not originally, an individual's will but a supraindividual "infinite will"[74] that acts in and through individual wills.

On Fichte's account, the presence of the infinite will in the finite wills takes the form of the law under which finite intelligence as such stands. In fact, the infinite will is nothing else than the "practical law, the law of the supersensible world."[75] Moreover, just as finite, individual will is nothing other than reason qua practical reason, infinite, supraindividual will is itself the "law of reason" (*Gesetz der Vernunft*),[76] understood as the law given to reason by reason, or as reason's own, self-given law. In line with the popular orientation of *The Vocation of Man*, the meditator deifies and worships original pure will as "sublime living will" and "the one who sees into the human heart" (*Herzenskündiger*).[77] More importantly, the infinite will is believed to function as the "universal mediator" (*allgemeiner Vermittler*) between finite wills, thus establishing the "system of . . . individual wills" that consists in the "unification and immediate reciprocal action [*Wechselwirkung*] of several free and independent wills.[78]

Fichte's account of noumenal interpersonal relations is remarkable for its insistence on the direct interaction between finite wills. The interpersonal relations in the noumenal realm are neither mediated by a Malebranchian respondent to occasions nor are they part of a Leibnizian preestablished harmony between totally self-enclosed finite wills. In interacting with each other the finite members of the noumenal realm reenact their original unity as so many individuations of the infinite will. The "synthesis of the world of spirits" that was to provide the capstone of the Jena *Wissenschaftslehre,* then, is the synthesis of an individual's will with every other individual's will under the universal law of reason. Still, membership in the noumenal realm and the specific relations in it are a matter of faith; they reflect the individual will's assent to the law of the pure will.

In the Third Book of *The Vocation of Man* the will thus exercises a double role. As individual will, it is the faculty of free assent to the law of reason, the latter manifesting itself in the voice of conscience. As pure will, it is the very legislation of the law of reason. With its two functions as free choice and pure rational autonomy, the will clearly occupies the central position in Fichte's thinking at the close of the Jena period. Yet there is also an indication in the concluding pages of *The Vocation of Man* that the systematic and existential primacy of the will was to be supplemented soon by an emphasis on the contemplative stand toward the noumenal world. Fichte's meditator moves from the interests of the heart that govern the practical relation to the world and that therefore still tie the will to the transitory and insubstantial to the dispassionate vision of the eternal order: "Now that my heart is closed against all desire for earthly things, now that I no longer have a heart for the transitory and perishable, the universe appears before my eyes in a transfigured [*verklärten*] shape.[79] VOM /50+

The shift in metaphor from the heart to the eyes marks the ascent from the infinitely striving finite will to the visionary union with the eternal will. Fichte's later work on the *Wissenschaftslehre* with its sustained philosophical contemplation of the absolute continues this development beyond the primacy of the practical. In going beyond the striving will Fichte also goes beyond willing's original double, discursive thinking. In *The Vocation of Man* the *Wissenschaftslehre,* that most rigorous and moralistic form of transcendental philosophy, prepares itself for the *sacrificium intellectus et volontatis.*

NOTES

Introduction

1   In line with the practice established by Fichte's foremost modern translator into English, Daniel Breazeale, the *terminus technicus "Wissenschaftslehre"* will be left untranslated.

2   Draft of a letter to Jens Baggesen, April or May 1795, GA III/2: 297–299 (no. 282a); EPW, 385.

3   See WLnmK, 184f., 189, 209, 211–212, 222, 227, 234, esp. 185 and 209. Breazeale renders *"Duplizität"* as "duality" (see FTP, 365 passim).

4   The Halle transcript (*Hallesche Nachschrift*) was discovered at the beginning of this century and first published in 1937 (Johann Gottlieb Fichte, *Nachgelassene Schriften*, Bd. II, ed. H. Jacob [Berlin: Junker und Dünnhaupt, 1937], 341–612). It has since been reprinted/reedited in GA IV/2: 17–267. A second transcript, named after its author, K. Chr. F. Krause (*Krause Nachschrift*), was discovered in 1980 and first published in 1982 (Johann Gottlieb Fichte, *Wissenschaftslehre nova methodo: Kollegnachschrift K. Chr. Fr. Krause 1798/99*, ed. E. Fuchs. 2d edition [Hamburg: Felix Meiner, 1994]). Since the Krause transcript is somewhat superior in care of execution and degree of detail to the Halle transcript, references to the *Wissenschaftslehre nova methodo* will be in the first instance to the Krause transcript, with the corresponding passages in the Halle transcript indicated where applicable.

5   Italian translation of the Halle transcript under the title *Teoria della scienza 1798 "nova methodo,"* trans. A. Cantoni (Milan: Biblioteca "Il pensiero," 1959); Spanish translation of the same text under the title *Doctrina de la Ciencia nova methodo,* trans. M. Ramos and J. L. Villacañas (Valencia: Universidad de Valencia, 1987); French translation of the Krause transcript with selected variants from the Halle transcript under the title *La Doctrine de la Science Nova Methodo: Suivi de Essai d'une nouvelle présentation de la Doctrine de la Science,* trans. I. Radrizzani (Lau-

127

sanne: L'Age d'homme, 1989); English translation of the Krause transcript with selected variants from the Halle transcript under the title *Foundations of Transcendental Philosophy (Wissenschaftslehre) Nova Methodo (1796/99)*, ed. and trans. D. Breazeale (Ithaca, N.Y.: Cornell University Press, 1992). See also my review of the English translation in *The Philosophical Review* 103 (1994): 585–588.

6 Ives Radrizzani, *Vers la fondation de l'intersubjectivité chez Fichte: Des Principes à la Nova Methodo* (Paris: Vrin, 1993). See also my review in *Philosophischer Literaturanzeiger* 47 (1994): 366–368.

7 See Peter Rohs, *Johann Gottlieb Fichte* (Munich: Beck, 1991), 65–85; and my essay "The Flowering of Idealism: Johann Gottlieb Fichte," in *The Columbia History of Philosophy*, ed. R. Popkin (New York: Columbia University Press, forthcoming).

8 The Fourth Biennial meeting of the North American Fichte Society at Marquette University in March 1997 was devoted to the new presentation of the *Wissenschaftslehre;* a volume with selected papers from that conference, edited by Daniel Breazeale and Tom Rockmore, is in preparation. Manfred Frank is editing a special issue of *Revue internationale de philosophie* on the *Wissenschaftslehre nova methodo.*

9 With respect to the *Wissenschaftslehre nova methodo,* the reading of Fichte's theory of interpersonality as a social ontology is reviewed and critiqued in Radrizzani, *Vers la fondation de l'intersubjectivité chez Fichte,* 34–41 and 185–188.

10 For a more detailed discussion of the systematic place of interpersonality in Fichte's transcendental theory of subjectivity, see my essays "Die Individualität des Ich in Fichtes zweiter Jenaer Wissenschaftslehre (1796–99)," *Revue internationale de philosophie* (forthcoming) and "Leib, Materie und gemeinsames Wollen als Anwendungsbedingungen des Rechts," in *Fichtes Grundlage des Naturrechts,* ed. J. C. Merle. Reihe Klassiker auslegen. (Berlin: Akademie Verlag, forthcoming).

11 The account of volition in the second edition of the *Attempt at a Critique of All Revelation* marks an important early stage in the development of Fichte's thinking about willing that predates the beginnings of the *Wissenschaftslehre* but does not significantly extend the time frame of the present study beyond the years 1794–1800, which best capture the scope of the study within the chronology of Fichte's works.

12 The year 1800 still marks the watershed in the development of the *Wissenschaftslehre,* whose first late version dates from 1801–1802.

13 GA, I/6: 189; VOM, 3.

Chapter 1

1 See, e.g., GA I/4: 231n.; IWL, 63f.n. On the difference between letter and spirit, see also the manuscript remains pertaining to the later, unpublished parts of Fichte's lectures on the vocation of the scholar held in Jena during the summer semester of 1794 (GA II/3: 291–342; partial translation in EPW, 192–215).

2 See *Critique of Pure Reason* B 370/A 314. On Fichte's interpretation of Kant, see Manfred Zahn, "Fichtes Kant-Bild," in *Erneuerung der Transzendentalphilosophie*

im Anschluß an Kant und Fichte, ed. K. Hammacher and A. Mues (Stuttgart –Bad Cannstatt: Frommann-Holzboog, 1979), 479–505.

3   *Critique of Pure Reason,* B 869/A 841.

4   See GA I/4: 230n.; IWL, 63n. (Fichte's emphases).

5   On Fichte's distinction between critique and system with respect to his own work, see GA I/2: 159f.; EPW, 97.

6   For an account of the overall nature and the modes of employment of reason in Kant in the context of the practical orientation of classical German philosophy in general and Kant's doctrine of the primacy of practical reason in particular, see my essay "Kant and the Unity of Reason" (unpublished manuscript; originally presented as an invited paper at the Central Division Meeting of the American Philosophical Association in Kansas City in May 1994). For an alternative account of the unity of reason in terms of the latter's practico-regulative function, cf. Susan Neiman, *The Unity of Reason: Rereading Kant* (New York: Oxford University Press, 1993). See also my review of Neiman's book in *Journal of the History of Philosophy* 34 (1996): 306–308.

7   The formulation of the critical task through the question "How are synthetic judgments a priori possible?" first occurs in section 5 of the *Prolegomena to Any Future Metaphysics* (1783; AA IV, 276; Immanuel Kant, *Prolegomena to Any Future Metaphysics,* introd. L. W. Beck [Indianapolis: Bobbs-Merrill, 1982], 23), from where it is taken over into the second edition of the *Critique of Pure Reason* (1787; B 19ff.).

8   For a reconstruction of Kant's systematic idealism in aesthetics, see my essay "Kant's Aesthetic Idealism," in *The Iowa Review* 21 (1991): 52–57.

9   On Kant's project of a practico-dogmatic metaphysics of postulates of pure practical reason, see AA XX, 252–332, esp. 296–301 (*Preisschrift über die Fortschritte der Metaphysik*); *What Real Progress Has Metaphysics Made in Germany since the Time of Leibniz and Wolff?* Trans. and introd. T. Humphrey (New York: Abaris, 1983), 127–137.

10   See *Critique of Pure Reason,* A 369 and B 519/A 491, respectively.

11   On the systematic place of transcendental idealism in the *Critique of Pure Reason,* see also my *Theoretische Gegenstandsbeziehung bei Kant* (Berlin and New York: de Gruyter, 1984), 289–296.

12   See AA II, 398–406 (*De mundi sensibilis atque intelligibilis forma et principiis*); Immanuel Kant, *Theoretical Philosophy, 1755–1770,* trans. and ed. D. Walford in collaboration with R. Meerbole (Cambridge: Cambridge University Press, 1992), 391–400. Although the term "ideal" (*ideale*) is applied to space in the *Inaugural Dissertation* (AA II, 403; *Theoretical Philosophy,* 397), Latin equivalents of the coinages "transcendental ideality" and "transcendental idealism" are not yet to be found in that work.

13   See *Critique of Pure Reason,* B 44/A 28 and B 52/A 36.

14   For an account of the role of reason in the generation of the feeling of pleasure, see my essay "Toward the Pleasure Principle: Kant's Transcendental Psychology of the Feeling of Pleasure and Displeasure," in *Akten des Siebenten Internationalen Kant-Kongresses,* ed. G. Funke (Bonn: Bouvier, 1991), 809–819.

15   See *Critique of Pure Reason,* B 160n.; B 176ff./A 137ff. For an account of Kant's controversial notion of "formal intuition" in the context of the relation between

sensibility and understanding, see my exchange with Patricia Kitcher in *The Southern Journal of Philosophy* 25 (1986), supp. (*The B-Deduction*): 137–155.

16   See AA IV, 293f. (*Prolegomena*, section 13, Remark III); *Prolegomena to Any Future Metaphysics*, 41.

17   The only exception to this is to be found in Kant's late, fragmentary reflections on the "highest standpoint of transcendental philosophy" in the *Opus postumum* (in the last, so-called first fascicle; see, e.g., AA XXI, 32ff.; Immanuel Kant, *Opus Postumum*, ed. E. Förster [Cambridge: Cambridge University Press, 1993], 235ff.). In those passages, Kant can be seen as a reacting to, and even participating in, the post-Kantian undertaking of completing transcendental philosophy in the idealist spirit.

18   See *Critique of Pure Reason*, B 86off./A 832ff.; AA V, 170–179 (*Critique of Judgment*, Introduction, I–III) and AA XX, 241–247 (*First Introduction to the Critique of Judgment*, XI); *Critique of Judgment: With the First Introduction*, trans. W. Pluhar (Indianapolis: Hackett, 1987), 9–18 and 431–437.

19   See *Critique of Pure Reason*, A 369 and B 519/A 491; see also B 37–40/A 22–25 and B 46–48/A 30–32.

20   For an account of the role of Reinhold in Fichte's conception of philosophy as system, see Wolfgang Schrader, "Philosophie als System – Reinhold und Fichte," in Hammacher and Mues, *Erneuerung der Transzendentalphilosophie im Anschluß an Kant und Fichte*, 331–344.

21   GA I/2: 112; EPW, 101.

22   See ibid.

23   See GA I/2: 113f.; EPW, 102.

24   On the architectonic of the first published presentation of the *Wissenschaftslehre*, see Chapter 3.

25   See GA IV/2: 16f. and WLnmK, 10f.; FTP, 85f.

26   GA I/2: 140; EPW, 125.

27   See, e.g., GA I/2: 146; EPW, 130.

28   GA I/4: 190; IWL, 13.

29   See GA I/4: 186; IWL, 7f.

30   GA I/2: 147; EPW, 131 (translation modified). See GA I/2: 365; SK, 198f. The contrast between ephemeral and pragmatic historiography can be traced back to Kant's identification of "pragmatic" (*pragmatisch*) with "prudential" (*klug*) and his conception of pragmatic history as instruction in pursuing one's advantage in the world. See AA IV, 416f. (*Grundlegung zur Metaphysik der Sitten*, II); *Foundations of the Metaphysics of Morals*, trans. L. W. Beck (Indianapolis: Bobbs-Merrill, 1983), 34. The transposition of the term "pragmatic history" from the political sphere to that of the philosophical account of the mind occurs in Ernst Platner's *Philosophical Aphorisms* (*Philosophische Aphorismen*, 3d edition of Part One; Leipzig: Schwickert, 1793), on which Fichte based the lectures on logic and metaphysics, which he offered during each of the eight semesters that he taught at Jena. For Platner's use of the phrase "pragmatic history of the human faculty of cognition" (*pragmatische Geschichte des menschlichen Erkenntnißvermögens*), see the reprint of his *Philosophical Aphorisms* in GA II/4 supp., 16. On Fichte's critical appropriation of Platner's term in the context of his Jena lectures on logic and metaphysics, see GA II/4: 46, 52; GA IV/1: 204f.

31 For an account of Fichte's alternative self-interpretation of the *Wissenschaftslehre* as a scientific experiment, see Chapter 2.

32 See GA I/4: 188, 190; IWL, 11 (translation modified), 13.

33 GA I/4: 191; IWL, 14.

34 See GA I/4: 189; IWL, 12.

35 For an account of the I's ideal-real double nature, see Chapter 6.

36 See GA I/4: 194; IWL, 18.

37 See GA I/4: 194f.; IWL, 18f.

38 GA I/4: 195; IWL, 20 (translation modified). See also the further discussion of the idealist and dogmatist standpoints in Chapter 2.

39 GA I/4: 201; IWL, 27 (translation modified).

40 GA I/4: 201; IWL, 27.

41 See GA I/4: 200; IWL, 26f.

42 GA I/4: 202; IWL, 29 (translation modified).

43 See GA I/4: 201f.; IWL, 27f.

44 GA I/4: 204; IWL, 30.

45 GA I/4: 203; IWL, 29 (translation modified).

46 See GA I/4: 203n.; IWL, 29n. (translation modified).

47 See GA I/2: 159; EPW, 97. The text under consideration is the preface to the second edition of this work, published in 1798.

48 Ibid.

49 GA I/2: 160; EPW, 98 (translation modified).

50 Kant's open letter, which is dated 7 August 1799, appeared in the *Intelligenzblatt* of the *Allgemeine Litteratur-Zeitung* on 28 August 1799. Jacobi's extensive, rhapsodic letter, which is dated 3 March 1799, was first sent to Fichte and subsequently published in expanded form in the fall of 1799. For Kant's letter, see *Fichte im Gespräch*, ed. E. Fuchs, 6 vols. (Stuttgart–Bad Cannstatt: Frommann-Holzboog, 1980), 2:217f.; for the early version of Jacobi's letter, cf. GA III/3: 224–281; for the printed version, see *Transzendentalphilosophie und Spekulation: Der Steit um die Gestalt einer Ersten Philosophie (1799–1807)*, ed. W. Jaeschke (Hamburg: Meiner, 1993), 3–43; English translation of the printed version under the title "Open Letter to Fichte", in *Philosophy of German Idealism*, ed. E. Behler (New York: Continuum, 1987), 119–141.

51 See *Fichte im Gespräch*, 245; see also ibid., 238, 240f.

52 GA I/7: 194; CCR, 47. Many of the metaphilosophical points of the *Crystal Clear Report* are already to be found in Fichte's unpublished draft of an essay entitled *Rückerinnerungen, Antworten, Fragen*, written in 1799 as part of his defense in the atheism dispute (see GA II/5: 103–186). On Fichte's related appropriation strategy with respect to Jacobi's notion of "faith" in *The Vocation of Man*, see Chapter 8.

53 On the concept of life in Fichte, see Wolfgang Schrader, *Empirisches und absolutes Ich* (Stuttgart–Bad Cannstatt: Frommann-Holzboog, 1972); id., "Philosophie und Leben im Denken Fichtes um 1800," in *Kategorien der Existenz: Festschrift für W. Janke*, ed. K. and J. Hennigfeld (Würzburg: Königshausen und Neumann, 1993), 77–86.

54 See GA I/7: 202, 204; CCR, 54f., 56.

55   GA I/7: 203ff.; CCR, 56ff.

56   GA I/7: 198f.; CCR, 51.

57   See GA I/7: 203f.; CCR, 56.

58   On Fichte's account, the guiding principle of the *Wissenschaftslehre* is first for-
     mulated on the basis of a "fortunate idea," which as such falls outside of the
     Wissenschaftslehre, and which is confirmed subsequently through the *Wis-
     senschaftlehre*'s complete derivation of the main features of experience from the
     first principle. Cf. GA I/7: 212, 217ff.; CCR, 63, 68ff.

59   See GA I/7: 210; CCR, 61.

60   See GA I/7: 216; CCR, 67.

61   See GA I/7: 218; CCR, 69 (translation modified).

62   See GA I/7: 218; CCR, 69 (translation modified).

63   See GA I/7: 232f.; CCR, 82f. Fichte's extended comparison between philo-
     sophical and geometrical method turns on the analogous role of intellectual
     intuition in the two disciplines. See GA I/7: 226ff.

64   See GA I/7: 232f.; CCR, 82–84.

65   GA I/7: 232, 233, 249; CCR, 82, 83, 98 (translation modified).

66   GA I/7: 249; CCR, 99.

67   GA I/7: 249; CCR, 98 (*Unsere bestehende Welt ist fertig. . . . Das Leben ist kein Erzeu-
     gen sondern ein Finden.*) (translation modified). It should be stressed that it is
     only the already existing world that is ready-made, not any future world that is
     to be brought about by human praxis. For Fichte's account of practical change,
     see Chapter 4.

68   On the role of the *Critique of Judgment* in German idealism in general and in
     Fichte in particular, see Rolf-Peter Horstmann, *Die Grenzen der Vernunft: Eine
     Untersuchung zu Zielen und Motiven des Deutschen Idealismus* (Frankfurt/M.: Anton
     Hain, 1991), 191–219.

Chapter 2

1   For an overview of Fichte's development up to and through his Jena years, see
    "Editor's Introduction: Fichte in Jena," in EPW, 1–49.

2   For a recent comprehensive account of Fichte's philosophy, see Peter Bau-
    manns, *J. G. Fichte: Kritische Gesamtdarstellung seiner Philosophie* (Freiburg and
    Munich: Karl Alber, 1990). Other comprehensive treatments are Wolfgang
    Janke, *Fichte: Sein und Reflexion – Grundlagen der kritischen Vernunft* (Berlin: de
    Gruyter, 1970), id., *Vom Bilde des Absoluten: Grundzüge der Phänomenologie Fichtes*
    (Berlin and New York: de Gruyter, 1993), and Günter Schulte, *Die Wis-
    senschaftslehre des späten Fichte* (Frankfurt/M.: Vittorio Klostermann, 1971). For
    a recent English-language account of Fichte's philosophy of subjectivity during
    his Jena period, see Frederick Neuhouser, *Fichte's Theory of Subjectivity* (Cam-
    bridge: Cambridge University Press, 1990). A concise assessment of Fichte's
    contribution to philosophy is Allen W. Wood, "Fichte's Philosophical Revolu-
    tion," *Philosophical Topics* 19 (1992): 1–28.

3   See GA I,2: 118; EPW, 106.

4   See WLnmK, 11; GA IV/2: 18; FTP, 87.

5   See GA I/4: 230; IWL, 62f. On Fichte's relation to Kant, see Chapter 1.

6   For an overview of the early reception of Kant's philosophy, see Frederick C.
Beiser, *The Fate of Reason: German Philosophy from Kant to Fichte* (Cambridge, Mass.:
Harvard University Press, 1987) and Claude Piché, *Kant et ses épigones: Le jugement critique en appel* (Paris: Vrin, 1995). An English translation of selected primary material from that first phase of post-Kantianism can be found in *Between
Kant and Hegel: Texts in the Development of Post-Kantian Idealism*, trans. G. di Giovanni and H. S. Harris (Albany: State University of New York Press, 1985).

7   See GA I/4: 187; IWL, 9.

8   See WLnmK, 4, 9; FTP, 79, 84. For a discussion of the systematic function of
the concept of objective validity in Kant, see my *Theoretische Gegenstandsbeziehung
bei Kant.* For an account of Fichte's theory of objective reference, see Wayne
Martin, *Idealism and Objectivity: Understanding Fichte's Jena Project* (Stanford: Stanford University Press, 1997).

9   See WLnmK, 13; GA IV/2: 18f.; FTP, 89.

10 See GA I/4: 219; IWL, 49. Among recent interpreters of Fichte, Peter Baumanns has especially stressed the foundational role of the conviction of freedom in Fichte's works from the Jena period. See his *Fichtes ursprüngliches System:
Sein Standort zwischen Kant und Hegel* (Stuttgart–Bad Cannstatt; Frommann-Holzboog 1972); and *Fichtes Wissenschaftslehre: Probleme ihres Anfangs. Mit einem Kommentar zu Par. 1 der "Grundlage der gesamten Wissneschaftslehre"* (Bonn: Bouvier,
1974). For earlier interpretations of Fichte as a theoretician of freedom, see
Wilhelm Weischedel, *Der frühe Fichte: Aufbruch der Freiheit zur Gemeinschaft*
(Stuttgart–Bad Cannstatt: Frommann-Holzboog: 1973; first published in 1939);
and Alexis Philonenko, *La liberté humaine dans la philosophie de Fichte* (Paris: Vrin,
1966).

11 See WLnmK, 10; GA IV/2: 17; FTP, 85.

12 See Introduction, note 2.

13 See WLnmK, 7; FTP, 82.

14 See Jakob Sigismund Beck, *Erläuternder Auszug aus den Kritischen Schriften des
Herrn Prof. Kant, auf Anraten desselben.* [vol. 3:] *Dritter Band, welcher den Standpunkt darstellt, aus welchem die Kritische Philosophie zu beurteilen ist: Einzig moeglicher
Standpunkt, aus welchem die Kritische Philosophie beurteilt werden muss* (Riga: Hartknoch, 1793; reprinted in *Aetas Kantiana* [Brussels: Culture et Civilisation,
1968]); excerpts in *Between Kant and Hegel,* 204–249.

15 GA I/4: 200; IWL, 26f.

16 See GA I/4: 194; IWL, 18. See also GA I/5: 43, 65.

17 See GA I/4: 192; IWL, 16. For a detailed dicussion of the standpoints of ideal-
ism and realism in Fichte, see Ingeborg Schüssler, *Die Auseinandersetzung von
Idealismus und Realismus in Fichtes Wissenschaftslehre* (Frankfurt/M.: Vittorio
Klostermann, 1972).

18 GA I/4: 195; IWL, 20 (*Was für eine Philosophie man wähle, hängt sonach davon ab,
was man für ein Mensch ist.*) (translation modified).

19 GA I/2: 326n.; SK, 162n.

20 See GA I/4: 201f.; IWL, 27f. See also GA I/3: 144f.; EPW 245f.

21 Draft of a letter to Jens Baggesen, April or May 1795, GA III/2: 297–299 (no.
282a); EPW, 385.

22   GA I/3: 313n. For a detailed treatment of the concept of activity in Fichte's
      work from the Jena period, see Martin Oesch, *Das Handlungsproblem: Ein sys-
      temgeschichtlicher Beitrag zur ersten Wissenschaftslehre Fichtes* (Hildesheim: Ger-
      stenberg, 1981).

23   See GA I/4: 254f.; IWL, 86f.

24   See GA I/2: 47; EPW, 64. GA I/2: 258ff.; SK, 95ff. WLnmK, 16; GA IV/2: 21f.;
      FTP, 94. GA I/4: 242, 272; IWL, 74, 108.

25   See WLnmK, 25; GA IV/2: 27; FTP, 106. GA I/4: 210n., 236n.; IWL, 38n., 68n.
      GA I/7: 246–252; CCR, 95–101. For a more detailed discussion, see Daniel
      Breazeale, "The 'Standpoint of Life' and the 'Standpoint of Philosophy' in the
      Context of the *Jena Wissenschaftslehre* (1794–1800)," in *Transzendentalphilosophie
      als System: Die Auseinandersetzung zwischen 1794 und 1806*, ed. A. Mues (Ham-
      burg: Felix Meiner, 1989), 81–104.

26   See WLnmK, 21, 34f.; FTP, 101, 120. GA I/4: 209f.; IWL, 37.

27   See GA I/2: 255; SK, 93. WLnmK, 10f., 25.; FTP, 86, 106.

28   GA I/4: 274; IWL 110 (translation modifed). See WLnmK, 28f.; GA IV/2: 32;
      FTP, 110. See also Johannes Römelt, " 'Merke auf dich selbst': Das Verhältnis
      des Philosophen zu seinem Gegenstand nach dem *Versuch einer neuen Darstel-
      lung der Wissenschaftslehre* (1797/98)," *Fichte-Studien* 1 (1990), 73–98.

29   See GA I/4: 213; IWL, 41. WLnmK, 28; FTP, 109f.

30   See GA I/2: 149; EPW, 133.

31   See GA I/2: 146; EPW, 131. WLnmK, 8f., 22f.; FTP, 83f., 102f. Fichte's idea of
      a history of self-consciousness is treated in detail in Ulrich Claesges, *Geschichte
      des Selbstbewußtseins: Der Ursprung des spekulativen Problems in Fichtes Wissenschafts-
      lehre von 1794–94* (The Haag: Martinus Nijhoff, 1974).

32   See the editor's preliminary overview of Fichte's presentations of the *Wis-
      senschaftslehre* in Johann Gottlieb Fichte, *Wissenschaftslehre 1805*, ed. H. Gliwitzky
      (Hamburg: Felix Meiner, 1984), LXXIf.

33   See WLnmK, 8; GA IV/2: 64, 76; FTP, 83.

34   See GA I/3: 342.

35   See GA I/3: 329ff. See also WLmnK, 149–152 and 236–239; FTP, 301–307
      and 461–464.

36   See GA I/4: 200f.; IWL, 27.

37   The earliest published text that gives evidence of Fichte's emerging second
      Jena system is "A Comparison between Prof. Schmid's System and the *Wis-
      senschaftslehre*" (GA I/3: 251–266; selections translated in EPW, 321–335). For
      an overview in English of Fichte's lecture and publication activity during his
      Jena period, see the editor's introduction in EPW, 46–49. The place, function
      and method of the *Wissenschaftslehre nova methodo* is discussed in Ives Radriz-
      zani, *Vers la fondation de l'intersubjectivité chez Fichte*, 49–115.

38   See GA I/2: 255ff.; SK, 93ff. See the further discussion of "*Tathandlung*" in
      Chapter 3, especially note 13.

39   See GA I/2: 261; SK, 99.

40   See GA I/2: 266; SK, 104.

41   See GA I/2: 272; SK, 110. For a more detailed discussion of the three prin-
      ciples in the context of Fichte's doctrines of positing and determining, see
      Chapter 3.

42　See GA I/2: 279; SK, 116f.

43　See GA I/2: 410; SK, 245.

44　For a more detailed account of the structure and the doctrinal core of the *Wissenschaftslehre* of 1794–1795, see Chapter 3.

45　See WLnmK, 27f.; GA IV/2: 28F.; FTP, 108–110.

46　See WLnmK, 24f.; GA IV/2: 27; FTP, 105f. On Fichte's transcendental theory of individuality in the new presentation of the *Wissenschaftslehre*, see my essay "Die Individualität des Ich in Fichtes zweiter Jenaer Wissenschaftslehre (1796–99)."

47　See GA I/4: 216f; IWL, 46. GA I/5: 60. On the development of Fichte's theory of intellectual intuition during his Jena period, see Jürgen Stolzenberg, *Fichtes Begriff der intellektuellen Anschauung: Die Entwicklung in den Wissenschaftslehren von 1793/94 bis 1801/02* (Stuttgart: Klett-Cotta, 1986). On the term and concept of intellectual intuition in German idealist and romantic thought, see Xavier Tilliette, *L'intuition intellectuelle de Kant à Hegel* (Paris: Vrin, 1995).

48　See *Critique of Pure Reason*, B 71f.

49　See GA I/4: 277f.; IWL, 114f. WLnmK, 34; GA IV/2: 31, 37; FTP, 119f.

50　See GA I/4: 224ff.; IWL, 55ff. WLnmK, 31f.; GA IV/2: 31; FTP, 115.

51　See *Critique of Pure Reason*, B310f./A254f.

52　See GA I/4: 271; IWL, 106.

53　See GA I/4: 273f.; IWL, 109f. WLnmK, 29f; GA IV/2: 30; FTP, 112.

54　On Fichte's account of the nonreflexive nature of the pure I, see Dieter Henrich, "Fichte's Original Insight," in *Contemporary German Philosophy*, vol. 1 (College Park, Penn.: Pennsylvania State University Press, 1982), 15–53.

55　GA I/4: 276; IWL, 113. See also WLnmK, 31; GA IV/2: 31; FTP, 114.

56　GA IV/2: 31; FTP, 114 (translation modified).

57　See GA I/4: 276; IWL, 113. WLnmK, 30; GA IV/2: 30; FTP, 113.

58　GA I/4: 276; IWL, 114. See also WLnmK, 34; FTP, 119f. For a detailed examination of Fichte's theory of self-consciousness throughout the Jena period, see Reinhard Friedrich Koch, *Fichtes Theorie des Selbstbewußtseins: Ihre Entwicklung von den "Eignen Meditationen über ElementarPhilosophie" 1793 bis zur "Neuen Bearbeitung der W.L." 1800* (Würzburg: Königshausen und Neumann, 1989).

59　A possible source of inspiration for Fichte's use of the ocular metaphor is Johann Heinrich Jacobi, *David Hume über den Glauben oder Idealismus und Realismus* (Breslau: Loewe, 1787; reprint, London and New York: Garland, 1983), 179, 184, 190 and especially 195. On Fichte's usage of the eye metaphor, see also Henrich, *Fichte's Original Insight*, 31–40 and 47–50.

60　See SW VII, 461f. (FW VII, 461f.) and NW III, 347 (FW XI, 347); for an English translation, see Henrich, *Fichte's Original Insight*, 39.

61　GA I/6: 254; VOM, 84 (translation modified). For Fichte's later usage of the eye metaphor, see Johann Gottlieb Fichte, *Darstellung der Wissenschaftslehre aus den Jahren 1801/02*, ed. Peter K. Schneider (Hamburg: Felix Meiner, 1977), 26, 33, 46–48, 118, 140.

62　WLnmK, 40; FTP, 130 (translation modified).

63　WLnmK, 54; FTP, 151 (translation modified). See GA IV/2: 49.

64　WLnmK, 54; FTP, 152 (translation modified).

65　See GA I/4: 214; IWL, 43 (translation modified).

66   Ibid. (emphasis added; translation modified).

67   GA II/5: 338 (*Das unmittelbare Selbstbewußtseyn ist das ewig unveränderlich subjective u. wird als solches, u. isoliert, nie Object eines Bewußtseyns.*). See also ibid., 335,
345.

68   GA II/5: 347 (*Es ist auch nicht's anderes, als das, [allem Bewußtseyn vorauszuset-
zende] – Bey sich selbst seyn u. für sich selbst seyn des Bewußtseyenden selbst – der reine
Reflex des Bewußtseyns.*). See also ibid., 349.

69   GA II/5: 335.

70   GA I/4: 276f.; IWL, 113f. See WLnmK, 7, 31; FTP, 82, 114.

71   See WLnmK, 34; FTP, 119.

72   See Fichte, *Darstellung der Wissenschaftslehre aus den Jahren 1801/02*, 4f. On the
presence of a theory of the absolute already in Fichte's Jena period, see Hans
Radermacher, *Fichtes Begriff des Absoluten* (Fankfurt/M.: Vittorio Klostermann,
1970). For an alternative view of Fichte's development that contrasts the striving toward an infinite ideal in the early Fichte with the repose in the idea of
God in the later Fichte, cf. Bernard Bourgeois, *L'idéalisme de Fichte*, 2d edition
(Paris: Vrin, 1995).

Chapter 3

1   An example of a composition in sonata form that lacks the reprise section would
be Beethoven's so-called second *Leonore* Overture (op. 72), which is now
assumed to have been composed before the three other overtures to his opera
in three versions, *Leonore* (1805, 1806) or *Fidelio* (1814). Unlike Beethoven's
composition, though, the *Foundation of the Entire Wissenschaftslehre* does not contain a concluding section or coda.

2   See GA I/3: 261; SK, 99 (*Das Ich setzt urspünglich schlechthin sein eigenes Seyn.*)
(translation modified).

3   See GA I/3: 266; SK, 103 (*Das Entgegengesetztseyn ist überhaupt schlechthin durch
das Ich gesetzt.*).

4   See GA I/3: 270; SK, 108 (*[Es] wird demnach schlechthin das Ich sowohl als das
Nicht-Ich theilbar gesetzt.*).

5   See GA I/3: 266; SK, 104.

6   See GA I/3: 268; SK, 105f.

7   Karl Leonhard Reinhold, *Beyträge zur Berichtigung bisheriger Mißverständnisse der
Philosophie.* 2 vols. (Jena: Manke, 1790–1794), 167.

8   Gottlob Ernst Schulze, *Aenesidemus oder über die Fundamente der von Herrn Professor Reinhold in Jena gelieferten Elementar-Philosophie*, ed. M. Frank (Hamburg:
Meiner, 1996).

9   GA, I/3: 41–67; EPW, 59–77.

10   See GA, I/3: 43; EPW, 60f.

11   On the relation of the *Foundation of the Entire Wissenschaftslehre*, especially its
First Part, to Reinhold's Elementary Philosophy, see Robert L. Benson,
"Fichte's Original Argument" (Ph.D. dissertation, Columbia University,
1974); Jörg-Peter Mittmann, *Das Prinzip der Selbstgewißheit: Fichte und die
Entwicklung der nachkantischen Grundsatzphilosophie* (Bodenheim: Athenäum

Hain Hanstein, 1993); and Marcelo Stamm, "Das Programm des methodologischen Monismus: Subjekttheoretische und methodologische Aspekte der Elementarphilosophie K. L. Reinholds," *Neue Hefte für Philosophie* 35 (1995): 18–31.

12   See GA I/3: 259f.; SK, 98.

13   GA I/3: 255, 257, 259, 260; SK, 93, 96, 97, 99. Heath and Lachs translate the term as "act." But this does not quite capture Fichte's daring variation on the German word for "fact" (*Tatsache*), which rather invites a Heideggerian – Derridean rendition such as "(f)act." See also the extensive use of the term "*Tathandlung*" in the recently discovered Lavater transcript of Fichte's Zurich lectures on the concept of the *Wissenschaftslehre* from February 1794: Johann Gottlieb Fichte, *Zürcher Vorlesungen über den Begriff der Wissenschaftslehre: Nachschrift Lavater*, ed. E. Fuchs (Neuried: Ars Una, 1995), 77, 79, 81, 131, 149, 169. In this text the plural form "*Thathandlungen*" occurs four times (77, 79). See also my discussion of the Zurich *Wissenschaftslehre* in "Funde, Verzeichnisse und Folgen: Neuere Resultate der Fichte-Forschung," *Philosophischer Literaturanzeiger* 49 (1996): 389–394.

14   On the relation between *Tatsache* and *Tathandlung* in Fichte, see Jürgen Stolzenberg, "Fichtes Satz 'Ich bin': Argumentanalytische Überlegungen zu Paragraph 1 der *Grundlage der gesamten Wissenschaftslehre* von 1794/95," in *Fichte-Studien* 6 (1994), 1–34. On the relation between *Tathandlung* and absolute I, see Lore Hühn, *Fichte und Schelling oder: Über die Grenze des menschlichen Wissens* (Stuttgart and Weimar: Metzler, 1994), 77–100.

15   See GA I/3: 259; SK, 97.

16   On the relation between *Tathandlung* and intellectual intuition – a term which, although conspicuously absent from the *Foundation of the Entire Wissenschaftslehre*, figures prominently in several of Fichte's other works from that period – see Jürgen Stolzenberg, *Fichtes Begriff der intellektuellen Anschauung*.

17   See GA I/3: 260; SK, 98.

18   See GA I/3: 279; SK, 116f.

19   On the status of the absolute I as a moment rather than an independently functioning entity, see Peter Baumanns, *Fichtes ursprüngliches System*, 168f.

20   See GA I/3: 282; SK, 119.

21   See GA I/3: 385; SK, 122.

22   See GA I/3: 271; SK, 109.

23   See GA I/3: 276f.; SK, 114f. On the systematic function of the thetic judgment in Fichte, see Wolfgang Janke, *Vom Bilde des Absoluten*, 204–212. For a critical assessment of Fichte's thetic judgments, see Peter Baumanns, *J. G. Fichte*, 78–82.

24   See GA I/3: 272; SK, 110.

25   See GA I/3: 272, 278F.; SK, 110, 116.

26   See GA I/3: 403f.; SK, 238.

27   GA I/3: 385; SK, 218 (*das Ich setzt sich, als bestimmt durch das Nicht-Ich* and *das Ich setzt sich als bestimmend das Nicht-Ich*, respectively).

28   Fichte's repeated use of the modal verb *sollen* in his discussion of the relationship of determination between I and Not-I is often not an expression of a command or obligation but indicates indirect discourse.

29   See GA I/3: 285; SK, 122.

30 See GA I/3: 283–285; SK, 120F.
31 See GA I/3: 309ff.; SK, 146ff.
32 See GA I/3: 279f.; SK, 117f.
33 See GA I/3: 355f.; SK, 189f.
34 See GA I/3: 361; SK, 195f.
35 See GA I/3: 371; SK, 204f.
36 See GA I/3: 245f.; SK, 217.
37 See GA I/3: 286; SK, 122f.
38 GA I/3: 389; SK, 222 (translation modified).
39 See GA I/3: 387f.; SK, 221.
40 GA I/3: 405; SK, 239 (*es muß sich, unbeschadet seines absoluten Setzens durch sich selbst, für ein anderes Setzen gleichsam offen erhalten.*) (translation modified).
41 See GA I/3: 400; SK, 233.
42 See GA I/3: 401, 419; SK, 235, 254F.
43 GA I/3: 409; SK, 243f. (*sich . . . selbst setzen für irgendeine Intelligenz ausser ihm* and *sich setzen, als durch sich selbst gesetzt,* respectively).
44 See GA I/3: 409; SK, 243 (translation modified).
45 GA I/3: 408; SK, 243 (*über sich selbst zu reflektieren*) (translation modified).
46 On the distinction between the absolute I and God, see Max Wundt, *Fichte-Forschungen,* 2d edition (Stuttgart: Frommann-Kurtz, 1976), 265–280.
47 See GA I/3: 407f.; SK, 242.
48 GA I/3: 409f.; SK, 244 (*Reihe des Idealen* and *Reihe . . . des Wirklichen,* respectively).
49 On the ideal-real double nature of the I in Fichte, see Chapter 6.
50 See GA I/3: 408f.; SK, 243f.
51 See GA I/3: 410; SK, 245.
52 See GA I/3: 451; SK, 286. On the idealist nature of Fichte's theory of action, see Chapter 4.

Chapter 4

1 See *Faust I,* v. 1224 (*Studierzimmer [I]*). In 1774 and 1775 Herder had already used the terms "will" (*Wille*) and "deed" (*That*) to improve upon Luther's translation of *logos* into "word" (*Wort*). See Albrecht Schöne, *Johann Wolfgang Goethe, Faust: Kommentare* (Frankfurt/M.: Deutscher Klassiker Verlag, 1994), 247.

2 The work's full title is "The System of Ethics according to the Principles of the *Wissenschaftslehre*" (*Das System der Sittenlehre nach den Principien der Wissenschafts-lehre*). Among Fichte's posthumously published writings, there is another text entitled "The System of Ethics" (*Das System der Sittenlehre*), which consists of lectures held in Berlin in 1812. See NW III, 1–118 (FW XI, 1–118). The two works are usually distinguished from each other by the addition of the year of publication or delivery, respectively. In what follows all references are to *The System of Ethics* of 1798.

3 See GA I/5: 34f.

4 See GA/5: 33–71.

5 See GA I/5: 73–146. The remainder of *The System of Ethics,* which contains the

"Systematic Application of the Principle of Morality or Ethics in the More Narrow Sense" (GA I/5: 147–317), will not be considered here.

6 On the architectonic of Fichte's philosophical system, see also Reinhard Lauth, "Die Frage der Vollständigkeit der Wissenschaftslehre im Zeitraum 1793–96," in id., *Vernünftige Durchdringung der Wirklichkeit: Fichte und sein Umkreis* (Neuried: Ars Una, 1994), 57–120; and id., "J. G. Fichtes Gesamtidee der Philosophie," in id., *Zur Idee der Transzendentalphilosophie* (Munich and Salzburg: Pustet, 1965), 73–123.

7 GA I/3: 313–460 and I/4: 5–165. A new English translation of the *Foundation of Natural Law* by Michael Baur, edited by Karl Ameriks, is in preparation for the series Cambridge Texts in the History of Philosophy, published by Cambridge University Press. On Fichte's pioneering transcendental theory of human bodily reality (*Leib*) in the *Foundation of Natural Law*, see my "Leib, Materie und gemeinsames Wollen als Anwendungsbedingungen des Rechts."

8 GA I/5: 21–317. I am preparing a new English translation of the *The System of Ethics* for the series Cambridge Texts in the History of Philosophy, published. by Cambridge University Press. On Fichte's practical philosophy in general, see Allen W. Wood, "Fichte's Philosophy of Law and Ethics," in *The Cambridge Companion to Fichte*, ed. Günter Zöller (Cambridge: Cambridge University Press, in preparation); and my essay "Fichtes Jenenser Naturrecht und Sittenlehre," in *Zur Geschichte der Philosophie*, ed. K. Bärthlein (Würzburg: Königshausen und Neumann, 1983), 2:55–62.

9 For an account of Fichte's philosophy of religion in general and the issue of the atheism implied by the *Wissenschaftslehre* in particular, see Hansjürgen Verweyen, "Fichte's Philosophy of Religion," in Zöller, *The Cambridge Companion to Fichte*.

10 For a reconstruction of Fichte's philosophy of nature, see Reinhard Lauth, *Die transzendentale Naturlehre Fichtes nach den Prinzipien der Wissenschaftslehre* (Hamburg: Meiner, 1984).

11 GA IV/2: 17–267 and WLnmK, 1–244.

12 For an account of Fichte's theory of subjectivity informed by current work in the philosophy of mind, see F. Neuhouser, *Fichte's Theory of Subjectivity*.

13 See GA I/5: 56, 70, 74, 125, 130.

14 For an account of Fichte's philosophical experiment with the I, see Chapter 1.

15 See GA I/5: 21f.

16 See GA I/5: 35f.

17 See GA I/5: 26.

18 GA I/5: 37 (*Ich finde mich selbst, als mich selbst, nur wollend.*).

19 See GA I/5: 38.

20 See GA I/5: 53f.

21 See GA I/5: 54f.

22 See GA I/5: 56.

23 GA I/5: 46. On Fichte's concept of positing, see Chapter 3.

24 GA I/5: 48 (*unter die Botmäßigkeit des Begriffs*).

25 GA I/5: 48 (*reis't sich selbst von sich selbst los*).

26 GA I/5: 27.

27 GA I/5: 63.

28   See GA I/5: 68.
29   See GA I/5: 51.
30   See GA I/5: 66.
31   GA I/5: 51f.
32   GA I/5: 66f.
33   GA I/5: 66.
34   GA I/5: 69 (*Das Princip der Sittlichkeit ist der nothwendige Gedanke der Intelligenz, daß sie ihre Freiheit nach dem Begriffe der Selbstständigkeit, schlechthin ohne Ausnahme, bestimmen sollte.*)
35   See GA I/5: 77.
36   See GA I/5: 78f.
37   See GA I/5: 79f.
38   See GA I/5: 80 (*Meine Welt wird verändert, heißt, Ich werde verändert; meine Welt wird weiter bestimmt, heißt, Ich werde weiter bestimmt.*).
39   GA I/5: 83–88.
40   GA I/5: 88–92.
41   GA I/5: 93–95.
42   GA I/5: 97–102.
43   GA I/5: 102–118.
44   See GA I/5: 105, 117. On the development of Fichte's theory of the will in relation to Reinhold and Kant and his theory of drives, see Chapter 7.
45   See GA I/5: 113.
46   See GA I/5: 108.
47   See GA I/5: 121, 125.
48   GA I/5: 129, 149.
49   See GA I/5: 126.
50   See GA I/5: 125f.
51   See Ga I/5: 142f.
52   GA I/5: 126.
53   For Fichte's response to the contemporary objection that there can be no progressive approximation with respect to a goal placed at an infinite distance, see GA I/5: 141.
54   GA I/5: 126.
55   See GA I/5: 140f.
56   GA I/5: 141 (*Erfülle jedesmal deine Bestimmung*).
57   GA I/5: 132 (*eine ganz neue Reihe der Handlungen ihrem Inhalte nach*).

Chapter 5

1   See GA I/2: 397, 399; SK, 231, 233.
2   GA I/4: 183–281; IWL, 1–118.
3   For further discussion of the core doctrines of the *New Presentation of the Wissenschaftslehre* and the *Wissenschaftslehre nova methodo*, see Max Wundt, *Fichte-Forschungen*, 77–141; Peter Baumanns, *J. G. Fichte*, 152–163; Peter Rohs, *Johann Gottlieb Fichte*, 65–85; and Ives Radrizzani, *Vers la fondation de l'intersubjectivité*, 117–184.

4 GA I/5: 19–317. See Chapters 4 and 7. For an account of Fichte's theory of practical self-determination in *The System of Ethics* in the context of the *Wissenschaftslehre* of 1794–1795, see Frederick Neuhouser, *Fichte's Theory of Subjectivity*, 117–166. The *Foundation of Natural Law* of 1795–1796 can also be counted among the works of the new presentation of the *Wissenschaftslehre*. But its account of willing in the context of a transcendental theory of right does not reach as far into the deep structure of transcendental subjectivity as either the *Wissenschaftslehre nova methodo* itself or *The System of Ethics*. On the latter's special status in the system of the *Wissenschaftslehre*, see GA I/5: 199.

5 GA I/5: 19–71. For Fichte's earlier theory of volition, see Chapter 7.

6 See the entries under *"Denken," "Wille"* and *"Wollen"* in the index of GA I/2: 472, 477.

7 See GA IV/2: 17; FTP, 85 (translation modified).

8 See GA I/4: 186–188; IWL, 7–10. See also WLnmK, 3–5 and 12–14; GA IV/2: 17–20; FTP, 77–79 and 88–91.

9 See GA I/4: 187; IWL, 9. See also WLnmK, 13; GA IV/2: 19; FTP, 90.

10 See GA I/4: 200; IWL, 26. See also WLnmK, 195; FTP, 387.

11 WLnmK, 154; FTP, 310.

12 See GA I/4: 211n.; IWL, 38n. WLnmK, 25; GA IV/**2: 27**; FTP, 106.

13 See GA I/4: 193, 195; IWL, 17, 19f.

14 GA I/4: 274; IWL, 110 (translation modified).

15 GA I/4: 248, 249n.; IWL, 80, 81n.

16 GA I/4: 261; IWL, 94 (translation modified).

17 On the experimental nature of Fichte's *Wissenschaftslehre*, see Chapter 2.

18 GA I/4: 276; IWL, 113 (translation modified). See WLnmK, 19; GA IV/2: 24; FTP, 99.

19 GA I/4: 216; IWL, 45 (translation modified).

20 See GA I/4: 254–258; IWL., 86–90.

21 See WLnmK, 9; FTP, 83f.

22 On the development and function of Fichte's notion of intellectual intuition, cf. Stolzenberg, *Fichtes Begriff der intellektuellen Anschauung*.

23 See GA I/4: 216f.; IWL, 46. WLnmK, 31; GA IV/2: 31; FTP, 113F.

24 See GA I/4: 279f.; IWL, 117. WLnmK, 32; GA IV/2: 31; FTP, 116.

25 WLnmK, 38; FTP, 125. See WLnmK, 98; FTP, 219. Breazeale renders the German term as "law of reflective opposition." See also the further discussion of this fundamental principle of Fichte's new presentation of the *Wissenschaftslehre* in Chapters 6, 7 and 8.

26 See WLnmK, 98; FTP, 219.

27 See also Kant's distinction between matter as the determinable and form as its determination in the Appendix on the Amphiboly of the Concepts of Reflection in the *Critique of Pure Reason* (B 322f./A 266f.) and the subsequent employment of the distinction in Salomon Maimon's *Versuch über die Transscendentalphilosophie* (1790), reprinted in id., *Gesammelte Werke*, ed. V. Verra, 7 vols. (Hildesheim: Olms, 1965), 2: 94.

28 WLnmK, 36; FTP, 123 (translation modified).

29 GA I/4: 255; IWL, 87. GA IV/2: 46; FTP, 114 (translation modified).

30 WLnmK, 32; GA IV/2: 101; FTP, 116.

31   WLnmK, 41; GA IV/2: 48; FTP, 131.

32   WLnmK, 7, 31; GA I/4: 277; FTP, 82, 115.

33   WLnmK, 54; FTP, 152 (*wir sehen nur uns, nur als handelnd*) (translation modified).

34   See WLnmK, 40f., 46; GA IV/2: 44f.; FTP, 129, 67f.

35   WLnmK, 54; GA IV/2: 49; FTP, 152.

36   WLnmK, 184f.; GA IV/2: 228; FTP, 365 (translation modified). See also the
discussion of Fichte's key notion of "original duplicity" in Chapter 8.

37   WLnmK, 119; FTP, 253 (*Das Ich kann nicht ideal sein ohne praktisch zu sein und
umgekehrt*) (translation modified).

38   WLnmK, 182; FTP, 359.

39   See WLnmK, 42; GA IV/2: 39; FTP, 132.

40   WLnmK, 54; FTP, 152 (translation modified).

41   WLnmK, 123; GA IV/2: 113; FTP, 259.

42   WLnmK, 124; FTP, 259 (translation modified).

43   WLnmK, 124; FTP, 260 (*Wollen ist bloß ein Denken*) (translation modified).

44   WLnmK, 125; FTP, 261 (translation modified).

45   See WLnmK, 123; FTP, 258f.

46   WLnmK, 124; FTP, 260 (*Ich will, in wiefern ich mich als Wollend denke, und ich
denke mich als wollend, in wiefern ich will.*) (translation modified).

47   For further discussion of Fichte's relation to Kant on the distinction between
Wille and *Willkür,* see Neuhouser, *Fichte's Theory of Subjectivity,* 144ff.

48   See WLnmK, 138; FTP, 285. There is a precursor to this problematic constellation in the possible circle between end-setting and object-cognition in the
Foundation of Natural Law (cf. GA I/3: 340). There the solution is provided by
the doctrine of solicitation (*Aufforderung*). On the relation between the two
circle situations, see Jürgen Stolzenberg, "Fichtes Begriff des praktischen Selbstbewußtseins," in *Fichtes Wissenschaftslehre 1794: Philosophische Resonanzen,* ed. W.
Hogrebe (Frankfurt/M.: Suhrkamp, 1995), 71–95, esp. 79–81 and 86–90.

49   WLnmK, 148; FTP, 300 (*Diese Bestimmtheit, die meinen Hauptcharakter ausmacht,
besteht darin, daß ich bestimmt bin, mich auf eine gewisse Weise zu bestimmen.*).

50   WLnmK, 142f.; GA IV/2: 136f.; FTP, 291f. See the further discussion of the
circle and its solution through "pure willing" in Chapters 6 and 7.

51   WLnmK, 140; FTP, 288 (translation modified).

52   WLnmK, 141.; FTP, 289 (*Unser synthetischer Begriff ist Freiheit und Bestimmtheit in
Einem, Freiheit in wiefern angefangen wird, Bestimmtheit in wiefern nur so angefangen werden kann.*) (translation modified).

53   WLnmK, 142; FTP, 291.

54   Ibid.

55   WLnmK, 142; FTP, 292. For further discussion of Fichte's conception of the
"pure will," see Franz Bader, "Fichtes Lehre vom prädeliberativen Willen," in
Mues, Transzendentalphilosophie als System, 212–241.

56   WLnmK, 144; GA IV/2: 135f.; FTP, 293.

57   WLnmK, 148; FTP, 300 (*Sonach entsteht das reine Wollen nicht durch das Denken,
sondern jenes wird diesem schon vorausgesezt.*) (translation modified). See GA IV/2:
140.

58 See WLnmK, 150; GA IV/2: 140; FTP, 302f.
59 WLnmK, 153; GA IV/2: 147; FTP, 309.
60 WLnmK, 150; GA IV/2: 141; FTP, 302.
61 On the central role of "synthetic thinking" in Fichte, see Chapter 8.
62 See *Critique of Pure Reason*, B176/A137-B187/A147.
63 WLnmK, 153f.; GA IV/2: 147; FTP, 310 (translation modified).
64 Ibid. (translation modified).
65 See WLnmK, 160; GA IV/2: 156; FTP, 321.
66 See WLnmK, 176ff.; GA IV/2: 176f.; FTP, 350ff.
67 WLnmK, 166f.; FTP, 332 (*Wir können nur nach unseren Denkgesetzen erklären, und nach diesen muß die Antwort auf unsere Frage ausfallen. Unsere Erklärung ist demnach auch nicht an sich gültig; denn die Frage ist, wie kann ein Vernunftwesen sein Bewußtsein erklären.*) (translation modified). See GA IV/2: 163f.

Chapter 6

1 See Chapter 3.
2 See Chapter 3.
3 See WLnmK, 25; FTP, 106.
4 See WLnmK, 14; FTP, 92.
5 See GA I/4: 216ff.; IWL, 46ff.
6 See WLnmK, 8f.; FTP, 83f.
7 See WLnmK, 23; FTP, 104.
8 See WLnmK, 21; FTP, 101. On Fichte's experimental reconstruction of the I, see Chapter 2.
9 The inevitable circle of presentation in Fichte's theory of subjectivity is not to be confused with the deficiently circular "reflection theory" of self-consciousness diagnosed by Dieter Henrich in "Fichte's Original Insight," 15–53.
10 GA I/4: 275; IWL, 112.
11 See WLnmK, 32; FTP, 116.
12 See WLnmK, 50, 60; FTP, 145, 160.
13 See WLnmK, 63; FTP, 167.
14 See WLnmK, 49; FTP, 143.
15 See WLnmK, 46, 51; FTP, 67.
16 WLnmK, 50; FTP, 145.
17 See WLnmK, 67; FTP, 174.
18 See WLnmK, 54; FTP, 151F.
19 See WLmmK, 84; FTP, 198. The German original states that the theoretical (based on limitation) and the practical (based on striving) are "right away" (*gleich*) originally connected. The point is that the two are equally original, none being prior to the other. This co-originality of the different is not to be confused with some identical origin in which what is different is reduced to one and the same.
20 See WLnmK, 62; FTP, 164.
21 See WLnmK, 182; FTP, 359.
22 See WLnmK, 48; FTP, 141f.

23 WLnmK, 53f.; FTP, 151 (translation modified).

24 See WLnmK, 138; FTP, 285.

25 See WKLnmK, 142; FTP, 292. On Fichte's theory of the will, see Chapter 7.

26 See WLnmK, 143; FTP, 293.

27 See WLnmk, 142; FTP, 291.

28 See Chapter 5, note 25.

29 See *Critique of Pure Reason*, B 322–324/A 266–268.

30 WLnmk, 39; FTP, 128 (translation modified).

31 WLnmK, 18; FTP, 97 (translation modified).

32 See WLnmK, 38; FTP, 125.

33 See WLnmK, 42; FTP, 132.

34 WLnmK, 185, 227; FTP, 365, 447 (translation modified). See the further discussion of this notion in Chapter 8.

35 See WLnmK, 42; FTP, 132.

36 See WLnmK, 182; FTP, 359.

37 Ibid.

38 WLnmK, 53; FTP, 149 (translation modified).

39 See WLnmK, 218; FTP, 431.

40 WLnmK, 146; FTP, 298. See the further discussion of "synthetic thinking" in Chapter 8.

41 WLnmK, 186; FTP, 368 (*Der Anfang alles Bewußtseins ist Synthesis und Analysis zugleich.*) (translation modified). See WLnmK, 184; FTP, 364f.

42 WLnmK, 124; FTP, 260.

43 See WLnmK, 176ff.; FTP, 350ff. For further discussion of Fichte's theory of interpersonality in the *Wissenschaftslehre nova methodo*, see Chapter 8.

44 See WLnmK, 124, 131f.; FTP, 260f., 271f.

45 See WLnmK, 124; FTP, 261.

46 See WLnmK, 134; FTP, 274.

47 See WLnmK, 176; FTP, 349f. For further discussion of the individuation of pure will in the *Wissenschaftslehre nova methodo*, see Chapter 8.

48 WLnmK, 176; FTP, 349 (translation modified).

49 On the relation between intellect and will in Fichte, see Chapter 5.

50 WLnmK, 167; FTP, 334.

Chapter 7

1 See AA XX, 246 (*First Introduction into the Critique of Judgment*, XI); *Critique of Judgment*, 436 (translation modified).

2 See AA IV, 391; *Foundations of the Metaphysics of Morals*, 8; AA V, 16; *Critique of Practical Reason*, trans. L. W. Beck (New York: Macmillan, 1993), 16.

3 Reinhold's *Briefe über die Kantische Philosophie* (Letters on the Kantian Philosophy) originally appeared in the journal *Teutscher Merkur* in the years 1786–1787, then in an enlarged edition in book form in 1790 and 1792 (reprint, ed. R. Schmidt [Leipzig, 1923]). The practical philosophy is first dealt with in the second volume, published in 1792. Reinhold's *Versuch einer neuen Theorie des menschlichen Vorstellungsvermögens* (Attempt at a New Theory of the Human Fac-

ulty of Representation) appeared in 1789 (reprint [Darmstadt: Wissenschaftliche Buchgesellschaft, 1963]). In the latter work practical philosophy only comes up in the concluding section, entitled *Grundlinien der Theorie des Begehrungvermögens* (Outline of the Theory of the Faculty of Desire) (560–579).

4   See GA I/2: 385–451 and 255–282, respectively; SK, 218–286 and 93–119.

5   For a detailed examination of Fichte's theories of thinking and willing in the *Wissenschaftslehre nova methodo*, see Chapters 5 and 6.

6   Fichte's last published treatment of the *Wissenschaftslehre* (*Die Wissenschaftslehre in ihrem allgemeinen Umrisse* [1810]) briefly refers to the concept of the will. See SW II, 708 (FW II, 708); "The Science of Knowledge in Its General Outline," trans. W. E. Wright, *Idealistic Studies* 6 (1976): 106–117, here 117. The concept of the will also figures in Fichte's late lectures on ethics, which were published postumously under the title *Das System der Sittenlehre* (1812) (*The System of Ethics*); see NW III, 1–119 (FW XI, 1–119). These two late Fichte texts are not considered here.

7   GA I/1: 135–153; ACR, 40–59: *Theorie des Willens, als Vorbereitung einer Deduction der Religion überhaupt*.

8   Reinhold, *Letters*, vol. 2, Seventh Letter: "Über den bisher verkannten Unterschied zwischen dem uneigennützigen Triebe und dem eigennützigen Triebe, und zwischen diesen beiden Trieben und dem Willen" ("On the Hitherto Unnoticed Difference between the Unselfish Drive and the Selfish Drive, and between Both and the Will"). Eighth Letter: "Erörterung des Begriffs von der Freiheit des Willens" ("Discussion of the Concept of the Freedom of the Will"). On Fichte's relation to Reinhold and his acquaintance with the latter's works, see Alfred Klemmt, *Karl Leonhard Reinholds Elementarphilosophie* (Hamburg: Felix Meiner, 1958), 479ff., as well as Daniel Breazeale, "Between Kant and Fichte: Karl Leonhard Reinhold's 'Elementary Philosophy,'" in *Review of Metaphysics* 35 (1982), 785–821, and the more recent work by Mittmann and Stamm referred to in note 11 of Chapter 3.

9   GA I/1: 135; ACR, 40 (*sich mit Bewußtseyn eigner Tätigkeit zur Hervorbringung einer Vorstellung bestimmen*).

10 Ibid.

11 See GA I/2: 64; EPW, 75 (translation modified).

12 See the discussion of Fichte's theory of drives in *The System of Ethics* in Chapter 4. For a systematic reconstruction and critique of Fichte's doctrine of the drive, see Wilhelm G. Jacobs, *Trieb als sittliches Phänomen* (Bonn: Bouvier, 1967). See also Alois Soller, *Trieb und Reflexion in Fichtes Jenaer Philosophie* (Würzburg: Königshausen und Neumann, 1984).

13 See GA I/1: 136; ACR, 41.

14 "Matter" (*Stoff*), "form" (*Form*) and "drive" (*Trieb*) are basic terms in Reinhold's *Versuch einer neuen Darstellung der Grundbegriffe und Grundsätze der Moral und des Naturrechts* (Attempt at a New Presentation of the Basic Concepts and Basic Principles of Morals and Natural Law) in the Sixth Letter of the second volume of the *Letters* as well as in the two immediately following Seventh and Eighth Letters on the relation between drive and will and will and freedom, respectively (*Briefe*, 430ff.).

15   See GA I/1: 139; ACR, 44.

16   GA I/1: 141; ACR, 47 (*zu wollen, schlechthin weil man will*).

17   See GA I/1: 143f.; ACR, 48f.

18   See GA I/1: 146; ACR, 52. Fichte here explicitly subjects prudential reasoning to free choice and thereby expands the latter's scope compared to Reinhold, who had restricted the choice to that between the determination according to the selfish drive and that according to the unselfish drive. See also Fichte's explicit critique of Reinhold on this matter in the Mirbach transcript of Fichte's lectures on morals from the summer semester of 1796 (GA IV/1, 76f.). Moreover, as early as in his theory of the will from 1793 Fichte finds fault with Reinhold's identification of the moral drive with the unselfish drive and of the immoral drive with the unselfish drive, arguing that the moral drive, too, must be referred to the self in order to bring about an actual willing (see GA I/1: 144).

19   GA I/1: 146; ACR, 53 (*absolut-ersten Äußerung der Freiheit durch das practische Vernunftgesetz*).

20   See GA I/1: 147; ACR, 53f. Reinhold, too, speaks of the "decision" that must be added to the prescription of reason in order to conclude the self-determination (*Briefe*, 487f.).

21   See also Fichte's use of that distinction in his review of L. Creuzer's *Skeptische Betrachtungen über die Freyheit des Willens* (GA I/2: 7f.).

22   The conception of free choice as faculty to choose for or against the moral law goes back to Reinhold and was criticized by Kant in the latter's *Metaphysics of Morals* (Part One, 1797), where he argued that the freedom to deviate from the moral law represents not a capacity (*Vermögen*) but an incapacity (*Unvermögen*) (AA VI, 226f. [Introduction, IV]; Immanuel Kant, *The Metaphysics of Morals*, trans. M. Gregor [Cambridge: Cambridge University Press, 1991], 52). For the late Kant, only the faculty of choice (*Willkür*) can be called "free," whereas the will can be termed neither "free" nor "unfree." Reinhold's response to Kant from 1797 is reprinted in *Materialien zu Kants "Kritik der praktischen Vernunft,"* ed. R. Bittner and K. Cramer (Frankfurt/M.: Suhrkamp, 1975), 310–324. On the debate between Kant and Reinhold, see also Henry E. Allison, *Kant's Theory of Freedom* (Cambridge: Cambridge University Press, 1990), 129–136.

23   For a discussion of the transcendental theories of practical subjectivity in *The System of Ethics*, see Chapter 4.

24   See GA I/5: 21.

25   GA I/5: 37 (in the German original emphasis on the whole phrase). See also GA I/3: 332: "Willing is the proper essential character of reason" (*Das Wollen ist der eigenthliche wesentliche Charakter der Vernunft*.).

26   GA I/5: 38.

27   GA I/5: 40 (emphasis in the original) (*reellen Selbstbestimmens seiner selbst durch sich selbst*).

28   GA I/5: 38.

29   GA I/5: 48 (emphasis in the original).

30   GA I/5: 62.

31 GA I/5: 45 (emphasis in the original); on the relation between drive and tendency, see also GA I/5: 54.

32 See GA I/5: 67.

33 GA I/5: 125.

34 See GA I/5: 125f. On Fichte's typology of drives, see Chapter 4.

35 On the pre-Kantian and post-Kantian search for the unitary origin of subjectivity, see Dieter Henrich, "On the Unity of Subjectivity," in id., *The Unity of Reason*, ed. R. Velkley (Cambridge, Mass.: Harvard University Press, 1994), 17–54.

36 See GA I/5: 126.

37 See GA I/5: 195f.

38 GA I/5: 127.

39 GA I/5: 353; IWL, 150 (*Unsre Welt ist das versinnlichte Material unsrer Pflicht.*) (translation modified).

40 See GA I/5: 77f.

41 See AA IV, 119ff. (*Critique of Practical Reason*).

42 GA I/5: 158.

43 See GA I/5: 154.

44 See Chapter 4, note 38.

45 GA I/5: 210 (emphasis in the original).

46 Cf. GA I/5: 148f.

47 See WLnmK, 7; FTP, 82.

48 WLnmK, 49; FTP, 142 (translation modified).

49 See WLnmK, 50; FTP, 144F.

50 See Chapter 6, note 34.

51 See WLnmK, 119; FTP, 253.

52 See WLnmK, 123ff.; FTP, 258ff.

53 See WLnmK, 124; FTP, 260 (translation modified).

54 On the relation between thinking and willing, see Chapter 6.

55 See WLnmK, 122f.; FTP, 258f.

56 See WLnmK, 126f.; FTP, 264 (translation modified). On the function of self-affection in Kant's transcendental theory of the subject, see my "Making Sense Out of Inner Sense," in *International Philosophical Quarterly* 29 (1989): 263–270.

57 See WLnmK, 138; FTP, 283f.

58 WLnmK, 143; FTP, 292f. On Fichte's doctrine of the pure will, see also Bader, "Fichtes Lehre vom prädeliberativen Willen."

59 See WLnmK, 140; FTP, 288.

60 WLnmK, 141; FTP, 289 (translation modified). The German original is quoted in note 52 of Chapter 5.

61 See WLnmK, 142; FTP, 291.

62 WLnmK, 148; FTP, 300. The German original is quoted in note 49 of Chapter 5.

63 See WLnmK, 130; FTP, 269. See the further discussion of the two-part structure of the *Wissenschaftslehre nova methodo* in Chapter 8.

64 See WLnmK, 161; FTP, 323.

65 See WLnmK, 166f.; FTP, 332f.

66 See Chapter 5, note 25.

67 Cf. WLnmK, 149ff.; FTP, 301ff. On Fichte's theory of noumena, cf. Chapter 8.
68 See WLnmK, 149; FTP, 302 (*Maße*).
69 WLnmK, 148; FTP, 300.
70 See WLnmK, 156; FTP, 313f.
71 See WLnmK, 167; FTP, 333f.
72 See WLnmK, 151; FTP, 305.
73 Ibid.
74 See WLnmK, 147; FTP, 298f.
75 WLnmK, 142; FTP, 291.
76 See GA I/5: 353; IWL, 150); GA I/6: 291f.; VOM, 96. For a further discussion of the role of the will in *The Vocation of Man*, see Chapter 8.
77 See Fichte's letter to Schelling from 27 December 1800 and his sketch for that letter (GA III/4: 405f.).

Chapter 8

1 See Chapter 6, note 34.
2 See Chapters 5 and 6.
3 WLnmK, 152; FTP, 72.
4 See Chapter 5, note 25.
5 See WLnmK, 36; FTP, 123 (translation modified).
6 WLnmK, 202; FTP, 401 (*Vermögen das Bestimmbare zu faßen*) (translation modified). See Fichte's detailed discussion of productive imagination in WLnmK, 201–218; FTP, 399–432.
7 See *Critique of Pure Reason*, B 294/A 235-B 315/A 260. See also AA II, 392–398 (*De mundi sensibilis atque intelligibilis forma et principiis*, Sectio II); Kant, *Theoretical Philosophy, 1755–1770*, 384–390.
8 On Fichte's critique of Kant's disjointed treatment of the "system of noumena," see WLnmK, 124; FTP, 26of.
9 WLnmK, 137; FTP, 282 (*Was heißt sich denken, sich etwas denken? Die Art, wodurch die Noumene zu Stande kommen, ist das sich denken? Das intelligible in das sinnliche hineinsetzen als Vereinigungsgrund, heißt: sich etwas Denken.*) (translation modified). I take the verbal form "*sich denken*" to be a medial construction indicating the self-reference involved in all thinking and not to denote a fictitious thinking up of something. The latter would be expressed in German as "*sich etwas ausdenken.*"
10 See *Critique of Pure Reason*, A 250, A 355.
11 To be sure, Kant explicitly critiques the terminological confusion between "intelligible" and "intellectual." See AA IV, 316 note (*Prolegomena*, Section 34); *Prolegomena to Any Future Metaphysics*, 63 note. It stands to reason that Fichte is not engaged in an illicit terminological quid pro quo but in a reconceptualization of the functions of the intellect.
12 See the discussion of Kant in Chapter 1.
13 The affinity between Fichte's will-centered transcendental philosophy and Schopenhauer's voluntaristic transformation of Kant is striking. Much in

Fichte's work on the relation between intelligence and will from the later Jena years, culminating in *The Vocation of Man*, could figure under the heading "How Fichte Almost Wrote *The World as Will and Representation*." The case for a far-reaching affinity between Kant's two principal heirs is further strengthened through a neo-Kantian reading of Schopenhauer such as the one by Rudolf Malter in his *Arthur Schopenhauer: Transzendentalphilosophie und Metaphysik des Willens* (Stuttgart–Bad Cannstatt: Frommann-Holzboog, 1991). See also my discussion of Schopenhauer's transcendentalism in "Schopenhauer and the Problem of Metaphysics: Critical Reflections on Rudolf Malter's Interpretation," *Man and World* 28 (1994): 1–10.

14 See Fichte's own remark about the two-part structure of the *Wissenschaftslehre nova methodo*, consisting of an ascent from the empirical to the nonempirical in sections 1 through 13 and a descent from the nonempirical to the empirical in sections 14 through 19 (WLnmK, 161; FTP, 323).

15 See WLnmK, 149; FTP, 302.

16 See WLnmK, 154; FTP, 310 (translation modified).

17 WLnmK, 176; FTP, 349f. (translation modified). On the notion of individuality in relation to the distinction between the intelligible and the sensible, see also WLnmK, 169, 177 and 220; FTP, 337f., 350f. and 436f.

18 See GA I/2: 365; SK, 198f. See also WLnmK, 172; FTP, 342 (*Geschichte des entstehenden Bewußtseins*).

19 On time as mediator between the intelligible and sensible in the *Wissenschaftslehre nova methodo*, see Peter Rohs, "Über die Zeit als das Mittelglied zwischen dem Intelligiblen und dem Sinnlichen," *Fichte-Studien* 6 (1994): 95–116.

20 WLnmK, 136; FTP, 280.

21 WLnmK, 155; FTP, 312 (translation modified).

22 WLnmK, 173; FTP, 344 (*Die Sinnlickeit ist nur Versinnlichung, nichts ursprüngliches.*) (translation modified).

23 WLnmK, 157; FTP, 314 (*Das Intelligible ist nur . . . hinzugedacht.*) (translation modified).

24 WLnmK, 176; FTP, 350 (*Das Intelligible ist das einzige ursprüngliche, die Sinnenwelt ist eine gewiße Ansicht des erstern.*) (translation modified).

25 See *Critique of Pure Reason*, B 129–131.

26 WLnmK, 184f.; FTP, 364f. (translation modified). See also WLnmK, 193; FTP, 382.

27 WLnmK, 183f.; FTP, 364 (translation modified).

28 WLnmK, 183; FTP, 360 (*Das Denken eines Zwecks und das eines Objects sind eigentlich daßelbe, nur sind sie es von verschiedenen Seiten angesehen.*) (translation modified).

29 WLnmK, 211; FTP, 420.

30 WLnmK, 212; FTP, 420 (*alles ist eins und daßelbe nur immer in verschiedenen Ansichten.*) (translation modified). See also "My thinking that my hand moves and the movement of my hand are one and the same; but it is thinking when I am immediately conscious of this thinking, whereas it is movement when I consider it viewed by means of the medium of the imagination" (WLnmK, 210; FTP, 418 [translation modified]).

31 On the distinction between the natural standpoint and the standpoint of philosophy, see Chapter 1.

32 WLnmK, 156; FTP, 314 (*Alles aber kommt her aus dem absoluten Sein, und aus dem absoluten Beschränktsein im Auffaßen dieses Seins. In realer Rücksicht bin ich nicht alles, in idealer kann ich was ich bin nicht auf einmal auffaßen.*)

33 WLnmK, 148; FTP, 300 (*Diese Bestimmtheit . . . besteht daher lediglich in einer Aufgabe zu einem Handeln, zu einem Sollen. Die Bestimmung des Menschen ist nicht etwas, das der Mensch sich giebt, sondern das wodurch der Mensch Mensch ist.*) (translation modified).

34 On Fichte's theory of freedom in action, see Chapter 4.

35 WLnmK, 156; FTP, 313.

36 WLnmK, 151; FTP, 306.

37 WLnmK, 155; FTP, 312.

38 WLnmK, 213; FTP, 423 (*alles Wollen ist Erscheinung, das reine Wollen wird bloß als Erklärungsgrund vorausgesetzt.*) (translation modified).

39 See WLnmK, 205; FTP, 408 (*Es ist alles Erscheinung, auch ich mir selbst.*) (translation modified).

40 WLnmK, 68; FTP, 176 (*das Gefühl ist factisch das erste ursrpüngliche.*) (translation modified).

41 WLnmK, 93; FTP, 213.

42 On the systematic function of positing in Fichte, see Chapter 3.

43 WLnmK, 179; FTP, 355. Breazeale translates *Aufforderung* as "summons." The fact that the appeal is addressed to the called-upon individual insofar as it is free to heed or not heed the call suggests a reading of *Aufforderung* closer to "invitation" and its social connotations. See also the title of Carl Maria von Weber's piano piece *Aufforderung zum Tanz* (now most often heard in the orchestration by Hector Berlioz), whose title is customarily rendered in English as "Invitation to the Dance." On Fichte's account of the relationship between solicitation and recognition (*Anerkennung*) in the *Foundation of Natural Law*, see my essay "Leib, Materie und gemeinsames Wollen als Anwendungsbedingungen des Rechts."

44 WLnmK, 176; FTP, 351 (*Die erste Vorstellung die ich habe ist die Aufforderung meiner als Individuum zu einem freien Handeln.*) (translation modified).

45 WLnmK, 150; FTP, 303 (translation modified).

46 WLnmK, 178; FTP, 352 (*Kein Individuum kann sich aus sich selbst erklären; wenn man also auf ein erstes Individuum kommt, worauf man kommen muß, so muß man auch noch ein höheres unbegreifliches Wesen annehmen.*). In the corresponding passage of the Halle transcript of the *Wissenschaftslehre nova methodo* (GA IV/2: 176) Fichte refers to the corollaries to § 3 of the *Foundation of Natural Law*, where the same thought is already expressed. See GA I/3: 347f.

47 On Fichte's pioneering theory of interpersonality, see Reinhard Lauth, "Le problème de l'interpersonalité chez J. G. Fichte," *Archives de philosophie* 35 (1962): 325–344; German translation as "Das Problem der Interpersonalität bei J. G. Fichte" in id., *Transzendentale Entwicklungslinien von Descartes bis zu Marx und Dostojewski* (Hamburg: Meiner, 1989), 180–195; and Ives Radrizzani, *Vers la fondation de l'intersubjectivité chez Fichte.*

48 See Chapter 7, note 77.

49 See the last section of this chapter.

50 WLnmK, 188; FTP, 371.

51 WLnmK, 195; FTP, 384.

52 See WLnmK, 238; FTP, 463.

53 GA I/6: 248ff.; VOM, 76ff. (translation modified).

54 On Jacobi's nihilism charge against Fichte and the latter's response, see also Chapter 1.

55 See GA I/6: 300; VOM, 144 (*practisch transcendentale Idealisten*).

56 Jacobi sent his open letter to Fichte in early 1799 and published it in revised, expanded form in the fall of that year. See the bibliographical information in Chapter 1, note 50.

57 There is evidence that Jacobi had actually based his understanding and critique of the *Foundation of the Entire Wissenschaftslehre* exclusively on that work's first two parts, thus omitting the crucial Third Part that solves the basic deficiency in the account of theoretical knowledge (*theoretisches Wissen*) by considering the knowledge of the practical (*Wissenschaft des Practischen*). See Fichte's letter to Reinhold from 8 January 1800 (GA III/4: 180).

58 See *Friedrich Heinrich Jacobi's Werke*, 6 vols. (Leipzig: Fleischer, 1812–1825), vol. 1 (*Allwill's Briefsammlung*), vol. 2 (*David Hume über den Glauben*), vol. 4 (*Ueber die Lehre des Spinoza*), vol. 5 (*Woldemar*).

59 See Reinhard Lauth, "Fichtes Verhältnis zu Jacobi unter besonderer Berücksichtigung der Rolle Friedrich Schlegels in dieser Sache," in id., *Transzendentale Entwicklungslinien von Descartes bis zu Marx und Dostojewski*, 266–296, esp. 269–274.

60 Fichte here trades on the linguistic proximity of the German words for "doubt" (*Zweifel*) and "despair" (*Verzweiflung*).

61 GA I/5: 257; VOM, 88 (translation modified).

62 GA I/6: 258; VOM, 90.

63 GA I/6: 257; VOM, 89 (*Entschluß des Willens, das Wissen gelten zu lassen*) (translation modified). For a comparison of the systematic function of faith in Kant, Jacobi and Fichte, see my essay "'Das Element aller Gewissheit': Jacobi, Kant und Fichte über den Glauben," forthcoming in *Fichte-Studien*.

64 GA I/6: 259; VOM, 91 (translation modified).

65 GA I/6: 257; VOM, 88 (translation modified).

66 GA I/6: 257; VOM, 89 (*freiwillige[s] Beruhen bei der sich uns natürlich darbietenden Ansicht*).

67 GA I/6: 259; VOM, 92 (translation modified).

68 See Chapters 3 and 4, respectively.

69 See GA I/5: 351: "the point that unites thinking and willing into one" (*der Punkt, der Denken und Wollen in Eins vereiniget*).

70 There is an alternative reading of *The Vocation of Man* as discontinous with Fichte's Jena writings; cf. Martial Gueroult, "La Destination de l'homme," in *Etudes sur Fichte* (Hildesheim and New York: Olms, 1974), 72–95. More recently the continuity of *The Vocation of Man* with Fichte's Jena writings has been stressed by Jean-Christophe Goddard in the introduction to his French translation of the work (*La destination de l'homme* [Paris: Garnier-Flammarion, 1996]).

71 GA I/6: 265; VOM, 98f.

72 GA I/6: 280; VOM, 118 (translation modified).

73 GA I/6: 284; VOM, 124 (translation modified).

74 GA I/6: 292; VOM, 134.

75 GA I/6: 295; VOM, 137 (translation modified).
76 GA I/6: 295; VOM, 137.
77 GA I/6: 296f.; VOM, 139 (translation modified).
78 GA I/6: 293; VOM, 135 (*Vereinigung, und unmittelbare Wechselwirkung mehrerer selbständiger und unabhängiger Willen mit einander*) (translation modified).
79 GA I/6: 306; VOM, 150f. (translation modified).

BIBLIOGRAPHY

Primary Sources

Beck, Jakob Sigismund. *Erläuternder Auszug aus den Kritischen Schriften des Herrn Prof. Kant, auf Anraten desselben.* Vol. 3: *Dritter Band, welcher den Standpunkt darstellt, aus welchem die Kritische Philosophie zu beurteilen ist: Einzig moeglicher Standpunkt, aus welchem die Kritische Philosophie beurteilt werden muss.* Riga: Hartknoch, 1793. Reprinted in Aetas Kantiana. Brussels: Culture et Civilisation, 1968.

Fichte, Johann Gottlieb. *Johann Gottlieb Fichte's sämmtliche Werke.* Ed. I. H. Fichte. 8 vols. Berlin: Veit and Co., 1845–1846. Reprinted as *Fichtes Werke.* 11 vols. Berlin: de Gruyter, 1971. Vols. 1–8.

Johann Gottlieb Fichte's nachgelassene Schriften. Ed. I. H. Fichte. 3 vols. Bonn: Adolph-Marcus, 1834–1835. Reprinted as *Fichtes Werke.* 11 vols. Berlin: de Gruyter, 1971. Vols. 9–11.

Nachgelassene Schriften. Bd. II. Ed. H. Jacob. Berlin: Junker und Dünnhaupt, 1937.

J. G. Fichte – Gesamtausgabe der Bayerischen Akademie der Wissenschaften. Ed. R. Lauth and H. Gliwitzky. Stuttgart–Bad Cannstatt: Frommann-Holzboog, 1962ff.

Darstellung der Wissenschaftslehre aus den Jahren 1801/02. Ed. P. K. Schneider. Hamburg: Felix Meiner, 1977.

Fichte im Gespräch. Ed. E. Fuchs. 6 vols. Stuttgart–Bad Cannstatt: Frommann-Holzboog, 1978–1992.

Wissenschaftslehre nova methodo: Kollegnachschrift K. Chr. Fr. Krause 1798/99. Ed. E. Fuchs. Hamburg: Felix Meiner, 1982; 2d edition 1994.

Wissenschaftslehre 1805. Ed. H. Gliwitzky. Hamburg: Felix Meiner, 1984.

Fichte in zeitgenössischen Rezensionen. Ed. E. Fuchs, W. G. Jacobs and W. Schieche. 4 vols. Stuttgart–Bad Cannstatt: Frommann-Holzboog, 1995.

Zürcher Vorlesungen über den Begriff der Wissenschaftslehre: Nachschrift Lavater. Ed. E. Fuchs. Neuried: Ars Una, 1995.

Jacobi, Johann Heinrich. *David Hume über den Glauben oder Idealismus und Realismus.* Breslau: Loewe, 1787. Reprint, London and New York: Garland, 1983.
Friedrich Heinrich Jacobi's Werke. 6 vols. Leipzig: Fleischer, 1812–1825.

Kant, Immanuel. *Kant's gesammelte Schriften.* Ed. Royal Prussian Academy of Sciences and Its Succesors. Berlin, later Berlin and New York: Reimer, later de Gruyter, 1900ff.
Kritik der reinen Vernunft. Ed. R. Schmidt. Hamburg: Felix Meiner, 1971.

Maimon, Salomon. *Gesammelte Werke.* Ed. V. Verra. 7 vols. Reprint, Hildesheim: Olms, 1970.

Reinhold, Karl Leonhard. *Versuch einer neuen Theorie des menschlichen Vorstellungsvermögens.* 1789. Reprint, Darmstadt: Wissenschaftliche Buchgesellschaft, 1963.
Briefe über die Kantische Philosophie. 2 vols. Leipzig: Goschen, 1790 and 1792. Reprint, Leipzig: Reclam, 1923.
Beyträge zur Berichtigung bisheriger Mißverständnisse der Philosophen. 2 vols. Jena: Mauke, 1790–1794.

Schulze, Gottlob Ernst. *Aenesidemus oder über die Fundamente der von Herrn Professor Reinhold in Jena gelieferten Elementar-Philosophie.* Ed. M. Frank. Hamburg: Felix Meiner, 1996.

Translations

Between Kant and Hegel: Texts in the Development of Post-Kantian Idealism. Trans. G. di Giovanni and H. S. Harris. Albany: State University of New York Press, 1985.

Fichte, Johann Gottlieb. *Teoria della scienza 1798 "nova methodo."* Trans. A. Cantoni. Milan: Biblioteca "Il pensiero," 1959.
"The Science of Knowledge in Its General Outline." Trans. W. E. Wright. *Idealistic Studies* 6 (1976): 106–117.
Attempt at a Critique of All Revelation. Trans. G. Green. Cambridge: Cambridge University Press, 1978.
Science of Knowledge with the First and Second Introductions. Trans. P. Heath and J. Lachs. Cambridge: Cambridge University Press, 1982.
The Vocation of Man. Ed. R. M. Chisholm. New York: Macmillan, 1986.
"A Crystal Clear Report to the General Public concerning the Actual Essence of the Newest Philosophy: An Attempt to Force the Reader to Understand." In *Philosophy of German Idealism.* Ed. E. Behler. New York: Continuum, 1987, 39–115.
Doctrina de la Ciencia nova methodo. Trans. M. Ramos and J. L. Villacañas. Valencia: Universidad de Valencia, 1987.
Early Philosophical Writings. Ed. and trans. D. Breazeale. Ithaca, N.Y.: Cornell University Press, 1988.
La Doctrine de la Science Nova Methodo: Suivi de Essai d'une nouvelle présentation de la Doctrine de la Science. Trans. I. Radrizzani. Lausanne: L'Age d'homme, 1989.
Foundations of Transcendental Philosophy (Wissenschaftslehre) Nova Methodo (1796/99). Ed. and trans. D. Breazeale. Ithaca, N.Y.: Cornell University Press, 1992.
Introductions to the Wissenschaftslehre and Other Writings. Ed. and trans. D. Breazeale. Indianapolis: Hackett, 1994.

La destination de l'homme. Trans. J.-C. Goddard. Paris: Garnier-Flammarion, 1996.
Jacobi, Friedrich Heinrich. "Open Letter to Fichte." In *Philosophy of German Idealism.*
Ed. E. Behler. New York: Continuum, 1987, 119–141.
Kant, Immanuel. *Critique of Pure Reason.* Trans. N. K. Smith. New York: St. Martin's,
1965.
Prolegomena to Any Future Metaphyics. Introduction by L. W. Beck. Indianapolis:
Bobbs-Merrill, 1982.
Foundations of the Metaphysics of Morals. Trans. L. W. Beck. Indianapolis: Bobbs-Mer-
rill, 1983.
What Real Progress Has Metaphysics Made in Germany since the Time of Leibniz and Wolff?
Trans. and introd. T. Humphrey. New York: Abaris, 1983, 127–137.
Critique of Judgment: Including the First Introduction. Trans. W. Pluhar. Indianapolis:
Hackett, 1987.
The Metaphysics of Morals. Trans. M. Gregor. Cambridge: Cambridge University
Press, 1991.
Theoretical Philosophy, 1755–1770. Trans. and ed. D. Walford in collaboration with
R. Meerbote. Cambridge: Cambridge University Press, 1992.
Critique of Practical Reason. Trans. L. W. Beck. New York: Macmillan, 1993.
Opus Postumum. Ed. E. Förster. Cambridge: Cambridge University Press, 1993.

Bibliographies

Baumgartner, Hans Michael, and Jacobs, Wilhelm G., eds. *J. G. Fichte-Bibliographie.*
Stuttgart–Bad Cannstatt: Frommann-Holzboog, 1968.
Breazeale, Daniel. "Fichte in English: A Complete Bibliography," In *Fichte: Historical
Contexts/Contemporary Controversies.* Ed. D. Breazeale and T. Rockmore. Atlantic
Heights, N.J.: Humanities Press, 1994, 235–263.
Doyé, Sabine. *Fichte-Bibliographie 1968–1992.* Fichte-Studien Supplementa. Amster-
dam and Atlanta: Rodopi, 1994.

Secondary Sources

Allison, Henry E. *Kant's Theory of Freedom.* Cambridge: Cambridge University Press,
1990.
Ameriks, Karl. "Kant, Fichte, and Short Arguments to Idealism." *Archiv für Geschichte
der Philosophie* 72 (1990): 63–85.
"Fichte's Appeal Today: The Hidden Primacy of the Practical." In *From Transcendental Philosophy to Metaphysics: The Emergence of German Idealism.* Ed. M. Baur
and D. Dahlstrom. Washington, D.C.: Catholic University of America Press,
1998, 129–152.
Bader, Franz. "Fichtes Lehre vom prädeliberativen Willen." In *Transzendentalphilosophie als System: Die Auseinandersetzung zwischen 1794 und 1806.* Ed. A. Mues. Hamburg: Felix Meiner, 1989, 212–241.
Baumanns, Peter. *Fichtes ursprüngliches System: Sein Standort zwischen Kant und Hegel.*
Stuttgart–Bad Cannstatt: Frommann-Holzboog, 1972.

Fichtes Wissenschaftslehre: Probleme ihres Anfangs. Mit einem Kommentar zu Par. 1 der "Grundlage der gesamten Wissenschaftslehre." Bonn: Bouvier, 1974.

J. G. Fichte: Kritische Gesamtdarstellung seiner Philosophie. Freiburg and Munich: Karl Alber, 1990.

Beiser, Frederick C. *The Fate of Reason: German Philosophy from Kant to Fichte.* Cambridge, Mass.: Harvard University Press, 1987.

Benson, Robert L. "Fichte's Original Argument." Ph.D. dissertation, Columbia University, 1974.

Bittner, Rüdiger, and Cramer, Konrad, eds. *Materialien zu Kants "Kritik der praktischen Vernunft."* Frankfurt/M.: Suhrkamp, 1975.

Bondelli, Martin. *Das Anfangsproblem bei Karl Leonhard Reinhold: Eine systematische und entwicklungsgeschichtliche Untersuchung zur Philosophie Reinholds in der Zeit 1789–1803.* Frankfurt/M.: Vittorio Klostermann, 1994.

Bourgeois, Bernard. *L'idéalisme de Fichte.* 2d edition. Paris: Vrin, 1995.

Breazeale, Daniel. "Fichte's *Aenesidemus* Review and the Transformation of German Philosophy." *The Review of Metaphysics* 34 (1981): 545–568.

"Between Kant and Fichte: Karl Leonhard Reinhold's 'Elementary Philosophy.'" *The Review of Metaphysics* 35 (1982): 785–822.

"How to Make an Idealist: Fichte's 'Refutation of Dogmatism' and the Problem of the Starting Point of the *Wissenschaftslehre.*" *Philosophical Forum* 19 (1988): 97–123.

"The 'Standpoint of Life' and the 'Standpoint of Philosophy' in the Context of the *Jena Wissenschaftslehre* (1794–1800)." In *Transzendentalphilosophie als System: Die Auseinandersetzung zwischen 1794 und 1806.* Ed. A. Mues. Hamburg: Felix Meiner, 1989, 81–104.

"Circles and Grounds in the Jena *Wissenschaftslehre.*" In *Fichte: Historical Contexts/Contemporary Perspectives.* Ed. D. Breazeale and T. Rockmore. Atlantic Heights, N.J.: Humanities Press, 1994. 43–70.

"Philosophy and the Divided Self: On the 'Existential' and 'Scientific' Tasks of the Jena *Wissenschaftslehre.*" *Fichte-Studien* 6 (1994): 117–147.

"Check or Checkmate? On the Finitude of the Fichtean Self." In *The Modern Subject: Conceptions of the Self in Classical German Philosophy.* Ed. K. Ameriks and D. Sturma. Albany: State University of New York Press, 1995, 87–114.

"De la *Thathandlung* à l'*Anstoß* et retour: Liberté et facticité dans les *Principes de la Doctrine de la Science.*" *Cahiers de Philosophie,* numéro hors série *Fichte* (1995): 69–87.

"The Theory of Practice and the Practice of Theory: Fichte and the Primacy of Practical Reason." *International Philosophical Quarterly* 36 (1996): 47–64.

Chansky, James. "The Conscious Body: Schopenhauer's Difference from Fichte in Relation to Kant." *International Studies in Philosophy* 24 (1992): 25–44.

Claesges, Ulrich. *Geschichte des Selbstbewußtseins: Der Ursprung des spekulativen Problems in Fichtes Wissenschaftslehre von 1794–95.* The Hague: Martinus Nijhoff, 1974.

Düsing, Edith. *Intersubjektivität und Selbstbewußtsein: Behavioristische, phänomenologische und idealistische Begründungstheorien bei Mead, Schütz, Fichte und Hegel.* Cologne: Dinter, 1986.

Düsing, Klaus. "C'è un circolo dell' autocoscienza? Uno schizzo delle posizioni paradigmatiche e dei modelli di autocoscienza da Kant a Heidegger." *Teoria* 12 (1992): 3–29.

Frank, Manfred. "'Intellectuale Anschauung': Drei Stellungnahmen zu einem Deutungsversuch von Selbstbewußtsein: Kant, Fichte, Hölderlin/Novalis." In *Die Aktualität der Frühromantik.* Ed. E. Behler and J. Hörisch. Paderborn: Schöningh, 1987, 96–126.

Girndt, Helmut. *Die Differenz des Fichteschen und Hegelschen Systems in der Hegelschen "Differenzschrift."* Bonn: Bouvier, 1965.

Gueroult, Martial. *L'évolution et la structure de la doctrine de la science chez Fichte.* 2 vols. Paris: Société de l'édition Les Belles Lettres, 1930.

Etudes sur Fichte. Hildesheim and New York: Olms, 1974.

Henrich, Dieter. "On the Unity of Subjectivity." In id., *The Unity of Reason.* Ed. R. Velkley. Cambridge, Mass.: Harvard University Press, 1994, 17–54. Originally published in German under the title "Über die Einheit der Subjektivität." *Philosophische Rundschau* 3 (1955): 28–69.

"Fichte's Original Insight." In *Contemporary German Philosophy.* 4 vols. College Park, Penn.: Pennsylvania State University Press, 1982–1984, 1: 15–53. Previously published in German as *Fichtes ursprüngliche Einsicht.* Frankfurt/M.: Vitterio Klostermann, 1967.

Selbstverhältnisse. Stuttgart: Reclam, 1982.

"Die Anfänge der Theorie des Subjekts (1789)." In *Zwischenbetrachtungen.* Ed. A. Honneth et al. Frankfurt/M.: Suhrkamp, 1989, 106–170.

"Noch einmal in Zirkeln: Eine Kritik von Ernst Tugendhats semantischer Erklärung von Selbstbewußtsein." In *Mensch und Moderne: Beiträge zur philosophischen Anthropologie und Gesellschaftskritik.* Ed. C. Bellut and U. Müller-Scholl. Würzburg: Königshausen und Neumann, 1989, 93–132.

Horstmann, Rolf-Peter. *Die Grenzen der Vernunft: Eine Untersuchung zu Zielen und Motiven des Deutschen Idealismus.* Frankfurt/M.: Anton Hain, 1991.

Hühn, Lore. *Fichte und Schelling oder: Über die Grenze menschlichen Wissens.* Stuttgart and Weimar: Metzler, 1994.

Jacobs, Wilhelm G. *Trieb als sittliches Phänomen.* Bonn: Bouvier, 1967.

Jaeschke, Walter, ed. *Transzendentalphilosophie und Spekulation: Der Steit um die Gestalt einer Ersten Philosophie (1799–1807).* Hamburg: Meiner, 1993.

Janke, Wolfgang. *Fichte: Sein und Reflexion – Grundlagen der kritischen Vernunft.* Berlin and New York: de Gruyter, 1970.

Vom Bilde des Absoluten: Grundzüge der Phänomenologie Fichtes. Berlin and New York: de Gruyter, 1993.

Kabitz, Willy. *Studien zur Entwicklungsgeschichte der Fichteschen Wissenschaftslehre aus der Kantischen Philosophie: Mit bisher ungedruckten Stücken aus Fichtes Nachlaß.* Berlin: Reuther und Reichard, 1902.

Klemmt, Alfred. *Karl Leonhard Reinholds Elementarphilosophie.* Hamburg: Meiner, 1958.

Koch, Reinhard. *Fichtes Theorie des Selbstbewußtseins: Ihre Entwicklung von den "Eignen Meditationen über ElementarPhilosophie" 1793 bis zur "Neuen Bearbeitung der W.L." 1800.* Würzburg: Königshausen und Neumann, 1989.

Lauth, Reinhard. "Le problème de l'interpersonalité chez J. G. Fichte." *Archives de philosophie* 35 (1962): 325–344.

Zur Idee der Transzendentalphilosophie. Munich and Salzburg: Pustet, 1965.

Die transzendentale Naturlehre Fichtes nach den Prinzipien der Wissenschaftslehre. Hamburg: Felix Meiner, 1984.

Transzendentale Entwicklungslinien von Descartes bis zu Marx und Dostojewski. Hamburg: Felix Meiner, 1989.

Vernünftige Durchdringung der Wirklichkeit: Fichte und sein Umkreis. Neuried: Ars Una, 1994.

Léon, Xavier. *Fichte et son temps.* 2 vols. Paris: Colin, 1922–1927.

Malter, Rudolf. *Arthur Schopenhauer: Transzendentalphilosophie und Metaphysik des Willens.* Stuttgart–Bad Cannstatt: Frommann-Holzboog, 1991.

Martin, Wayne. *Idealism and Objectivity: Understanding Fichte's Jena Project.* Stanford: Stanford University Press, 1997.

Metz, Wilhem J. *Kategoriendeduktion und produktive Einbildungskraft in der theoretischen Philosophie Kants und Fichtes.* Stuttgart–Bad Cannstatt: Frommann-Holzboog, 1991.

Mittmann, Jörg-Peter. *Das Prinzip der Selbstgewißheit: Fichte und die Entwicklung der nachkantischen Grundsatzphilosophie.* Bodenheim: Athenäum Hain Hanstein, 1993.

Neiman, Susan. *The Unity of Reason: Rereading Kant.* New York: Oxford University Press, 1993.

Neuhouser, Frederick. *Fichte's Theory of Subjectivity.* Cambridge: Cambridge University Press, 1990.

Oesch, Martin. *Das Handlungsproblem: Ein systemgeschichtlicher Beitrag zur ersten Wissenschaftslehre Fichtes.* Hildesheim: Gerstenberg, 1981.

Philonenko, Alexis. *La liberté humaine dans la philosophie de Fichte.* Paris: Vrin, 1966.

Piché, Claude. *Kant et ses épigones: Le jugement critique en appel.* Paris: Vrin, 1995.

Pippin, Robert. "Kant on the Spontaneity of Mind." *Canadian Journal of Philosophy* 17 (1987): 449–475.

"Fichte's Contribution." *Philosophical Forum* 19 (1988): 74–96.

Hegel's Idealism: The Satisfactions of Self-consciousness. Cambridge: Cambridge University Press, 1989.

Radermacher, Hans. *Fichtes Begriff des Absoluten.* Frankfurt/M.: Vittorio Klostermann, 1970.

Radrizzani, Ives. *Vers la fondation de l'intersubjectivité chez Fichte: Des Principes à la Nova Methodo.* Paris: Vrin, 1993.

"Der Übergang von der *Grundlage* zur *Wissenschaftslehre nova methodo.*" *Fichte-Studien* 6 (1994): 355–366.

Renaut, Alain. *Le système du droit: Philosophie et droit dans la pensée de Fichte.* Paris: Presses Universitaires de France, 1986.

Rohs, Peter. *Johann Gottlieb Fichte.* Munich: Beck, 1991.

"Über die Zeit als das Mittelglied zwischen dem Intelligiblen und dem Sinnlichen." *Fichte-Studien* 6 (1994): 95–116.

Römelt, Johannes. "'Merke auf dich selbst': Das Verhältnis des Philosophen zu seinem Gegenstand nach dem *Versuch einer neuen Darstellung der Wissenschaftslehre* (1797/98)." *Fichte-Studien* 1 (1990): 73–98.

Schöne, Albrecht. *Johann Wolfgang Goethe, Faust: Kommentare.* Frankfurt/M.: Deutscher Klassiker Verlag, 1994.

Schrader, Wolfgang, *Empirisches und absolutes Ich. Zur Geschichte des Begriffs Leben in der Philosophie J. G. Fichtes.* Stuttgart–Bad Cannstatt: Frommann-Holzboog, 1972.

"Philosophie als System: Reinhold und Fichte." In *Erneuerung der Transzendentalphilosophie im Anschluß an Kant und Fichte.* Ed. K. Hammacher and A. Mues. Stuttgart–Bad Cannstatt: Frommann-Holzboog, 1979, 331–344.

"Nation, Weltbürgertum und Synthesis der Geisterwelt." *Fichte-Studien* 2 (1990): 27–36.

"Philosophie und Leben im Denken Fichtes um 1800." In *Kategorien der Existenz: Festschrift für W. Janke.* Ed. K. Held and J. Hennigfeld. Würzburg: Königshausen und Neumann, 1993, 77–86.

Schulte, Günter. *Die Wissenschaftslehre des späten Fichte.* Frankfurt/M.: Vittorio Klostermann, 1971.

Schulz, Walter. *J. G. Fichte: Vernunft und Freiheit.* Pfullingen: Neske, 1962.

Schüssler, Ingeborg. *Die Auseinandersetzung von Idealismus und Realismus in Fichtes Wissenschaftslehre. Grundlage der Gesamten Wissenschaftslehre 1794/95. Zweite Darstellung der Wissenschaftslehre 1804.* Frankfurt/M.: Vittorio Klostermann, 1972.

Siep, Ludwig. *Hegels Fichtekritik und die Wissenschaftslehre von 1804.* Freiburg and Munich: Karl Alber, 1970.

Soller, Alois K. *Trieb und Reflexion in Fichtes Jenaer Philosophie.* Würzburg: Königshausen und Neumann, 1984.

"Die Unbegreiflichkeit der Wechselwirkung der Geister: Das Problem einer 'Interpersonalitätslehre' bei Fichte." *Fichte-Studien* 6 (1994): 215–227.

Stamm, Marcelo. "Das Programm des methodologischen Monismus: Subjekttheoretische und methodologische Aspekte der Elementarphilosophie K. L. Reinholds." *Neue Hefte für Philosophie* 35 (1995): 18–31.

Stolzenberg, Jürgen. *Fichtes Begriff der intellektuellen Anschauung: Die Entwicklung in den Wissenschaftslehren von 1793/94 bis 1801/02.* Stuttgart: Klett-Cotta, 1986.

"Fichtes Satz 'Ich bin': Argumentanalytische Überlegungen zu Paragraph 1 der *Grundlage der gesamten Wissenschaftslehre* von 1794/95." *Fichte-Studen* 6 (1994): 1–34.

"Fichtes Begriff des praktischen Selbstbewußtseins." In *Fichtes Wissenschaftslehre 1794: Philosophische Resonanzen.* Ed. W. Hogrebe. Frankfurt/M.: Suhrkamp, 1995, 71–95.

Tilliette, Xavier, *L'intuition intellectuelle de Kant à Hegel.* Paris: Vrin, 1995.

Tugendhat, Ernst. *Self-consciousness and Self-determination.* Trans. P. Stern. Cambridge, Mass.: MIT Press, 1986.

Verweyen, Hansjürgen. *Recht und Sittlichkeit in J. G. Fichtes Gesellschaftslehre.* Freiburg and Munich: Karl Alber, 1975.

"Fichte's Philosophy of Religion." In *The Cambridge Companion to Fichte.* Ed. G. Zöller. Cambridge: Cambridge University Press, forthcoming.

Weischedel, Wilhelm. *Der frühe Fichte: Aufbruch der Freiheit zur Gemeinschaft.* Leipzig: Meiner, 1939. 2d edition. Stuttgart–Bad Canstatt: Frommann-Holzboog, 1973.

Der Zwiespalt im Denken Fichtes. Berlin: de Gruyter, 1962.

Wood, Allen W. "Fichte's Philosophical Revolution." *Philosophical Topics* 19 (1992): 1–28.

"Fichte's Philosophy of Law and Ethics." In *The Cambridge Companion to Fichte.* Ed. G. Zöller. Cambridge: Cambridge University Press, forthcoming.

Wundt, Max. *J. G. Fichte.* Stuttgart: Frommann-Kurtz, 1927.

Fichte-Forschungen. Stuttgart: Frommann-Kurtz, 1929. 2d edition. Stuttgart–Bad Cannstatt: Frommann-Holzboog, 1976.

Zahn, Manfred. "Fichtes Kant-Bild." In *Erneuerung der Transzendentalphilosophie im Anschluß an Kant und Fichte.* Ed. K. Hammacher and A. Mues. Stuttgart–Bad Cannstatt: Frommann-Holzboog, 1979, 479–505.

Zimmermann, Bruno. "Freiheit und Reflexion: Untersuchungen zum Problem des Anfangs bei Joh. G. Fichte." Doctoral dissertation, University of Cologne, 1969.

Zöller, Günter. "Fichtes Jenenser Naturrecht und Sittenlehre." In *Zur Geschichte der Philosophie.* Ed. K. Bärthlein. 2 vols. Würzburg: Königshausen und Neumann, 1983, 2:55–62.

Theoretische Gegenstandsbeziehung bei Kant: Zur systematischen Bedeutung der Termini "objektive Realität" und "objektive Gültigkeit" in der "Kritik der reinen Vernunft." Berlin and New York: de Gruyter, 1984.

"Comments on Professor Kitcher's 'Connecting Intuitions and Concepts at B 160n.'" *The Southern Journal of Philosophy* 25 (1987), supp. (*The B-Deduction*): 151–155.

"Making Sense Out of Inner Sense," *International Philosophical Quarterly* 29 (1989): 263–270.

"Kant's Aesthetic Idealism." *The Iowa Review* 21 (1991): 52–57.

"Toward the Pleasure Principle: Kant's Transcendental Psychology of the Feeling of Pleasure and Displeasure." In *Akten des Siebenten Internationalen Kant-Kongresses.* Ed. G. Funke. Bonn: Bouvier, 1991, 809–819.

"Lichtenberg and Kant on the Subject of Thinking." *Journal of the History of Philosophy* 30 (1992): 417–441.

"Main Developments in Recent Scholarship on the *Critique of Pure Reason.*" *Philosophy and Phenomenological Research* 53 (1993): 445–466.

Review of Fichte, *Foundations of Transcendental Philosophy (Wissenschaftslehre) Nova Methodo (1796/99), The Philosophical Review* 103 (1994): 585–588.

Review of Ives Radrizzani, *Vers la fondation de l'intersubjectivité chez Fichte: Des Principes à la Nova Methodo. Philosophischer Literaturanzeiger* 47 (1994): 366–368.

"Schopenhauer and the Problem of Metaphysics: Critical Reflections on Rudolf Malter's Interpretation." *Man and World* 28 (1994): 1–10.

"Funde, Verzeichnisse und Folgen: Neuere Resultate der Fichte-Forschung." *Philosophischer Literaturanzeiger* 49 (1996): 389–394.

Review of Susan Neiman, *The Unity of Reason: Rereading Kant. Journal of the History of Philosophy* 34 (1996): 306–308.

ed., with D. Klemm. *Figuring the Self: Subject, Individual, and Others in Classical German Philosophy.* Albany: State University of New York Press, 1997.

ed. *The Cambridge Companion to Fichte.* Cambridge: Cambridge University Press, forthcoming.

"'Das Element aller Gewissheit': Jacobi, Kant und Fichte über den Glauben." *Fichte-Studien,* forthcoming.

"Die Individualität des Ich in Fichtes zweiter Jenaer Wissenschaftslehre (1796–99)." *Revue internationale de philosophie,* forthcoming.

"The Flowering of Idealism: Johann Gottlieb Fichte." In *The Columbia History of Philosophy.* Ed. R. Popkin. New York: Columbia University Press, forthcoming.

"Kant and the Unity of Reason," unpublished manuscript.

"Leib, Materie und gemeinsames Wollen als Anwendungsbedingungen des Rechts." In *Fichtes Grundlage des Naturrechts*. Ed. J. C. Merle. Reihe Klassiker auslegen. Berlin: Akademie Verlag, forthcoming.

INDEX